JBoss AS 7 Configuration, Deployment, and Administration

Build a fully-functional, efficient application server using JBoss AS

Francesco Marchioni

PUBLISHING

open source*
community experience distilled

BIRMINGHAM - MUMBAI

JBoss AS 7 Configuration, Deployment, and Administration

First published: December 2011

Production Reference: 1091211

Published by Packt Publishing Ltd.
Livery Place
35 Livery Street
Birmingham B3 2PB, UK.

ISBN 978-1-84951-678-5

www.packtpub.com

Cover Image by Charwak A (charwak86@gmail.com)

Credits

Author
Francesco Marchioni

Reviewers
Jaikiran Pai

Deepak Vohra

Acquisition Editor
Sarah Cullington

Development Editors
Dayan Hyames

Reshma Sundaresan

Technical Editors
Lubna Shaikh

Mohd. Sahil

Indexers
Hemangini Bari

Tejal Daruwale

Monica Ajmera Mehta

Project Coordinator
Jovita Pinto

Proofreaders
Jonathan Todd

Lesley Harrison

Graphics
Manu Joseph

Production Coordinator
Shantanu Zagade

Cover Work
Shantanu Zagade

About the Author

Francesco Marchioni is a Sun Certified Enterprise Architect employed by an Italian company based in Rome. He started learning Java in 1997, and since then he has followed the path to the newest Application Program Interfaces released by Sun. He joined the JBoss Community in 2000, when the application server was running the release 2.X.

He has spent many years as a software consultant, where he has overseen many successful software migrations from vendor platforms to open source products such as JBoss AS, fulfilling the tight budget requirements of current times.

Over the last five years, he started authoring technical articles for O'Reilly Media and running an IT portal focused on JBoss products (http://www.mastertheboss.com).

In December 2009, he published the title "JBoss AS 5 Development", which describes how to create and deploy Java Enterprise applications on JBoss AS: http://www.packtpub.com/jboss-as-5-development/book.

In December 2010, he published his second title, "JBoss AS 5 Performance Tuning", which describes how to deliver fast and efficient applications on JBoss AS: http://www.packtpub.com/jboss-5-performance-tuning/book

I need to thank a lot of people for this book. First, I owe my hearty thanks to the JBoss community which helped me through this journey in developing a completely new product. In particular, I'd like to thank Jaikiran for sharing his experience as a reviewer of the book, improving its quality substantially.

I'd like also to express my gratitude to Packt Publishing team that shared with me the challenge to write a book which was already rewritten many times as application server changed its skin.

Last but not least, I'd like to thanks my wife Linda, who has kept doing housework patiently while I was writing the book, just asking when that damned JBoss thing will end.

About the Reviewers

Jaikiran Pai works at Red Hat and is part of the JBoss AS and EJB3 development team. In his role as a software developer, Jaikiran has been mainly involved in Java language and Java EE technologies. He completed his graduation in 2004 and started working in a software company in Pune, India. During this period, he developed an interest in JBoss Application Server and has been active in the JBoss community ever since. Subsequently, he joined Red Hat to be part of the JBoss EJB3 team.

Jaikiran is one of the co-authors of JBoss AS Getting Started DZone RefCard (`http://refcardz.dzone.com/refcardz/getting-started-jboss`). When he's not doing anything JBoss related, you'll find him at his other favorite and friendly place - JavaRanch (`http://www.javaranch.com`), where he has been a moderator since 2007.

Deepak Vohra is a consultant and a principal member of the NuBean.com software company. Deepak is a Sun Certified Java Programmer and Web Component Developer and has worked in the fields of XML and Java programming and J2EE for over five years. Deepak is the co-author of the Apress book Pro XML Development with Java Technology, and he was the technical reviewer for the O'Reilly book WebLogic: The Definitive Guide. Deepak was also the technical reviewer for the Course Technology PTR book Ruby Programming for the Absolute Beginner and the technical editor for the Manning Publications book Prototype and Scriptaculous in Action. Deepak is also the author of the Packt Publishing books JDBC 4.0 and Oracle JDeveloper for J2EE Development, Processing XML Documents with Oracle JDeveloper 11g, and EJB 3.0 Database Persistence with Oracle Fusion Middleware 11g.

www.PacktPub.com

Support files, eBooks, discount offers, and more

You might want to visit www.PacktPub.com for support files and downloads related to your book.

Did you know that Packt offers eBook versions of every book published, with PDF and ePub files available? You can upgrade to the eBook version at www.PacktPub.com and as a print book customer, you are entitled to a discount on the eBook copy. Get in touch with us at service@packtpub.com for more details.

At www.PacktPub.com, you can also read a collection of free technical articles, sign up for a range of free newsletters and receive exclusive discounts and offers on Packt books and eBooks.

http://PacktLib.PacktPub.com

Do you need instant solutions to your IT questions? PacktLib is Packt's online digital book library. Here, you can access, read and search across Packt's entire library of books.

Why Subscribe?

- Fully searchable across every book published by Packt
- Copy & paste, print and bookmark content
- On demand and accessible via web browser

Free Access for Packt account holders

If you have an account with Packt at www.PacktPub.com, you can use this to access PacktLib today and view nine entirely free books. Simply use your login credentials for immediate access.

This book is dedicated to my family who have always been there for me and in particular to my child Alessandro who's only four but wants to be an actor in theater. Never doubt about your dreams Alessandro, no matter how crazy they might be.

– Francesco Marchioni

Table of Contents

Preface

As the Java EE standard has evolved and matured, the API has become increasingly rich and complex. The next generation of application servers needs to be modular and configurable to run only specific services or containers. JBoss AS 7 promises to meet those requirements but the configuration of a complex application server is composed of a mix of administrative and management tasks which often overlap, generating confusion.

JBoss AS 7 Configuration, Deployment and Administration will give you an expert's understanding of every component that makes up the JBoss application server, and will show you how to use them, helping you to cut down the learning curve for this exciting product dramatically.

This book will guide you through configuration, management, deployment, and advanced administration of JBoss AS 7 in a logical order to avoid the common pitfalls of setting up a new AS. At first, we will The book dives into the new application server structure and shows you how to install it. You will then learn how to configure the core AS services, including thread pools, the messaging system, and the transaction service. Finally, you will learn how to deploy and manage your applications through all possible configuration variants, including standalone or domain servers, through a single node or a cluster of application servers. and then tune the performance of your AS to achieve an efficient, indispensible application server. In the last part of this book, we will show also how to deliver your applications on the cloud as a service.

What this book covers

Chapter 1, Installing JBoss AS 7, will introduce you to the new application server, depicting its most important features and showing how to install it on your machine.

Chapter 2, Configuring the Application Server, covers the application server main configuration file and some core parts of it, such as like the Thread pool configuration and the Logging subsystem.

Chapter 3, Configuring Enterprise Services, will teach the reader how to model the core Java Enterprise services using the standalone configuration file.

Chapter 4, JBoss Web Server Configuration, completes the standalone server configuration by looking at the Web subsystem. This chapter also includes a full Java EE example which teaches the reader how to create and configure a Java EE 6 application on JBoss AS 7.

Chapter 5, Configuring a JBoss AS Domain, teaches the reader how to shape the domain server configuration and which is the criteria behind the choice of a standalone or domain server configuration.

Chapter 6, Deploying Applications on JBoss AS, covers all the nuts and bolts related to the application deployment. It also discusses the class loading mechanism which that is used by the application server when applications are loaded.

Chapter 7, Managing the Application Server, teaches the reader which management tools can be used to control the application server instances.

Chapter 8, Clustering, covers the AS 7 clustering capabilities that serve as an essential component to providing scalability and high availability to your applications.

Chapter 9, Load Balancing Web Applications, discusses the second important concern of clustering, which is the ability to make several servers participate in the same service and do the same work. In other words, it discusses how to load balance the number of requests across the available servers.

Chapter 10, Securing JBoss AS 7, covers the foundation of JBoss Security framework and how to secure Enterprise applications and the server management interfaces.

Chapter 11, Taking JBoss AS 7 into the cloud, shows how to deliver Java EE applications on a cloud environment using the Red Hat OpenShift platform.

Appendix, provides a quick reference for the most common commands and operations that can be used to manage the application server with the CLI.

What you need for this book

Some prior knowledge of Java Enterprise is expected, but no prior knowledge of JBoss application server is needed. However, the book contains many hints to upgrading your existing JBoss AS configuration in the new server release, so affectionate JBoss users will surely gain better dividends from reading this book.

Who this book is for

Java system administrators, developers, and application testers will benefit from this book. The brand new features in AS 7 mean that everyone can get something from this book, whether you have used JBoss AS or not.

Conventions

In this book, you will find a number of styles of text that distinguish between different kinds of information. Here are some examples of these styles, and an explanation of their meaning.

Code words in text are shown as follows: " Next, you need to state the path to the JDBC driver resource and finally the `module dependencies`."

A block of code is set as follows:

```
<module xmlns="urn:jboss:module:1.0" name="com.mysql"> <resources>
  <resource-root path="mysql-connector-java-5.1.17-bin.jar"/>
  </resources>
  <dependencies>
    <module name="javax.api"/>
    <module name="javax.transaction.api"/>
  </dependencies>
</module>
```

When we wish to draw your attention to a particular part of a code block, the relevant lines or items are set in bold:

```
Connection result = null;
try {
  Context initialContext = new InitialContext();
  DataSource datasource =
    (DataSource)initialContext.lookup("java:/MySqlDS");
  result = datasource.getConnection();
}
catch ( Exception ex ) {
  log("Cannot get connection: " + ex);
}
```

Any command-line input or output is written as follows:

```
[disconnected /] connect

Connected to localhost:9999

[localhost:9999 /] :reload
```

New terms and **important words** are shown in bold. Words that you see on the screen, in menus or dialog boxes for example, appear in the text like this: " Now, you should be able to see the JBoss AS 7 enlisted as a server by choosing **New | Server** from the upper menu and expanding the JBoss Community option:".

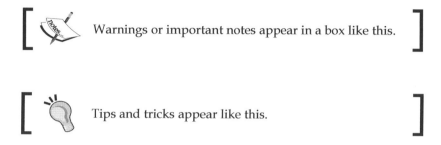

Warnings or important notes appear in a box like this.

Tips and tricks appear like this.

Reader feedback

Feedback from our readers is always welcome. Let us know what you think about this book—what you liked or may have disliked. Reader feedback is important for us to develop titles that you really get the most out of.

To send us general feedback, simply send an e-mail to feedback@packtpub.com, and mention the book title via the subject of your message.

If there is a book that you need and would like to see us publish, please send us a note in the **SUGGEST A TITLE** form on www.packtpub.com or e-mail suggest@ packtpub.com.

If there is a topic that you have expertise in and you are interested in either writing or contributing to a book on, see our author guide on www.packtpub.com/authors.

Customer support

Now that you are the proud owner of a Packt book, we have a number of things to help you to get the most from your purchase.

Downloading the example code for this book

You can download the example code files for all Packt books you have purchased from your account at http://www.PacktPub.com. If you purchased this book elsewhere, you can visit http://www.PacktPub.com/support and register to have the files e-mailed directly to you.

Errata

Although we have taken every care to ensure the accuracy of our content, mistakes do happen. If you find a mistake in one of our books—maybe a mistake in the text or the code—we would be grateful if you would report this to us. By doing so, you can save other readers from frustration and help us improve subsequent versions of this book. If you find any errata, please report them by visiting http://www.packtpub.com/support, selecting your book, clicking on the **let us know** link, and entering the details of your errata. Once your errata are verified, your submission will be accepted and the errata will be uploaded on our website, or added to any list of existing errata, under the Errata section of that title. Any existing errata can be viewed by selecting your title from http://www.packtpub.com/support.

Piracy

Piracy of copyright material on the Internet is an ongoing problem across all media. At Packt, we take the protection of our copyright and licenses very seriously. If you come across any illegal copies of our works, in any form, on the Internet, please provide us with the location address or website name immediately so that we can pursue a remedy.

Please contact us at copyright@packtpub.com with a link to the suspected pirated material.

We appreciate your help in protecting our authors, and our ability to bring you valuable content.

Questions

You can contact us at questions@packtpub.com if you are having a problem with any aspect of the book, and we will do our best to address it.

1
Installing JBoss AS 7

Java continues to be the most widely-used single-programming language today, edged out only by all scripting languages grouped together. Java remains also the language and/or platform of choice for Enterprise and Web application development, especially large-scale application development.

Nevertheless the Java language has changed a lot since its first appearance and will possibly continue to change in the future. Oracle, who has acquired Sun, the home of the Java language, has stated that its high-level Java strategy is to enhance and extend the reach of Java to new and emerging software development paradigms: **simplify**, **optimize**, and **integrate** the Java platform into new deployment architectures; and invest in the Java developer community allowing for increased participation.

At this point, one question arises: are application servers ready to meet these new paradigms? Originally designed as web containers for supporting web applications and, later, as EJB containers for remotely accessible services, application servers have expanded considerably from their simple origins. Today, most application servers provide a comprehensive service layer, which delivers support for distributed transactions, clustering, security, and so on.

In addition, a large number of open source building blocks have been added to the application server and they are heavily used in today's products. However, integrating all these libraries does not come without a price because each library has, in turn, evolved with complexity, following its own unsynchronized evolution path and requiring more and more additional libraries to work.

As most IT experts agree, the challenge for today's application server is to combine a rich set of features requested by the customers along with a lightweight and flexible container configuration.

The 7.0 release of JBoss AS is designed around a brand new kernel, which is now based on two main projects:

- **JBoss Modules**: This handles class loading of resources in the container. You can think about JBoss Modules as a thin bootstrap wrapper for executing an application in a modular environment.

- **Modular Service Container (MSC)**: This one provides a way to install, uninstall, and manage services used by a container. MSC further enables resources injection into services and dependency management between services.

The following picture depicts the basic architecture of the new application server kernel:

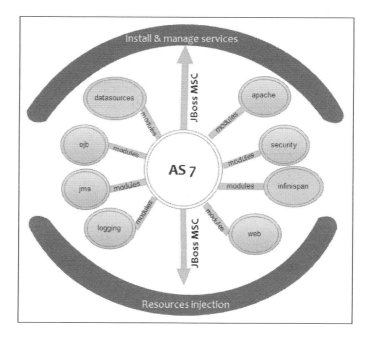

Understanding the details of the new modular kernel may be a little invasive at the beginning of the book, however, we will smoothly introduce some useful concepts within this chapter, just to make sure you get acquainted with the server configuration basics.

For the time being, let's just start installing the core server components and their required dependencies.

Getting started with the application server

The first step in learning about the application server will be installing all the necessary stuff on your machine in order to run it. The application server itself requires just a Java Virtual Machine environment installed.

As far as the hardware requirements are concerned, you should be aware that the server distribution, at the time of writing, requires about 75MB of hard-disk space and allocates a minimum of 64MB and a maximum of 512MB for a standalone server.

In order to get started, this is our checklist:

1. Install the Java Development Kit where JBoss AS 7 will run.
2. Install JBoss AS 7.0.
3. Install Eclipse development environment.

At the end of this chapter, you will have all the instruments to get started with the application server.

Installing the Java environment

JBoss AS is a full Java application server and hence it requires a Virtual Machine for the Java Platform to run on.

> At the time of writing, the J2SE 1.7 has been finally released and it's available for download. Although, there are no known issues with this Java release, there are still a few users who have tested it intensively with the new application server.
>
> For this reason, at the moment, we suggest you start with J2SE 1.6 and consider moving to the new Java platform in the near future.

So, let's move on the Oracle download page, which now hosts all JDK downloads: `http://www.oracle.com/technetwork/java/javase/downloads/index.html`

Choose to download the latest JDK/JRE which is, at the time of writing, the JDK 1.6 Update 26.

Java SE Development Kit 6 Update 26		
Product / File Description	File Size	Download
Linux x86 - RPM Installer	76.85 MB	⬇ jdk-6u26-linux-i586-rpm.bin
Linux x86 - Self Extracting Installer	jdk-6u2611 MB	⬇ jdk-6u26-linux-i586.bin
Linux Intel Itanium - RPM Installer	76.85 MB	⬇ jdk-6u26-linux-ia64-rpm.bin
Linux Intel Itanium - Self Extracting Installer	81.11 MB	⬇ jdk-6u26-linux-ia64.bin
Linux x64 - RPM Installer	77.06 MB	⬇ jdk-6u26-linux-x64-rpm.bin
Linux x64 - Self Extracting Installer	81.36 MB	⬇ jdk-6u26-linux-x64.bin
Solaris x86 - Self Extracting Binary	81.00 MB	⬇ jdk-6u26-solaris-i586.sh
Solaris x86 - Packages - tar.Z	136.67 MB	⬇ jdk-6u26-solaris-i586.tar.Z
Solaris SPARC - Self Extracting Binary	85.96 MB	⬇ jdk-6u26-solaris-sparc.sh
Solaris SPARC - Packages - tar.Z	141.11 MB	⬇ jdk-6u26-solaris-sparc.tar.Z
Solaris SPARC 64-bit - Self Extracting Binary	12.24 MB	⬇ jdk-6u26-solaris-sparcv9.sh
Solaris SPARC 64-bit - Packages - tar.Z	15.58 MB	⬇ jdk-6u26-solaris-sparcv9.tar.Z
Solaris x64 - Self Extracting Binary	8.49 MB	⬇ jdk-6u26-solaris-x64.sh
Solaris x64 - Packages - tar.Z	12.25 MB	⬇ jdk-6u26-solaris-x64.tar.Z
Windows x86	76.66 MB	⬇ jdk-6u26-windows-i586.exe
Windows Intel Itanium	67.27 MB	⬇ jdk-6u26-windows-ia64.exe
Windows x64	67.27 MB	⬇ jdk-6u26-windows-x64.exe

The download will take a few minutes depending how fast your network is. Once the download is complete, run the executable file to start the installation. (The actual name of the installer varies, also if you are on a 32-bit system or 64-bit. However, the steps will be the same, just the name will change).

```
jdk-6u26-windows-i586.exe       # Windows
sh jdk-6u26-linux-i586.bin      # Linux
```

If you are installing on a Linux/Unix box, you can safely accept all the defaults given to you by the setup wizard. The Windows users should stay away from the installation paths that include empty spaces, such as `C:\Program Files`, as this leads to some issues when you are referencing the core libraries. An installation path such as `C:\Software\Java` or simply `C:\Java` is a better alternative.

When the installation is complete, we need to update a couple of settings on the computer so it can interact with Java. The most important setting is `JAVA_HOME`, which is directly referenced by JBoss startup script.

If you are running Windows XP-2000, follow these steps:

1. Right-click on **My Computer** and select **Properties** from the context menu.

2. On the **Advanced** tab, click on the **Environment Variables** button.

3. Then, in the **System Variables** box, click on **New**.

4. Name the new variable as `JAVA_HOME`, and give a value of the path to your JDK installation; I would recommend something like: `C:\Java\jdk1.6.0_26`.

Windows Vista tip

Because of increased security in Windows Vista, standard users must have **User Account Control** (UAC) turned on to change the environment variables, and the change must be completed via user accounts. In the User Accounts window, under Tasks, select **Change my environment variables**. Use the **New**, **Edit** or **Delete** buttons to amend environment variables

5. Now it's time to modify the system's `PATH` variable. Double-click on the `PATH` system variable. In the box that pops up, navigate to the end of the **Variable Value** line, add a semicolon to the end, and then add the path to your JDK. This will be something like `%JAVA_HOME%\bin`.

Unix/Linux users can add the following commands in the user's profile scripts:

```
export JAVA_HOME=/installDir/jdk1.6.0_26
export PATH=$JAVA_HOME/bin:$PATH
```

Installing JBoss AS 7

JBoss application server can be freely downloaded from the community site:
`http://www.jboss.org/jbossas/downloads/`.

As you can see from the above picture, as I'm writing this book, you can
choose between the 7.0.2 final release (Arc) and the newer 7.1.0 Beta. If
you plan to use JBoss AS 7 in production, we suggest you using the former
stable release which provides all the functionalities contained in this book
except for one mentioned in *Chapter 4* ("Adding a Remote EJB client").

The 7.0.2 release is available in the Web profile certified distribution and
in the full distribution, which contains all the available server modules.

On the other hand, if you are on a learning path to the new server, just
proceed to the new 7.1.0 Beta release, which is available in the single EE6
server release."

Choose to download the full server distribution. You will be then warned that this
download is part of a community release and, as such, it is not yet fully supported.
As said before, RedHat maintains the Enterprise releases of JBoss middleware and,
hopefully, the AS 7 will be soon part of it.

JBoss AS 7 does not come with an installer; it is simply a
matter of extracting the compressed archive.

Windows users can simply use any uncompress utility, such as WinZip, or WinRAR
taking care to choose a folder, which doesn't contain empty spaces. Unix /Linux
should use the `unzip` shell command to explode the archive:

```
unzip jboss-as-7.0.2.Final.zip
```

Security warning

Unix/Linux users should be aware that JBoss AS does not require root privileges as none of the default ports used by JBoss are below the privileged port range of 1024. To reduce the risk of users gaining root privileges through the JBoss AS, install and run JBoss as a non-root user.

Starting up JBoss AS

After you have installed JBoss, it is wise to perform a simple startup test to validate that there are no major problems with your Java VM/operating system combination. To test your installation, move to the `bin` directory of your JBOSS_HOME directory and issue the following command:

```
standalone.bat      # Windows users

$ standalone.sh    # Linux/Unix users
```

Here's a sample JBoss AS 7 startup console:

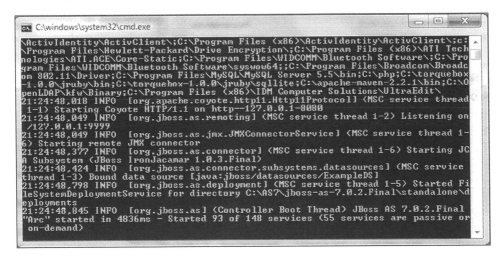

The above command starts up a JBoss standalone instance that's equivalent of starting the application server with the `run.bat`/`run.sh` script used by earlier AS releases. You will notice how amazingly fast is starting the new release of the application server; this is due to the new modular architecture, which only starts up necessary parts of the application server container needed by loaded applications.

If you need to customize the startup properties of your application server, then you need to open the `standalone.conf` (or `standalone.conf.bat` for the Windows users) where the memory requirements of JBoss are declared. Here's the Linux core section of it:

```
if [ "x$JAVA_OPTS" = "x" ]; then
    JAVA_OPTS="-Xms64m -Xmx512m -XX:MaxPermSize=256m -Dorg.jboss.resolver.
warning=true -Dsun.rmi.dgc.client.gcInterval=3600000 - Dsun.rmi.dgc.
server.gcInterval=3600000"
fi
```

So, by default, the application server starts with a minimum memory requirement of 64MB of heap space and a maximum of 512MB. This will be just enough to get started, however, if you need to run a core Java EE application on it, you will likely require at least 1GB of heap space or 2GB or more depending on your application type. Generally speaking, 32-bit machines cannot execute a process whose space exceeds 2GB, however on 64 bit machines, there's essentially no limit to process size.

You can verify that the server is reachable from the network by simply pointing your browser to the application server's welcome page, which is reachable by default at the well-known address: `http://localhost:8080`.

Connecting to the server with the command line interface

If you have been using previous releases of the application server you might have heard about the **twiddle** command-line utility that queried the MBeans installed on the application server. This utility has been replaced by a more sophisticated interface named the **Command Line Interface (CLI)**, which can be found in the `JBOSS_HOME/bin` folder.

Just launch the `jboss-admin.bat` script (or `jboss-admin.sh` for Linux users) and you will be able to manage the application server via a shell interface.

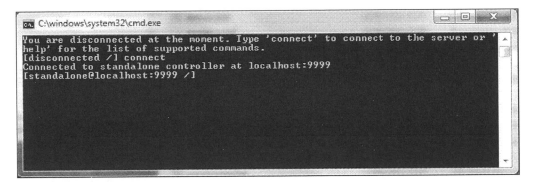

We have just started an interactive shell session which is also able to use the command-line completion (by pressing the *Tab* key) to match partly-typed command names. No more searches for finding the exact syntax of commands!

 In the previous screenshot, we have just connected to the server using the `connect` command, which by default uses the loopback server address and plugs into the port 9999.

The command-line interface is discussed in depth in Chapter 7, *Managing the Application Server*, which is all about the server-management interfaces; We will, however, have an initial taste of its basic functionalities in the following sections to get you accustomed to this powerful tool.

Stopping JBoss

Probably the easiest way to stop JBoss is by sending an interrupt signal with *Ctrl+C*.

However, if your JBoss process was launched in the background or rather is running on another machine (see next), then you can use the CLI interface to issue an immediate shutdown command:

```
[disconnected /] connect
Connected to localhost:9999
[localhost:9999 /] :shutdown
```

Locating the shutdown script

There is actually one more option to shutdown the application server, which is pretty useful if you need to shut down the server from within a script. This option consists of passing the `--connect` option to the admin shell, thereby switching off the interactive mode:

```
jboss-admin.bat --connect command=:shutdown        # Windows

jboss-admin.sh --connect command=:shutdown         # Unix / Linux
```

Stopping JBoss on a remote machine

Shutting down the application server, which is running on a remote machine, is just a matter of connecting and providing the server's remote address to the CLI:

```
[disconnected /] connect 192.168.1.10
Connected to 192.168.1.10:9999
[192.168.1.10:9999 /] :shutdown
```

 Since JBoss AS 7.1.0 Beta1 accessing remotely the CLI requires authentication. Check out Chapter 10 for more information about it.

Restarting JBoss

The command-line Interface contains a lot of useful commands. One of the most interesting options is the ability to reload all or parts of the AS configuration using the `reload` command.

When issued on the **root node path** of the AS server, it is able to reload the services configuration:

```
[disconnected /] connect
Connected to localhost:9999
[localhost:9999 /] :reload
```

Installing Eclipse environment

Although the main focus of this book is the administration of the application server, we are also concerned with the application packaging and deploying. For this reason, we will sometimes add examples that require a development environment to be executed.

The development environment used in this book is Eclipse known by Java developers worldwide and contains a huge set of plugins to expand its functionalities. Besides this, Eclipse is the first IDE that is compatible with the new application server.

So, let's move to the downloading page of Eclipse which is located at: `http://www.eclipse.org`.

From there, download the latest Enterprise Edition (at the time of this writing, it's version 3.7 and is also known as Indigo). The compressed package contains all the Java EE plugins already installed and requires about 210MB of disk space:

Once you have unzipped the previously downloaded file, you will see a folder named `eclipse`. In that folder, you will find the eclipse application (a big blue dot). We recommend you create a shortcut on the desktop to simplify the launching of Eclipse. Note that just like JBoss AS, Eclipse does not have an installation process. Once you have unzipped the file, you are done!

Installing JBoss tools

The next step will be installing the JBoss AS plugin, which is a part of the suite of plugins named JBoss tools. Installing new plugins in Eclipse is pretty simple; just follow these steps:

1. From the menu, choose **Help | Install New Software**.

2. Then, click on the **Add** button where you will enter the JBoss tools' download URL (along with a description): `http://download.jboss.org/jbosstools/updates/development/indigo/`.

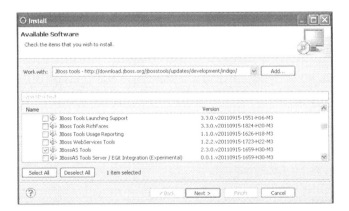

As you can see from the previous screenshot, you need to check the **JBossAS Tools** plugin and move forward to the next options where you will complete the installation process. Once done, restart when prompted.

Now, you should be able to see the JBoss AS 7 enlisted as a server by choosing **New | Server** from the upper menu and expanding the **JBoss Community** option:

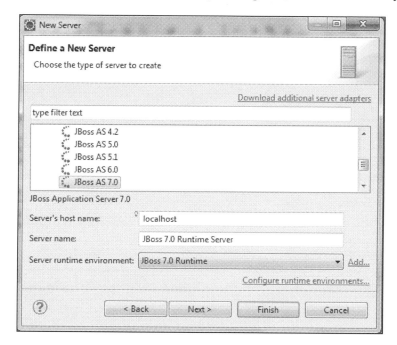

Completing the server installation into the Eclipse is quite straightforward as it just requires pointing to the folder where your server distribution, hence we will leave this to the reader as a practical exercise.

Exploring the application server file system

Once done with the installation of all the necessary tools, we will concentrate on the new application server structure. The first thing you'll notice when you browse through the application server folders is that its file system is basically divided into two core parts: the dichotomy reflects the distinction between **standalone** servers and **domain** servers.

The concept of the domain server is not new in the market of application servers, however, it is introduced for the first time in JBoss AS as a way to *manage and coordinate* a set of instances of the application server. An application server node which is not configured as part of a domain is qualified as standalone server and it resembles in practice to a single instances of the application server you used in earlier releases.

We will discuss the concept of domains in detail in *Chapter 5, Configuring a JBoss AS Domain*, of this book; for the time being, we will explore the different file system structures for both kinds of servers.

From a bird's eye perspective, we can see the one that the main file system is split in two: one section which is pertinent to **domain servers** and another which is relative to **standalone servers**. The following screenshot depicts the new tree of the application server:

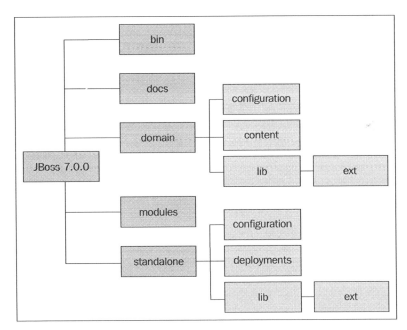

In the next section, we will enter into the single folders of the new AS infrastructure, dissecting their content and what they are used for in the application server.

The bin folder

This is where you start your application server instances. You can start a standalone server by launching the `standalone.bat` (`standalone.sh` for Linux users). In addition to the startup scripts, you can find the `standalone.bat`, which can be used to customize JBoss' bootstrap processIf you are going to use a domain of servers, you will use the `domain.bat` script (`domain.sh` for Linux users). This shell script starts up a set of application server instances as specified by the domain configuration file.

The `bin` folder also includes another useful script command, named `jboss-admin.bat`   (`jboss-admin.sh` for Linux users), which starts the new interactive command-line interface.

In addition, this folder contains the web services utility scripts (`wsconsume.sh` and `wsprovide.sh`) used to generate the web services definition language and the corresponding Java interfaces.

The docs folder

In spite of its name, this folder does not contain the server documentation, but two subfolders: the first one named `licenses` barely contains the licenses information for the application server and its dependencies. You might use the `licenses.xml` file as quick reference for finding out which are the version shipped with the default application server modules or dependencies. For example, JBoss AS 7 ships with the release 4.0.0.CR2 of Hibernate core libraries.

```
<dependency>
        <groupId>org.hibernate</groupId>
        <artifactId>hibernate-core</artifactId>
        <version>4.0.0.CR2</version>
        <licenses>
          <license>
            <name>GNU Lesser General Public License</name>
            <url>http://www.gnu.org/licenses/lgpl-2.1.html</url>
            <distribution>repo</distribution>
            <comments>See discussion at http://hibernate.org/license
for more details.</comments>
          </license>
        </licenses>
</dependency>
```

The other subfolder named `schema` contains the .xsd files which are used by the configuration as schema.

The domain folder

The next folder is the domain folder, which contains the domain structure, split across a set of folders:

The `configuration` folder contains as you might imagine the configuration files. The main configuration file is `domain.xml` which contains all services which are used by the nodes of the domain. It also configures the socket-binding interfaces for all services.

Along with it, the other key file is `host.xml` which is used to define the management aspects of the domain.

The last file contained in the configuration folder is `logging.properties` which are used to define the logging format of the bootstrap process.

The `content` folder is used as a repository to store deployed modules.

The `lib` folder hosts the sub-folder `ext`, which is there to support Java SE/EE style "extensions". Some of the application server deployers are able to scan this folder for additional libraries which are picked up by the local class loader; nevertheless this approach is not recommended and maintained only for compliance with the language specifications. The `modules` folder should be the one and only path for your libraries.

The `log` folder contains as you might imagine the logging output of the domain. The file, by default, is truncated every time the server is rebooted.

The **servers** folder holds a set of sub-folders for each server defined in the configuration file. The most useful directory contained beneath each server is the `log` folder which is the location where single instances emit their log. The `data` folder is used by the application server to store its runtime data, such as the transaction logging The `tmp` folder is a temporary location for some resource artifacts which is not a big issue for any of you.

The standalone folder

If you are running the application server in standalone mode, this is the part of the AS file system you will be interested in. Its structure is quite similar to the **domain** folder with the notable exception of a **deployment** folder. Let's proceed with order. Just below the domain folder, you will find the following set of subdirectories.

The **configuration** folder contains also the application server configuration files. As a matter of fact the application server ships with a set of different configuration files, each one using a different set of functionalities. Launching the standalone start-up script, by default, the `standalone.xml` configuration file will be used.

Besides `standalone.xml`, this folder contains the `logging.properties` file, which is also about the logging of bootstrap process. The other file you will find within it, `mgmt-users.properties`, can be used to secure the management interfaces. The security is discussed in detail in *Chapter 10, Securing JBoss AS,* of this book.

The `data` folder is used by the application server to store its runtime data, such as the transaction logging.

The `deployments` folder is the location in which users can place their deployment content (for example, WAR, EAR, JAR, SAR files) to have it automatically deployed into the server runtime. Users, particularly those running production systems, are encouraged to use the JBoss AS management APIs to upload and deploy deployment content instead of relying on the deployment scanner subsystem that periodically scans this directory. See *Chapter 6, Deploying Applications on JBoss AS 7,* for more details.

The `lib` folder hosts the sub folder `ext`, which is used to define extensions of the application server. The same considerations for the domain's `lib` path apply here.

The `log` folder contains the logs emitted by the standalone instance of the application server. The default log file, named `server.log`, is truncated every time the server is rebooted.

The `tmp` folder holds is used by JBoss **Virtual File System** as a temporary location for resource artifacts.

The welcome-content folder:

This directory contains the default page which is loaded when you surf on the home of your application server (`http://localhost:8080`). In terms of web server configuration, this is the **Web root context**.

The modules folder

Beneath the `modules` folder, you will find the application server's set of libraries, which are a part of the server distribution.

Historically, JBoss AS releases used to manage their set of libraries in different ways. Lets recap to make some order. Earlier, Release 4.x was used to define the core server libraries into the `JBOSS_HOME/server` libraries. Thereafter, each server definition had its specific library into the `server/<servername>/lib` folder.

This approach was pretty simple this way; however, it led to a useless proliferation of libraries which were replicated in the `default/all` server distribution.

The release 5.x and 6.x had the concept of the `common/lib` folder which was the main repository for all modules that were common to all server definitions. Each server distribution still contained a `server/<servername>/lib` path for the libraries that were specific to that server definition. Unchanged from the earlier release was the repository for core server modules comprised by `JBOSS_HOME/server`.

JBoss AS 7 follows a real modular approach deprecating all earlier approaches. The server bootstrap libraries are now located at the root of the application server. There you can find the `jboss-modules.jar` archive, which is all you need to bootstrap the new application server kernel, based on the JBoss modules.

The application server modules are now defined beneath the `modules` folder, grouped in a set of subfolders each one dedicated to a set of resources. At first sight, this approach might seem less intuitive than previous releases; however, once accustomed to it, you will find it much easier to handle module installation/updates.

The following table resumes the diverse approaches used across different server releases:

AS Release	Bootstrap libs	Server libs
4.x	`JBOSS_HOME/server`	`JBOSS_HOME/server/<server>/lib`
5.x – 6.x	`JBOSS_HOME/server`	`JBOSS_HOME/common/lib` and `JBOSS_HOME/server/<server>/lib`
7.x	`JBOSS_HOME/jboss-modules.jar`	`JBOSS_HOME/modules` subfolders

Listing all the modules will take up too much space; however, the module repository layout is pretty much the same as the module name. For example, the `org.jboss.as.ejb3` module will be found in `org/jboss/as/ejb3` subfolder of the `modules` folder. In the last section of this chapter, we will see how modules are actually loaded by the application server.

Loading application server modules

Learning more about JBoss module is essential if you want to understand the next chapters that discuss about the server configuration. Basically, each module is a pluggable unit. As depicted by the following picture. JBoss modules can load libraries using two approaches:

- Using a static file system
- Using direct JAR execution

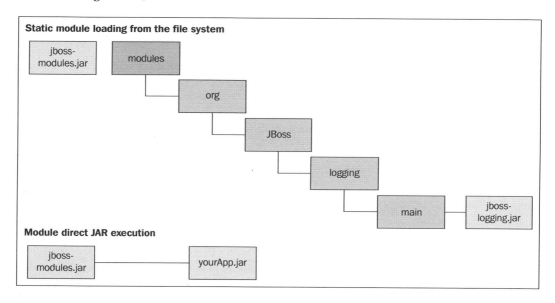

Using a **static file system** approach is the simplest way to load a module, and it's used as a default when starting up the application server. It is based on the assumption that the filesystem reflects the name and version of modules used. All you need to provide to the environment is the location where modules are stored. So, for example, you could start a standalone instance of JBoss AS 7 using the following command:

```
java -jar jboss-modules.jar -mp "%JBOSS_HOME%\modules" org.jboss.
as.standalone
```

The argument module path (-mp) actually points to the root directory (or directories), which will be searched by the default module loader for module definitions. A module is defined using a simple XML descriptor, like this:

```
<module xmlns="urn:jboss:module:1.0" name="org.jboss.msc">

    <main-class name="org.jboss.msc.Version"/>
    <resources>
        <resource-root path="jboss-msc-1.0.0.Beta8.jar"/>
    </resources>
    <dependencies>
        <module name="javax.api"/>
        <module name="org.jboss.logging"/>
        <module name="org.jboss.modules"/>
    </dependencies>
</module>
```

Basically, a module definition contains two main elements: the **resources** defined in the module (and their path) and the module **dependencies**. The previous example is the module definition for the JBoss MSC module which is contained in the `jboss-msc-1.0.0.Beta8.jar file` and bears a dependency on `javax.api`, `org.jboss.logging` and `org.jboss.modules` module.

 A module which is defined with a `main-class` element is said to be **executable**. In other words, the module name can be listed on the command line, and the standard static `main(String[])` method in the named module's `main-class` will be loaded and executed.

The other way to approach the module repository is by using **direct JAR execution**. This means that the module information, such as its dependencies, is contained in the `MANIFEST` file.

When the module is executed as a JAR file you just need to provide the name of your application module, which is packed in JAR file, and it will be picked up by JBoss modules:

```
java -jar jboss-modules.jar -jar your-app.jar
```

Then, in your `application.jar`, you might specify a set of module definitions, much the same way you did for flat filesystem modules. These definitions are contained in the `META-INF/MANIFEST.MF` file:

```
Main-Class: mypackage/MyClass
Dependencies: org.jboss.logging
```

Summary

In this chapter, we introduced the new application server, its new features, and the reasons which are behind these changes.

The release 7.0 of the JBoss application server provides the foundation for a new generation of application server, which will deliver the truly modular services.

The outcome of this is a lighter platform based on a tiny modular kernel that is able to load and extend its components from the filesystem and activate them just when they are required by the user.

The physical structure of the application server has been modified to reflect the dichotomy between standalone servers and domain servers, the former being basically a single node instance and the latter a set of managed resources controlled by a Domain Controller and a Host Controller.

In the next chapter we will enter into the details of the application server configuration, focusing our attention on the standalone server configuration file, which holds both core application server configuration and the stack of Enterprise services running on top of it.

2
Configuring
the Application Server

The first chapter has given us the initial groundwork to get started with JBoss AS 7. It is time for us to dive right into the new configuration and see how to shape a standalone instance of the application server. As you will see, the application configuration has also been renewed, moving from a large set of XML files to a single monolithic file.

The new configuration file is made up of a list of subsystems, which include the application server core services and standard Java EE services. By the end of this chapter, we will have covered the following topics:

- Introducing the server configuration file
- Configuring the application server's Thread Pool
- Configuring the application server's logging subsystem

Configuring the application server

The structure of the application server is maintained into a single file, which acts as a main reference for all server configurations. This file is not a static file, as it reflects the changes that are made when the server is running, for example, adding a new component, such as a JMS destination, or deploying an application.

The default configuration files are named `standalone.xml` for standalone servers and `domain.xml` for an application server domain. An application server domain can be seen as a specialized server configuration, which also includes the **Domain** and **Host controller** set-up. We will discuss the application server domain in *Chapter 5, Configuring a JBoss AS Domain*. However, as far as the core services configuration is concerned, what we learn here will be suitable for the domain configuration as well.

You can define as many configuration files as you need. For example, the AS 7.0.2 release provides a few variants of the `standalone.xml`, such as `standalone-preview.xml` (which includes JMS and web services subsystems) and the `standalone-ha.xml` (which can be used to start a cluster-aware application server). If you want to switch to another configuration file, just issue:

```
standalone.bat --server-config customConfiguration.xml
```

The `standalone.xml` file is located under the `JBOSS_HOME/standalone/configuration` folder. This configuration file consists of a large XML file, which is validated by a set of `.xsd` files mentioned in the `<server>` element.

If you want to check the single `.xsd` files, you can find them in the `JBOSS_HOME/docs/schema` folder of your server distribution. You can get to know all the available server parameters with a simple inspection of these files or by importing them into your Eclipse environment. Once they are located in your project, right-click your file and choose **Generate | XML File**.

The application server configuration follows a tree-like structure that contains, at the root element, the server definition.

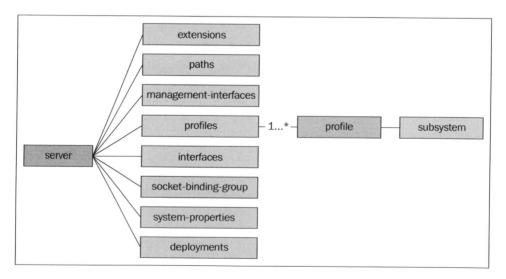

In the following sections, we will show in detail each part of the server configuration. This will be helpful to understand the role of each single component in the application server, although we warn you from manually changing the configuration file, since this can lead to unchecked data modifications that can easily corrupt the file.

> The best practice for changing the server configuration is to use the **Command Line Interface** (**CLI**) or the web admin console, which are described in *Chapter 7, Managing the Application Server*.

Extensions

The application server contains a list of basic modules, called extensions, which are shared by all of its services. Extensions can be seen as a special type of module, which are used to extend the functionalities of the application server. Much like standard modules, they are stored in the JBOSS_HOME/modules folder. Each extension is in turn picked up by the AS classloader at boot time, before any deployment. Here's an extract from the server configuration:

```
<extensions>
  <extension module="org.jboss.as.clustering.infinispan"/>
  <extension module="org.jboss.as.messaging"/>
</extensions>
```

> The application server detects that a module is an extension by scanning into the META_INF/services folder of the library. Modules that are qualified as Extensions contain in the META_INF/services folder a placeholder file named org.jboss.as.controller.Extension. This file simply declares the name of the Extension. For example, for the EJB3 subsystem, it will contain org.jboss.as.ejb3.subsystem. EJB3Extension.

Paths

Beneath module extensions, you can find the definition of paths that can be defined as logical names for file system paths. For example, the following bit of configuration defines a path relative to the AS log directory named log.dir, which translates for standalone servers into JBOSS_HOME/standalone/log/mylogdir:

```
<paths>
  <path name="log.dir" path="mylogdir" relative-to=
    "jboss.server.log.dir"/>
</paths>
```

Now, this path can be referenced in other sections of the configuration file, for example, we are using it as a folder for storing the logging rotating file handler:

```
<periodic-rotating-file-handler name="FILE" autoflush="true">
  <file relative-to="log.dir" path="myserver.log"/>
</periodic-rotating-file-handler>
```

 Please note that the property `relative-to` is not mandatory. If you don't include it in your path configuration, the path is meant as an absolute path.

By default, the application server provides a set of system paths that are available for use as relative paths and cannot be overridden by the user:

Path	Meaning
jboss.home	The root directory of the JBoss AS distribution
user.home	The user's home directory
user.dir	The user's current working directory
java.home	The Java installation directory
jboss.server.base.dir	The root directory for an individual server instance
jboss.server.data.dir	The directory the server will use for persistent data file storage
jboss.server.log.dir	The directory the server will use for logfile storage
jboss.server.tmp.dir	The directory the server will use for temporary file storage
jboss.domain.servers.dir	The directory under which a host controller will create the working area for individual server instances

Management interfaces

One of the innovating features of the application server is the powerful administration and management channels that include a CLI and a web-based administration console. The native CLI interface, by default, runs on port 9999, while the web console is bound on port 9990.

```
<socket-binding-group name="standard-sockets" default-
interface="public">
. . . . . . .
  <socket-binding name="management-native" interface="management"
port="9999"/>
  <socket-binding name="management-http" interface="management"
port="9990"/>
. . . . . .
</socket-binding-group>
```

Management interfaces are discussed in detail in *Chapter 7, Managing the Application Server*, which provides a detailed coverage of the application server management tools.

Profiles

Letting the configuration file flow, you can find the definition of the server's profiles, which is one of the core concepts introduced in AS. A profile can be seen as a collection of subsystems: each subsystem in turn contains a subset of functionalities used by the application server. For example, the web subsystem contains the definition of a set of connectors used by the container, the messaging subsystem defines the JMS configuration and modules used by the AS's messaging provider, and so on.

> One important difference between a standalone and a domain configuration file is the number of profiles contained in it. When using a standalone configuration, there's a single profile that contains the set of subsystem configurations. Domain configuration can, on the other hand, provide multiple profiles.

Interfaces

The interfaces section contains the network interfaces/IP addresses or host names where the application server can be bound.

By default, the standalone application server defines two available network interfaces: the `management` and the `public` interface:

```
<interfaces>
    <interface name="management">
        <inet-address value="${jboss.bind.address.
        management:127.0.0.1}"/>
    </interface>
    <interface name="public">
        <inet-address value="${jboss.bind.address:127.0.0.1}"/>
    </interface>
</interfaces>
```

The `public` network interface is intended to be used for the application server core services:

```
<socket-binding-group name="standard-sockets" default-
interface="public">

    . . . . . .

</socket-binding-group>
```

The `management` network interface is referenced by the AS management interfaces, as shown in the `management` interfaces section.

Both network interfaces resolve, by default, to the loop back address `127.0.0.1`. This means that, by default, the application server public services and the management services are accessible only from the local machine. By changing the `inet-address` value, you can bind the network interface to another IP address, which is available on the machine:

```
<interface name="public">
    <inet-address value="192.168.1.1"/>
</interface>
```

If, on the other hand, you want to bind the network interface to all available sets of IP address, you can use the `<any-address />` element:

```
<interface name="public">
    <any-address />
</interface>
```

Another useful variation of network interface is the **Network Interface Card (NIC)** element, which gathers the address information from the network card name:

```
<interface name="public">
    <nic name="eth0" />
</interface>
```

> **Using command-line options to change network interface bindings**
>
> In earlier releases of the application server, you used to launch the startup script with the additional -b parameter, followed by a valid host/IP address. This would cause the server to bind on the host/IP address provided. This option was not available in the initial AS 7 release however it has been restored in the AS 7.1.0 release.

Socket binding groups

A socket binding makes up a named configuration of a socket. Within this section, you are able to configure the network ports, which will be open and listening for incoming connections. As we have just seen, every socket binding group references a network interface through the `default-interface` attribute:

```
<socket-binding-group name="standard-sockets"
 default-interface="public">
 <socket-binding name="jndi" port="1099"/>
 <socket-binding name="jmx-connector-registry" port="1090"/>
```

```
    <socket-binding name="jmx-connector-server" port="1091"/>
    <socket-binding name="http" port="8080"/>
    <socket-binding name="https" port="8447"/>
    <socket-binding name="osgi-http" port="8090"/>
    <socket-binding name="remoting" port="4447"/>
    <socket-binding name="txn-recovery-environment" port="4712"/>
    <socket-binding name="txn-status-manager" port="4713"/>
    <socket-binding name="txn-socket-process-id" port="4714"/>
    <socket-binding name="messaging" port="5445"/>
    <socket-binding name="messaging-throughput" port="5455"/>
</socket-binding-group>
```

In order to change the ports where services are bound, you can change the `port` attribute of its service. A definitely better approach is, however, to use management interfaces that provide an immediate outcome of the affected change. In the following example, we are changing the default port for the `http` connector using the CLI:

```
[standalone@localhost:9999 /] /socket-binding-group=
  standard-sockets/socket-binding=http:write-attribute(name="port",
  value="8090")
{
  "outcome" => "success",
  "response-headers" => {
    "operation-requires-reload" => true,
    "process-state" => "reload-required"
  }
}
```

System properties

This section contains a set of system-wide properties, which can be added to the application server as part of the booting process. The following configuration snippet sets the property named example to `dummyvalue`:

```
<system-properties>
  <property name="myproperty" value="dummyvalue"/>
</system-properties>
```

The property can be later retrieved on the application server using:

```
String s = System.getProperty("myproperty");
```

Deployments

The last section of the configuration file contains the deployed application, which has been registered on the application server. Each time a new application is deployed or un-deployed, this section is updated to reflect the new application stack.

Configuring core subsystems

Now that you have grasped the basic concepts of the new configuration file, we will have a look at the peculiarities of single services. Discussing all single subsystems in a single chapter is a daunting task for both the author and for those who will read it later. That's why we had to find a criteria for approaching all subsystems gradually to make reading interesting and easy-to-understand.

In the following image, you can find a rough representation of core JBoss AS 7 subsystems (for the sake of simplicity we are including just the subsystems that are covered throughout this book):

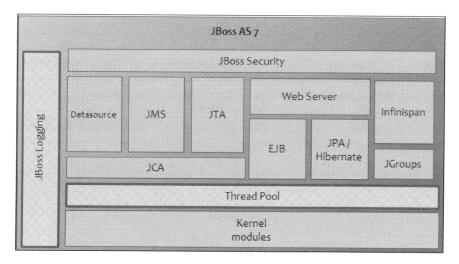

So, as a first taste of the application server, we will explore the areas that are highlighted in bold in this screenshot. These include the following core application server subsystems:

- The **Thread Pool** subsystem
- The **JBoss Logging** subsystem

Let's see each subsystem in a separate section.

Configuring the Thread Pool subsystem

Thread Pools address two different problems: they usually deliver improved performance when executing large numbers of asynchronous tasks, due to reduced per-task invocation overhead, and they provide a means of bounding and managing the resources, including Threads, consumed when executing a collection of tasks.

In the earlier releases of the application server, the Thread Pool configuration was centralized in a single file or deployment descriptor. This approach was maintained up to the first snapshots of the new application server. Since the 7.0.0 CR1 release, the individual subsystems that use Thread Pools manage their own Thread configuration.

By appropriately configuring the Thread Pool section, you can effectively tune the specific areas that use that kind of Pool to deliver new tasks. The application server Thread Pool configuration can include the following elements:

- Thread factory configuration
- Bounded Threads configuration
- Unbounded Threads configuration
- Queueless Thread Pool configuration
- Scheduled Thread configuration

Let's see in detail each single element:

Configuring the Thread factory

A **Thread factory** (implementing `java.util.concurrent.ThreadFactory`) is an object that creates new Threads on demand. Using Thread factories removes hardwiring of calls to new Thread, enabling applications to use special Thread subclasses, priorities, and so on.

The Thread factory is not included by default in the server configuration as it relies on defaults, which you will hardly need to modify. Nevertheless, we will provide a sample configuration of it for the experienced user who requires complete control of the Thread configuration.

So, here's an example of a custom Thread factory configuration:

```
<thread-factory name="MyThreadFactory"
   thread-name-pattern="My Thread %t"
   group-name="dummy" />
```

And here are the possible attributes that you can use when defining a Thread factory.

The `name` attribute is the name of the created Thread factory.

- The optional `priority` attribute may be used to specify the Thread priority of created Threads.
- The optional `group-name` attribute specifies the name of the Thread group to create for this Thread factory.

The `thread-name-pattern` is the template used to create names for Threads. The following patterns may be used:

Pattern	Output
`%%`	Emits a percent sign
`%g`	Emits the per-factory Thread sequence number
`%f`	Emits the global Thread sequence number
`%i`	Emits the Thread ID
`%G`	Emits the Thread group name

Bounded Thread Pool

A bounded Thread Pool is the most common kind of Pool used by the application server, as it helps prevent resource exhaustion by defining a constraint on the Thread Pool's size; the other side of the medal is that this kind of Pool is also the most complex to use. Its inherent complexity derives from the fact that it maintains both a fixed-length queue and two Pool sizes: a **core size** and a **maximum size**.

Each time a new task is submitted, if the number of running Threads is less than the core size, a new Thread is created. Otherwise, if there is room in the queue, the task is queued.

If none of these options are viable, the executor needs to evaluate if it can still create a new Thread. If the number of running Threads is less than the maximum size, a new Thread is created. Otherwise, the `blocking` attribute comes into play. If `blocking` is enabled, the caller blocks until room becomes available in the queue.

If `blocking` is not enabled, the task is assigned to the designated `hand-off` executor, if one is specified. In the absence of a designated `hand-off`, the task will be rejected.

The following image summarizes the whole process, showing how all the pieces fit together:

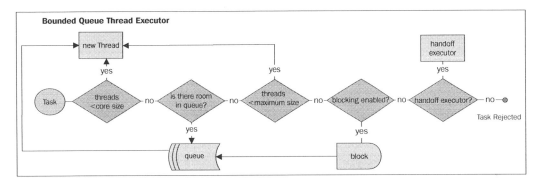

And here's a sample of bounded Thread Pools, which is included in the configuration:

```
<bounded-queue-thread-pool
  name="jca-short-running" blocking="true">
  <core-threads count="10" per-cpu="20"/>
  <queue-length count="10" per-cpu="20"/>
  <max-threads count="10" per-cpu="20"/>
  <keepalive-time time="10" unit="seconds"/>
</bounded-queue-thread-pool>
```

This is a short description of each attribute:

Attribute	Description
name	Specifies the bean name of the created executor
allow-core-timeout	Specifies whether core Threads may time out or not; if false, only Threads above the core size will time out
blocking	Specifies whether the submitter Thread will block if no space is available in this executor
core-threads	Specifies the core Thread Pool size, which is smaller than the maximum Pool size
max-threads	Specifies the maximum Thread Pool size
queue-length	Specifies the executor queue length
keepalive-time	Specifies the amount of time that Threads beyond the core Pool size should be kept running, when idle
thread-factory	Specifies the bean name of a specific Thread factory to use to create worker Threads
handoff-executor	Specifies an executor to delegate tasks to in the event that a task cannot be accepted

Performance focus

Queue size and **Pool size** are two samples of performance trade-off for each other. When using a small Pool with a large queue, you cause to minimize the CPU usage, OS resources, and context-switching overhead. It can, however, produce an artificially low throughput. If tasks are strongly I/O bound (and thus frequently blocked), a system may be able to schedule time for more Threads than you otherwise allow. Use of small queues generally requires larger Pool sizes, which keeps the CPUs busier but may encounter unacceptable scheduling overhead, which also decreases throughput.

Unbounded Thread Pool

This other kind of Thread Pool executor follows a simpler (but more risky!) approach; that is, it always accepts new tasks.

In practice, the unbounded Thread Pool has a core size and a queue with no upper bound. When a task is submitted, if the number of running Threads is less than the core size, a new Thread is created. Otherwise, the task is placed in a queue. If too many tasks are allowed to be submitted to this type of executor, an out of memory condition may occur.

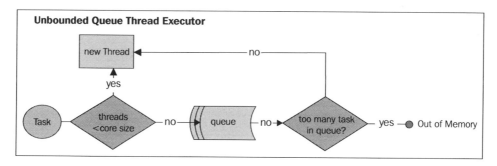

Due to its inherent risk, unbounded Thread Pools are not included by default in the server configuration. We will provide a sample here, with only one recommendation: don't try this at home, kids!

```
<unbounded-queue-thread-pool name="unbounded-threads"   >
   <max-threads count="10" per-cpu="20"/>
   <keepalive-time time="10" unit="seconds"/>
</unbounded-queue-thread-pool>
```

If you want to know more about the meaning of each Thread Pool element, you can refer to the bounded Thread Pool table.

Queueless Thread Pool

As its name implies, this is a Thread Pool executor with no queue. Basically, this executor short-circuits the same logic of the bounded Thread executor, as it does not attempt to store the task in a queue.

So, when a task is submitted, if the number of running Threads is less than the maximum size, a new Thread is created. Otherwise, if `blocking` is enabled, the caller blocks until another Thread completes its task and accepts the new one. If `blocking` is not enabled, the task is assigned to the designated `hand-off` executor, if one is specified. Without any designated `hand-off`, the task will be rejected.

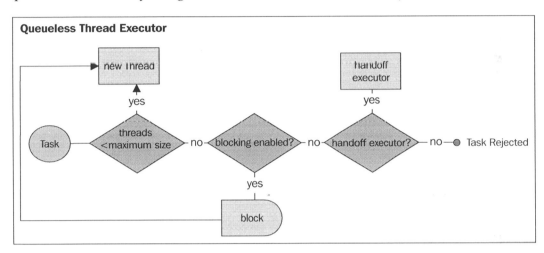

Queueless executors are also not included by default in the configuration file; we will, however, provide a sample configuration here:

```
<queueless-thread-pool
  name="queueless-thread-pool" blocking="true">
  <max-threads count="10" per-cpu="20"/>
  <keepalive-time time="10" unit="seconds"/>
</queueless-thread-pool>
```

Scheduled Thread Pool

The server-scheduled Thread Pool is used for activities on the server-side that require running periodically or with delays. It maps internally to a `java.util.concurrent.ScheduledThreadPoolExecutor` instance.

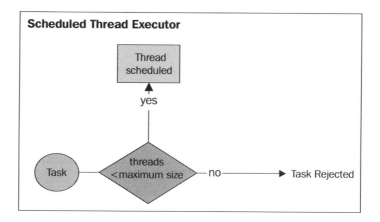

This type of executor is configured with the `scheduled-thread-pool` executor element:

```
<scheduled-thread-pool name="remoting">
  <max-threads count="10" per-cpu="20"/>
  <keepalive-time time="10" unit="seconds"/>
</scheduled-thread-pool>
```

 The scheduled Thread Pool is used by the remoting framework and by HornetQ subsystem, which uses both a bounded JCA Thread executor and a scheduled Pool for delayed delivery.

Configuring the application server logging

Every application needs to trace logging statements. At the moment, there are several implementations of logging libraries for Java applications, the most popular ones are:

- **Log4j**: It is a flexible open source logging library from Apache. Log4j is widely used in the open source community, and it was the default logging implementation on earlier releases of JBoss AS.

- **J2SE logging libraries (JUL)**: It provides the logging classes and interfaces as part of the J2SE platform's standard libraries.

Log4j and JUL are indeed very similar APIs. They differ conceptually only in small details, and in the end do more or less the same thing, except Log4j has more features that you may or may not need.

JBoss logging framework is substantially based on JUL, which is built around three main concepts: **loggers**, **handlers**, and **formatters**. These concepts allow developers to log messages according to their type and priority, to control where messages end up and how they look when they get there.

The following image shows the logging cycle using the JUL framework. **Applications** make logging calls on **Logger** objects. These **Logger** objects allocate LogRecord objects, which are passed to **Handler** objects for publication. Both the **Logger** and the **Handler** may use the **Formatter** to arrange the layout of logs and **Filter** to decide if they are interested in a particular LogRecord.

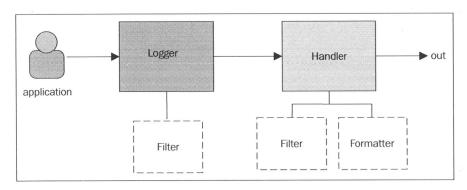

Choosing your logging implementation

JBoss AS, through its releases, has used different frameworks to handle application server logs. In JBoss AS 5 and earlier, log4j was the default logging API used by the application server, and it was defined in the server/<server>/conf/jboss-log4j. xml file.

Since JBoss AS 6, the logging provider switched to JBoss's own implementation, which is based on the JDK 1.4 logging system. However, it provides several fixes or works around many serious problems in the default JDK implementation.

For example, the default implementation of java.util.logging provided in the JDK is too limited to be useful. A limitation of JDK logging is the inability to have per-web application logging, as the configuration is per-VM.

As a result, JBoss AS replaces the default JUL LogManager implementation with its own implementation, which addresses these shortcomings. The following image illustrates the modules that make up the JBoss AS 7 logging subsystem:

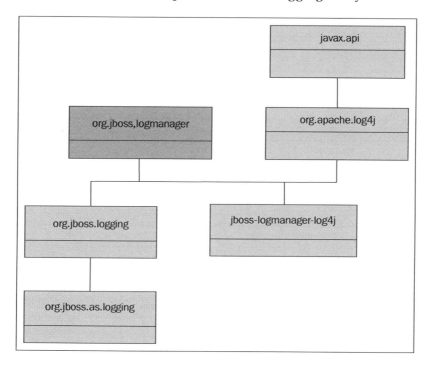

At the top of the hierarchy there's the `org.jboss.logmanager` module, which is the top-level library that manages logs for the `jboss` logging subsystem. Beneath the `jboss logmanager`, you can find the concrete implementations, such as the `org.jboss.logging` or the `jboss-logmanager-log4j` module. By default, the application server uses the former module (`org.jboss.logging`), which is implemented in its turn by `org.jboss.as.logging` to manage your logs inside the application server. However, if you want to switch to `log4j` implementation, the `jboss-logmanager-log4j` module is what you need (in the last section of this chapter, we will include an example of how to use `log4j` in your application).

Configuring the logging subsystem

The logging subsystem contains a set of log handlers out of the box. A handler object takes log messages from a logger and exports them. It might, for example, write them to a console or write them to a file, or send them to a network logging service, or forward them to an OS log, or whatever. By default, the following handlers are defined:

The console-handler

The `console-handler` defines a handler, which simply writes log messages to the console.

```
<console-handler name="CONSOLE" autoflush="true">
  <level name="INFO"/>
  <formatter>
    <pattern-formatter pattern="%d{HH:mm:ss,SSS} %-5p [%c] (%t)
      %s%E%n"/>
  </formatter>
</console-handler>
```

The attributes of the `console-handler` are common to all other handlers. We will shortly describe their meaning here:

The optional `autoflush` attribute determines if buffered logs are flushed automatically. The default value for this option is `true`.

The following element, `level`, defines the log level associated with the handler, ranging from FINEST (lower level) to FATAL (highest value).

Then, the `formatter` element provides support for formatting LogRecords. The log formatting inherits the same pattern strings for layout pattern of `log4j`, which was in turn inspired by dear old C's `printf` function.

For an exhaustive list of logging formats, you can check the `log4j` documentation at `http://logging.apache.org/log4j/1.2/apidocs/org/apache/log4j/PatternLayout.html`.

Here, we will just mention that `%d{HH:mm:ss,SSS}` outputs the date of the logging event using the conversion included in brackets.

- The string `%-5p` will output the priority of the logging event
- The string `[%c]` is used to output the category of the logging event
- The string `(%t)` outputs the Thread that generated the logging event
- The string `%s` outputs the log message
- Finally, the `%n` string outputs the platform-dependent line separator character or characters

The periodic-rotating-file-handler

The `periodic-rotating-file-handler` defines a handler that writes to a file, rotating the log after a time period derived from the given suffix string, which should be in a format understood by `java.text.SimpleDateFormat`.

Here's the definition of it:

```
<periodic-rotating-file-handler name="FILE" autoflush="true">
  <level name="INFO"/>
  <formatter>
    <pattern-formatter pattern="%d{HH:mm:ss,SSS} %-5p [%c] (%t)
      %s%E%n"/>
  </formatter>
  <file relative-to="jboss.server.log.dir" path="server.log"/>
   <suffix value=".yyyy-MM-dd"/>
</periodic-rotating-file-handler>
```

This handler introduces the file element containing the path, which is the actual filename and its `relative-to` position. In our case, the relative position corresponds to the `jboss.server.log.dir` application server parameter.

 With the default suffix configuration, logs are rolled at 12 PM. By changing the `SimpleDateFormat`, you can also change the period when logs are rotated, for example, the suffix `yyyy-MM-dd-HH` will rotate the logs every hour.

The size-rotating-file-handler

The `size-rotating-file-handler` defines a handler that writes to a file, rotating the log after the size of the file grows beyond a certain point. It also keeps a fixed number of backups.

There's no size handler defined in the standard configuration. However, we can find out its basic configuration from the `JBOSS_HOME/docs/schema/jboss-as-logging.xsd` file:

```
<size-rotating-file-handler name="FILESIZE" autoflush="true" >
  <rotate-size value="500k" />
  <level name="INFO"/>
  <formatter>
    <pattern-formatter pattern="%d{HH:mm:ss,SSS} %-5p [%c] (%t)
      %s%E%n"/>
  </formatter>
  <file relative-to="jboss.server.log.dir" path="server.log"/>
</size-rotating-file-handler>
```

The asynchronous handler

The asynchronous handler is a composite handler, which attaches to other handlers to produce asynchronous logging events. Behind the scenes, this handler uses a bounded queue to store events. Every time a log is emitted, the asynchronous handler appends the log into the queue and returns immediately. Here's an example of asynchronous logging for the FILE appender:

```
<async-handler name="ASYNC" >
  <level name="INFO" />
  <queue-length>1024</queue-length>
  <overflow-action>block</overflow-action>
  <sub-handlers>
    <handler-ref name="FILE" />
  </sub-handlers>
</async-handler>
```

In this handler, we are also specifying the size of the queue where events are sent and the action to take when the async queue overflows. You can opt between **blocked** where the calling Thread is blocked, and **discard** where the message will be discarded.

When should I use the asynchronous handler?

The asynchronous handler produces a substantial benefit to applications, which are heavily I/O bound, since an asynchronous logging event might be fired at times where Threads are blocked on intensive I/O operations. At the opposite end, CPU-bound applications might not benefit at all from asynchronous logging as it will put additional stress on the CPU.

Custom handlers

So far, we have seen just a few basic log handlers, which are usually included in your server configuration. If you need a more advanced approach to your logs, you can define a custom logging handlers. In order to add a custom handler, you need to define class that extends the java.util.logging.Handler interface and overrides its abstract methods. For example, this class named JdbcLogger is used to write the logs on a database storage (full code is available at: http://community.jboss.org/wiki/CustomLogHandlersOn701).

```
public class JdbcLogger extends Handler{
  @Override
  public void publish(LogRecord record){
    try{
      insertRecord(record);
```

```
      }
    catch (SQLException e)  {
      e.printStackTrace();
    }
  }
  @Override
  public void flush() {     . . . .      }
  @Override
  public void close() {     . . . .      }
}
```

Once compiled, this class needs to be packaged in an archive (for example, `logger.jar`) and installed as a module into the application server. We will name the module `com.JDBCLogger`, which requires the following structure under the modules folder:

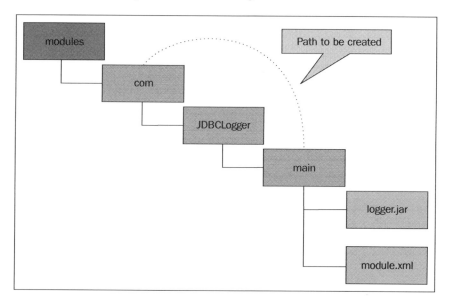

The label **Path to be created** shows off the directory structure under which we will place the **logger.jar** archive and its configuration file (**module.xml**), which follows here:

```xml
<module xmlns="urn:jboss:module:1.0" name="com.JDBCLogger">
  <resources>
    <resource-root path="logger.jar"/>
  </resources>
  <dependencies>
    <module name="javax.api"/>
    <module name="org.jboss.logging"/>
    <module name="com.mysql"/>
  </dependencies>
</module>
```

Please notice that this module has a dependency on another module named `com.mysql`. In the next chapter, we will show how to connect to a database by installing the appropriate module.

We are almost done. Now, insert the handler in the logging subsystem, which contains within its properties the database connection strings and the statement that will be used to insert logs into the database:

```
<custom-handler name="DB" class="com.sample.JdbcLogger"
  module="com.JDBCLogger">
  <level name="INFO"/>
  <formatter>
    <pattern-formatter pattern="%d{HH:mm:ss,SSS} %-5p [%c] (%t)
      %s%E%n"/>
  </formatter>
  <properties>
    <property name="driverClassName" value="com.mysql.jdbc.Driver"/>
    <property name="jdbcUrl"
      value="jdbc:mysql://localhost:3306/mydb"/>
    <property name="username" value="root"/>
    <property name="password" value="admin"/>
    <property name="insertStatement" value="insert into log_table
      values (?, $TIMESTAMP, $LEVEL, $MDC[ip], $MDC[user], $MESSAGE,
      hardcoded)"/>
  </properties>
</custom-handler>
<root-logger>
  <level name="INFO"/>
  <handlers>
    <handler name="CONSOLE"/>
    <handler name="FILE"/>
    <handler name="DB"/>
  </handlers>
</root-logger>
```

The new `handler`, named DB, is enlisted in the `root-logger` to collect all logging statements that have a priority of INFO or above. Before testing the logger, don't forget to create the required tables on your MySql database:

```
CREATE TABLE log_table(
  id INT(11) NOT NULL AUTO_INCREMENT,
  `timestamp` VARCHAR(255) DEFAULT NULL,
  level VARCHAR(255) DEFAULT NULL,
  mdc_ip VARCHAR(255) DEFAULT NULL,
  mdc_user VARCHAR(255) DEFAULT NULL,
  message VARCHAR(1500) DEFAULT NULL,
```

```
  hardcoded VARCHAR(255) DEFAULT NULL,
  PRIMARY KEY (id)
)
ENGINE = INNODB
AUTO_INCREMENT = 1
```

If you have carefully followed all the required steps, you will notice that the
`log_table` contains the logging events that have been triggered since server startup:

id	timestamp	level	mdc_ip	mdc_user	message
40	2011-09-16	INFO	*(null)*	*(null)*	11:35:33,425 INFO [org.jboss.as.connector.subsystems.datasources] (Controller Boot Thread) Deploying JDBC-compliant driver d...
41	2011-09-16	INFO	*(null)*	*(null)*	11:35:33,831 INFO [org.jboss.as.clustering.infinispan.subsystem] (Controller Boot Thread) Activating Infinispan subsystem.
42	2011-09-16	INFO	*(null)*	*(null)*	11:35:34,004 INFO [org.jboss.as.naming] (Controller Boot Thread) Activating Naming Subsystem
43	2011-09-16	INFO	*(null)*	*(null)*	11:35:34,044 INFO [org.jboss.as.naming] (MSC service thread 1-5) Starting Naming Service
44	2011-09-16	INFO	*(null)*	*(null)*	11:35:34,047 INFO [org.jboss.as.osgi] (Controller Boot Thread) Activating OSGi Subsystem
45	2011-09-16	INFO	*(null)*	*(null)*	11:35:34,109 INFO [org.jboss.as.security] (Controller Boot Thread) Activating Security Subsystem
46	2011-09-16	INFO	*(null)*	*(null)*	11:35:34,116 INFO [org.jboss.remoting] (MSC service thread 1-3) JBoss Remoting version 3.2.0.Beta2
47	2011-09-16	INFO	*(null)*	*(null)*	11:35:34,163 INFO [org.xnio] (MSC service thread 1-3) XNIO Version 3.0.0.Beta3
48	2011-09-16	INFO	*(null)*	*(null)*	11:35:34,211 INFO [org.xnio.nio] (MSC service thread 1-3) XNIO NIO Implementation Version 3.0.0.Beta3

Record 6 of 39

Configuring loggers

A **Logger** object is used to log messages for a specific system or application
components. Loggers are normally named, using a hierarchical dot-separated
namespace. Logger names can be arbitrary strings, but they should normally be
based on the package name or class name of the logged component. For example,
the logger instructs the logging system to emit logging statements for the package
`com.sample`, if they have the log level `"WARN"` or higher:

```
<logger category="com.sample">
  <level name="WARN"/>
</logger>
```

At the top of the hierarchy, there's the `root-logger`. It is exceptional in two ways:

- It always exists
- It cannot be retrieved by name

In the default server configuration, the root-logger defines two handlers, which are
connected to the `CONSOLE` and to the `FILE` handler:

```
<root-logger>
  <level name="INFO"/>
  <handlers>
    <handler name="CONSOLE"/>
    <handler name="FILE"/>
  </handlers>
</root-logger>
```

Configuring log4j in your application

So far, we have seen how to configure the application server logs operating on the main configuration file (`standalone.xml`). Chances are, however, that users will want to provide a log configuration on an application basis, using the widely adopted `log4j` framework. This section shows the simple steps needed to adopt `log4j` in your application.

Let's create a basic web application named `LogExample`. For this purpose, you can start a **New Dynamic Web** project from the Eclipse IDE. In order to configure `log4j`, we will need to provide a `log4j` configuration file, which, by default, is named `log4j.properties` or `log4j.xml`, and place it at the root of the Java sources (named `src` in Eclipse).

The following sample, `log4j.properties`, defines two appenders: the first one (`stdout`) prints messages on the console, while the second one(`R`) is connected with a `RollingFileAppender`:

```
log4j.rootLogger=warn, stdout, R

# stdout is set to be a ConsoleAppender.
log4j.appender.stdout=org.apache.log4j.ConsoleAppender

# stdout uses PatternLayout.
log4j.appender.stdout.layout=org.apache.log4j.PatternLayout

# Pattern to output the caller's file name and line number.
log4j.appender.stdout.layout.ConversionPattern=%5p [%t] (%F:%L) - %m%n

# R is set to be a RollingFileAppender.
log4j.appender.R=org.apache.log4j.RollingFileAppender
log4j.appender.R.File=example.log

# Max file size is set to 100KB
log4j.appender.R.MaxFileSize=100KB

# Keep one backup file
log4j.appender.R.MaxBackupIndex=1

# R uses PatternLayout.
log4j.appender.R.layout=org.apache.log4j.PatternLayout
log4j.appender.R.layout.ConversionPattern=%p %t %c - %m%n

log4j.logger.com.packtpub=DEBUG, stdout, R
```

As we said, this file will be placed at the root of your web project, so that when the project is built, it will be moved in the WEB-INF/classes folder of your web application that is visible to the application's classpath.

Additionally, place the log4j libraries in the WEB-INF/lib folder of your application. Here's how the Web application should look:

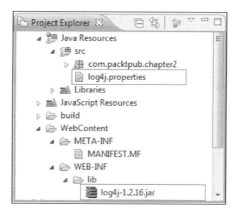

Now, you can add logging statements to your classes, and they will be intercepted by the console appender and by the file appender. For example, the following Servlet prints out the value of the System variable named myproperty, which has been added earlier in the server configuration file:

```
@WebServlet("/LoggerServlet")
public class LoggerServlet extends HttpServlet {
  private static org.apache.log4j.Logger logger =
    org.apache.log4j.Logger.getLogger(LoggerServlet.class);
  protected void doGet(HttpServletRequest request,
    HttpServletResponse response) throws ServletException,
    IOException {
    logger.info("System variable
      myproperty="+System.getProperty("myproperty"));
    PrintWriter out = response.getWriter();
    out.println("The Servlet just logged.");
  }
}
```

Why have we added log4j library to the application?

If you try to deploy your application without the `log4j` library, you will find that the deployer raises a `ClassNotFoundException` on the classes using the `log4j` package. This can be a bit surprising, since `log4j` libraries are indeed included in the application server modules.

The explanation to it is that JBoss AS 7 is not based any more on a hierarchical class loader, but it is entirely based on module classloading. This means that in practice, each deployment unit is itself a module, which is isolated from other modules, such as `.jars` that are included in the application server.

The first good news is that you will not face any more conflicts between the application classes and the server classes, also known with the infamous epithet *classpath hell*.

The second good news is that you can easily override the default (isolating) behavior by simply adding a dependency on other modules installed. For example, in this case, you would need to add a dependency on `org.apache.log4j` module so that `log4j` libraries are automatically linked by your application. *"Chapter 6, Deploying Applications on JBoss AS 7*, which is about deploying applications, covers all the steps required to solve classloader issues.

Summary

In this chapter, we've gone through the basics of the application server configuration, which is now composed by a single monolithic file that contains information about all the services installed.

It is important to stress again that the server configuration will be your main reference to get a full understanding on the new AS infrastructure, although it is recommended to use a management interface to modify parts of it.

So, after a detailed examination of each section, we have covered the Thread Pool configuration, which relies on the J2SE Thread Executor API to define a set of Pools that are used by the application server core services.

Next, we have discussed the JBoss logging framework, which is built around the **Java Util Logging** framework, addressing some known shortcomings of it. We have described how to customize the logging configuration and how to use, as an alternative, the well-known **log4j** framework in your applications.

In the next chapter, we will take a look at some core enterprise services configurations, such as datasource and messaging subsystems, which are the backbone of many enterprise applications.

3
Configuring Enterprise Services

This chapter completes the configuration of the application server, by adding a comprehensive description of the Java Enterprise services that can be run on top of the application server. Each service itself is a core subsystem, which can be included or removed, depending on the kind of applications you are delivering. Here, we will describe the most interesting ones, which have been increasingly adopted by the application server end-users, going in the following order of topics:

- Configure the database connectivity
- Configure the enterprise Java Bean container
- Configure the messaging service
- Configure the transaction service

Configuring database connectivity

In any application server, you can configure database connectivity by adding datasources to your server configuration. Each datasource contains a pool of database connections that are reserved as soon as the server is started up. Applications acquire a database connection from the datasource by looking it up on the JNDI tree and then calling getConnection().

```
Connection result = null;
try {
  Context initialContext = new InitialContext();
  DataSource datasource =
    (DataSource)initialContext.lookup("java:/MySqlDS");
```

```
result = datasource.getConnection();
  }
  catch ( Exception ex ) {
    log("Cannot get connection: " + ex);
  }
```

Once the connection is established, the application should call `connection.close()` as early as possible, which returns the database connection to the pool for other applications to use.

Earlier JBoss AS releases needed a well-known datasource configuration file (ending in `-ds.xml`), which had to be deployed in order to be used by applications. Since the release 7 of JBoss AS, you need to use a different approach, because of the modular nature of the application server.

Out of the box, the application server ships with the H2 open source database engine (`http://www.h2database.com`), which can be used for testing purposes because of its small footprint and its useful browser-based console.

However, a real world application requires an industry standard database, such as Oracle database or MySQL. In the following section, we will show how to configure a datasource for the MySQL database.

Basically, any database configuration requires a two-step procedure:

1. Installing the JDBC driver.
2. Adding the datasource to your configuration.

Let's see each section in detail:

Installing the JDBC driver

In JBoss AS 5 and 6, you used to install the JDBC driver into the `common/lib` folder of your server distribution. In the new modular server architecture, you have more than one option to install your JDBC driver. The first and recommended approach consists of installing the driver as a module.

> In the section named *Installing the driver as a deployment unit*, we will account for another approach, which is usually a bit faster. However, it has a few limitations.

As we have seen in the previous chapter, the procedure for installing a new module requires copying the `.jar` libraries in the appropriate modules path and adding a `module.xml` file, which declares the module and its dependencies.

The actual path for the module will be: JBOSS_HOME/modules/<module>/main

The main folder is where all key module components are installed. So, in our example, we will add the following units:

- JBOSS_HOME/modules/com/mysql/main/mysql-connector-java-5.1.17-bin.jar
- JBOSS_HOME/modules/com/mysql/main/module.xml

Here's an image of the module tree:

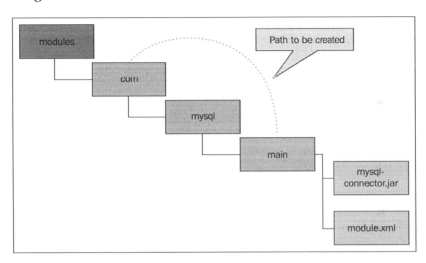

The JDBC driver used in this example, also known as Connector/J can freely be downloaded from the MySQL site: (http://dev.mysql.com/downloads/connector/j/).

The module.xml contains the actual module definition. The most interesting part of it is the module name (com.mysql), which corresponds to the module attribute defined in the your datasource.

Next, you need to state the path to the JDBC driver resource and finally the module dependencies.

```
<module xmlns="urn:jboss:module:1.0" name="com.mysql">
  <resources>
  <resource-root path="mysql-connector-java-5.1.17-bin.jar"/>
  </resources>
  <dependencies>
    <module name="javax.api"/>
    <module name="javax.transaction.api"/>
  </dependencies>
</module>
```

Adding a local datasource

Once the JDBC driver is installed, you need to configure the datasource in the application server. In JBoss AS 7, you can configure two kind of datasources, **local datasources** and **xa-datasources**.

 A local datasource does not support two phase commit using a `java.sql.Driver`. On the other hand, an xa-datasource supports two phase commit using a `javax.sql.XADataSource`.

Adding a datasource definition can be completed in several ways: you can just add the datasource definition within the server configuration file, or you can use the management interfaces that will accurately do the work for you.

Showing all possible approaches in this section would maybe add too much information at once, so we will let you digest at first the most intuitive approach, that is cutting and pasting the datasource definition into your server configuration file. In the *Chapter 7, Managing the Application Server*, which is about server management, we will show the other available options in more detail.

So, here's a sample MySQL datasource configuration:

```
<datasources>
  <datasource jndi-name="java:/MySqlDS" pool-name="MySqlDS_Pool"
    enabled="true" jta="true" use-java-context="true" use-ccm="true">
    <connection-url>
      jdbc:mysql://localhost:3306/MyDB
    </connection-url>
    <driver>mysql</driver>
    <pool />
    <security>
      <user-name>jboss</user-name>
      <password>jboss</password>
    </security>
    <statement/>
    <timeout>
      <idle-timeout-minutes>0</idle-timeout-minutes>
      <query-timeout>600</query-timeout>
    </timeout>
  </datasource>
  <drivers>
    <driver name="mysql" module="com.mysql"/>
  </drivers>
</datasources>
```

As you can see, the new configuration file borrows the same XML schema definition from the earlier `-*.ds.xml` file, so it should not be difficult to migrate to the new configuration. Basically, you would define the connection path to the database using the `connection-url` and the JDBC driver class with the `driver` section.

 Since JBoss AS 7.1.0, it's mandatory that the datasource is bound into the `java:/` or `java:jboss/` JNDI namespace.

The `pool` section can be used to define the JDBC Connection pool properties, leaving in this case to the default values. Then the `security` section lets you configure the connection credentials.

The `statement` section as well is added just as place holder for statement caching options.

The optional `timeout` section contains a set elements, such as the `query-timeout`, which is a static configuration of the maximum of seconds before a query times out. Also the included `idle-timeout-minutes` element indicates the maximum time a connection may be idle before being closed. Setting to `0` disables it. Default is `15` minutes.

Configuring the connection pool

One key aspect of the datasource configuration is the `pool` section. Strictly speaking, in order to use connection pooling, no configuration is required, because without any configuration JBoss AS will choose some default settings. However, if you want to customize how pooling is done, such as to control the size of the pools and which types of connections are pooled, you would be better learning about its available attributes.

Here's an example of pool configuration, which can be added to your datasource configuration:

```
<pool>
  <min-pool-size>5</min-pool-size>
  <max-pool-size>10</max-pool-size>
  <prefill>true</prefill>
  <use-strict-min>true</use-strict-min>
</pool>
```

The attributes included in the `pool` configuration are actually borrowed from earlier releases, so we include them here for your reference:

Attribute	Meaning
min-pool-size	The minimum number of connections in the pool (default 0 - zero)
max-pool-size	The maximum number of connections in the pool (default 20)
prefill	Attempt to pre-fill the connection pool to the minimum number of connections
use-strict-min	Whether idle connections below the min-pool-size should be closed

Configuring the statement cache

For each connection in a connection pool in your system, JBoss AS Server is able to create a statement cache. When a prepared statement or callable statement is used on a connection, JBoss AS caches the statement so that it can be reused. In order to activate the statement cache, you have to specify a value of `prepared-statement-cache-size` greater than `0`:

```
<statement>
  <track-statements>true</track-statements>
  <prepared-statement-cache-size>10</prepared-statement-cache-size>
  <share-prepared-statements/>
</statement>
```

Notice, we have also included the `track-statements` to `true` in the `statement` section, which enable automatic closing of `statements` and `ResultSets`. This is important if you want to use prepared statement caching and/or don't want to leak cursors in your database.

The last element, `share-prepared-statements`, can be used only with prepared statement cache enabled and determine whether the two requests in the same transaction should return the same statement (default `false`).

Adding an xa-datasource

Adding an `xa-datasource` requires some tweaks in the datasource configuration. As a matter of fact, the connection information is now acquired as `xa-datasource` properties. Also the `xa-datasource` class needs to be specified in the driver section.

In the following code, we are adding the equivalent configuration for our MySQL JDBC driver, which now is used to set up an `xa-datasource`:

```
<datasources>
  <xa-datasource jndi-name="java:/XAMySqlDS" pool-name="MySqlDS_Pool"
    enabled="true" use-java-context="true" use-ccm="true">
    <xa-datasource-property name="URL">
      jdbc:mysql://localhost:3306/MyDB
    </xa-datasource-property>
    <xa-datasource-property name="User">jboss
    </xa-datasource-property>
    <xa-datasource-property name="Password">jboss
    </xa-datasource-property>
    <driver>mysql-xa</driver>
  </xa-datasource>
  <drivers>
    <driver name="mysql-xa" module="com.mysql">
      <xa-datasource-class>
        com.mysql.jdbc.jdbc2.optional.MysqlXADataSource
      </xa-datasource-class>
    </driver>
  </drivers>
</datasources>
```

A shortcut for installing a datasource

As we said at the beginning of the book, with the new release of the application server, every library is a module. Thus simply deploying the JDBC driver to the application server will trigger its installation.

When using this option, we will just copy the `mysql-connector-java-5.1.17-bin.jar` driver into the `JBOSS_HOME/standalone/deployments` folder of your installation as shown in the following image:

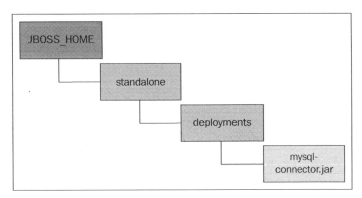

Once deployed, you need to add the datasource configuration to your server. You can do it in various ways. The most intuitive approach is pasting the datasource definition into the configuration file:

```
<datasource jndi-name="java:/MySqlDS" pool-name="MySqlDS_Pool"
  enabled="true" jta="true" use-java-context="true" use-ccm="true">
  <connection-url>
    jdbc:mysql://localhost:3306/MyDB
  </connection-url>
  <driver>mysql-connector-java-5.1.17-bin.jar</driver>
  <pool />
  <security>
    <user-name>jboss</user-name>
    <password>jboss</password>
  </security>
</datasource>
```

Alternatively, you can use the new Command Line Interface or the Web administration console to achieve the same result. *Chapter 7, Managing the Application Server*, details some practical examples of adding datasources using the management interfaces.

What about domain deployment?

In this chapter, we are discussing about the configuration of standalone servers and, as we said, the services configuration can be applied also to domain servers. Domain servers, however, don't have a specified folder which is scanned for deployment, rather the management interfaces are used to inject resources in the domain. *Chapter 5, Configuring a JBoss AS Domain*, will detail all the steps to deploy a module when using a domain server.

Choosing the right driver deployment strategy

At this point, you might wonder which is the best practice for deploying the JDBC driver. Actually, installing the driver as a deployment unit is an handy shortcut, however, it has a couple of limitations that might limit is usage within development bounds. At first, it requires a JDBC 4-compliant driver.

Deploying a non JDBC 4-compliant driver is, however, possible and it just requires a simple patching procedure. Create a `META-INF/services` structure containing the file `java.sql.Driver`. The content of the file will be the driver name, for example, supposing you had to patch a MySQL driver, the content will be: `com.mysql.jdbc.Driver`

Once you have created your structure, you can update your JDBC driver with any zipping utility or the `.jar` command: `jar -uf your-jdbc-driver.jar META-INF/services/java.sql.Driver`

Most current JDBC drivers are JDBC 4-compliant, although curiously, not everyone is recognized as such by the application server. The following table describes some of the most used drivers and their JDBC compliance:

DB	Driver	JDBC 4 compliant	Contains java. sql.Driver
MySQL	`mysql-connector-java-5.1.17-bin.jar`	Yes, though not recognized compliant by AS 7	Yes
PostgreSQL	`postgresql-9.1-901.jdbc4.jar`	Yes, though not recognized compliant by AS 7	Yes
Oracle	`ojdbc6.jar` / `ojdbc5.jar`	Yes	Yes
Oracle	`ojdbc4.jar`	No	No

As you can see, the most notable exception to the list of drivers is the older Oracle `ojdbc4.jar`, which is not JDBC 4-compliant and does not contain the driver info in `META-INF/services/java.sql.Driver`.

The second issue with driver deployment is related to the specific case of `xa-datasources`. As a matter of fact, by installing the driver as deployment means that the application server by itself cannot deduct the information about the `xa-datasource` class used in the driver. Since this information is not contained inside the `META-INF/services`, you are forced to specify information about the `xa-datasource` class for each `xa-datasource` you are going to create.

If you recall the earlier example, where we installed a driver as a module, the `xa-datasource` class information can be shared for all installed datasources.

```
<driver name="mysql-xa" module="com.mysql">
  <xa-datasource-class>
    com.mysql.jdbc.jdbc2.optional.MysqlXADataSource
  </xa-datasource-class>
</driver>
```

So, in definitive, if you are not too limited by these issues, installing the driver as deployment is a handy shortcut, which can be adopted in your development environment or as well, if you feel more adventurous, also in production.

Configuring a datasource programmatically

For the happiness of programmers, we will account for one more option to configure a datasource which requires zero file configuration. In fact, one cool feature of Java EE 6 is support for configuring a datasource programmatically, which can be done through the @DataSourceDefinition annotation:

```
@DataSourceDefinition(name = "java:/OracleDS",
  className = " oracle.jdbc.OracleDriver",
  portNumber = 1521,
  serverName = "192.168.1.1",
  databaseName = "OracleSID",
  user = "scott",
  password = "tiger",
  properties = {"createDatabase=create"})
@Singleton
public class DataSourceEJB {
  @Resource(lookup = "java:/OracleDS")
  private DataSource ds;
}
```

In this example, we have defined a DataSource for an Oracle database into a Singleton EJB 3.1. It's important to note that when configuring a datasource programmatically, you will actually bypass JCA, which proxies requests between the client and the connection pool.

The advantage of this approach is that you might obviously move your application from one application server to another without the need of re-configuring its datasources. On the other hand, by using JBoss' own datasource configuration, you will be able to leverage a larger set of options and tweaks, which are required for many kinds of application.

Configuring Enterprise Java Beans

The **Enterprise Java Bean (EJB)** container is a fundamental part of the Java Enterprise architecture. In a nutshell, the EJB container provides the environment used to host and manage the EJB components deployed in the container. The container is responsible for providing a standard set of services, including caching, concurrency, persistence, security, transaction management, and locking services.

The container also provides distributed access and lookup functions for hosted components, and it intercepts all method invocations on hosted components to enforce declarative security and transaction contexts.

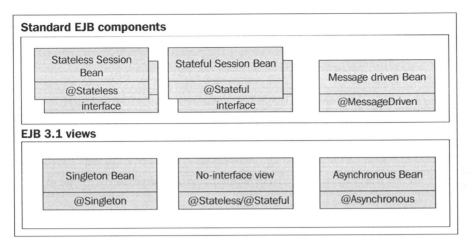

As depicted in this image, with JBoss AS 7, you will be able to deploy a rich set of EJB components:

- **Stateless session beans (SLSB)**: SLSB are objects whose instances have no conversational state. This means that all bean instances are equivalent when they are not servicing a client.

- **Stateful session beans (SFSB)**: SFSB support conversational services with tightly coupled clients. A stateful session bean accomplishes a task for a particular client. It maintains state for the duration of a client session. After session completion, state is not retained.

- **Message-driven beans (MDB)**: MDB are a kind of Enterprise Beans that are able to asynchronously process messages sent by any JMS producer.

 EJB components, which don't keep conversional states (SLSB, MDB), can be optionally configured to emit timed notifications. See the section named *Configuring the timer service* for more information about it.

Besides the standard EJB components, the application server also supports the new EJB 3.1 variants introduced by Java EE 6, which are:

- **Singleton EJB**: This is essentially similar to a stateless session bean, however, it uses a single instance to serve the client requests. Thus, you are guaranteed to use the same instance across invocations. Singletons can use a richer life-cycle set of events and a stricter locking policy to control concurrent access to the instance. In the next chapter, which is about Web applications, we will illustrate a Java EE 6 application that makes use of a Singleton to hold some cached data.

- **No-interface EJB**: This is just another view of the standard session bean except that local clients do not require a separate interface, that is, all public methods of the bean class are automatically exposed to the caller.

- **Asynchronous EJB**: These are able to process client requests asynchronously just like MDBs, except that they expose a typed interface and follow a more complex approach for processing client requests, which is composed of:

  ° `fire-and-forget` asynchronous void methods, which are invoked by the client

  ° `retrieve-result-later` asynchronous methods having `Future<?>Return` type

 In the next chapter, which is about Web applications, we will illustrate a Java EE 6 application, which makes uses of a **Singleton** to hold some cached data.

Configuring the EJB components

Now that we have shortly resumed the basic types of EJB, we will enter in the specific details of the application server configuration. We will therefore examine the following components:

- The SLSB configuration
- The SFSB configuration
- The MDB configuration
- The Timer service configuration

Let's see them all in detail:

Configuring Stateless Session Beans

By default, no Stateless Session Bean instances exist in JBoss AS at start-up time. As individual beans are invoked, the EJB container initializes new SLSB instances.

These instances are maintained in a free pool, which will be used to service EJB method calls. The EJB remains active for the duration of the client's method call. After the method completes, the EJB instance is returned to the free pool. Because the EJB container unbinds Stateless Session Beans from clients after each method call, the actual bean class instance that a client uses may be different from invocation to invocation.

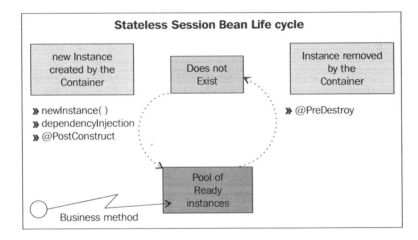

If all instances of an EJB class are active and the pool's `max-pool-size` has been reached, new clients requesting the EJB class will be blocked until an active EJB completes a method call. Depending on how you have configured your stateless pool, an acquisition timeout can be triggered, if you are not able to acquire an instance from the pool within a maximum time.

You can either configure your Session Pool through your main configuration file or programmatically. Let's see both approaches:

EJB are part of the `ejb3.1.2` subsystems; in order to configure your pool, you can operate on two parameters: the **maximum size of the pool** (`max-pool-size`)and the **instance acquisition timeout** (`instance-acquisition-timeout`). Let's see an example:

```
<subsystem xmlns="urn:jboss:domain:ejb3:1.2">
 <session-bean>
  <stateless>
   <bean-instance-pool-ref pool-name="slsb-strict-max-pool"/>
  </stateless>
  . . . . . . . . . .
 </session-bean>
  . . . . . . . . . . .
 <pools>
  <bean-instance-pools>
   <strict-max-pool name="slsb-strict-max-pool" max-pool-size=
   "25" instance-acquisition-timeout="5" instance-acquisition-
   timeout-unit="MINUTES"/>
  </bean-instance-pools>
 </pools>
  . . . . . . . . . .
</subsystem>
```

In this example, we have configured the SLSB pool with a **strict** upper limit of 25 elements. The strict pool implementation is the only available at the time of writing, and it allows a fixed number of concurrent requests to run at one time. If there are more requests running than the pool's strict size, those requests will block until an instance becomes available. Within the pool configuration, we have also set an `instance-acquisition-timeout` of 5 minutes, which will come into play if your requests are larger than the pool size.

You can configure as many pools as you like; the pool which will be used by the EJB container is indicated by the attribute `pool-name` of the `bean-instance-pool-ref` element. For example, here we have added one more pool configuration named `largepool`, and set it as the EJB container's pool implementation:

```
<subsystem xmlns="urn:jboss:domain:ejb3:1.2">
  <session-bean>
    <stateless>
   <bean-instance-pool-ref pool-name="large-pool"/>
    </stateless>
  </session-bean>
  <pools>
    <bean-instance-pools>
 <strict-max-pool name="large-pool" max-pool-size="100" instance-
 acquisition-timeout="5" instance-acquisition-timeout-
 unit="MINUTES"/>
    <strict-max-pool name="slsb-strict-max-pool" max-pool-size="25"
      instance-acquisition-timeout="5" instance-acquisition-timeout-
      unit="MINUTES"/>
    </bean-instance-pools>
  </pools>
</subsystem>
```

Using the CLI to configure the Stateless pool size

We have detailed the steps necessary to configure the SLSB pool size, through the main configuration file. However, the suggested best practice is to use the Command Line Interface to alter the server model.

Here's how you can add a new pool named `large-pool` to your EJB 3 sub-system:

```
/subsystem=ejb3/strict-max-bean-instance-pool=large-pool:add(max-pool-
  size=100)
```

Now you can set this pool as the default used by the EJB container:

```
/subsystem=ejb3:write-attribute(name=default-slsb-instance-pool,
  value=large-pool)
```

Finally, you can, at any time, change the pool size property by operating on the `max-pool-size` attribute:

```
/subsystem=ejb3/strict-max-bean-instance-pool=large-pool:write-
  attribute(name="max-pool-size",value=50)
```

Configuring Stateful session beans

SFSB are bound to particular client instances: the application server uses a cache to store active EJB instances in memory, so that they are immediately available for client requests. The cache contains EJBs that are currently in use by a client and instances that were recently in use.

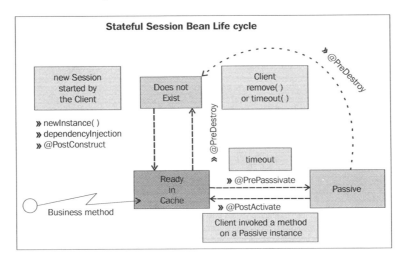

Having EJBs in memory is a costly operation, so you should move as soon as possible out of it, either by passivating them or removing them.

Passivation is a process by which the EJB container ensures that idle SFSB instances are freed from the cache, but save their state on disk.

Removing a bean from the cache, on the other hand, is a process, which can be either triggered by the user or by the EJB container. When triggered by the user, it is accomplished by adding a @javax.ejb.Remove annotation on a method of your EJBs, which will actually remove the EJB when invoked:

```
@Remove
public void remove() {}
```

At the moment, the configuration tweaks available for the stateful session beans include just the access timeout for the stateful instances.

```
<subsystem xmlns="urn:jboss:domain:ejb3:1.2">
  <session-bean>
  . . . . . . .
   <stateful default-access-timeout="5000"/>
  </session-bean>
  . . . . . .
</subsystem>
```

However, thanks to the help of the JBoss Team, and in particular of Paul Ferraro, we are able to share a preview of the Stateful cache configuration in AS 7 future releases. Cache definitions in AS 7.1 will be defined within the ejb3.1 subsystem. Within the definition of a cache, you'll have the option to specify a passivation store, which can optionally define a **max-size**.

```
<subsystem xmlns="urn:jboss:domain:ejb3:1.2">
  <session-bean>
   <stateful default-access-timeout="5000" cache-ref=
   "passivating" clustered-cache-ref="clustered"/>
  </session-bean>
  . . . . . . . . . . .
  <caches>
   <cache name="simple"/>
   <cache name="passivating" passivation-store-ref="file"/>
   <cache name="clustered" passivation-store-ref="infinispan"/>
  </caches>
  <passivation-stores>
   <file-passivation-store name="file" max-size="500" />
   <cluster-passivation-store name="infinispan" backing-cache=
   "sfsb" max-size="500"/>
  </passivation-stores>
  . . . . . . . . . . .
</subsystem>
```

As you can see, the stateful bean element references a cache definition, which in turn is connected with a passivation-store. In this configuration example, the file-based passivating cache is used for non-clustered SFSBs. Notice the optional max-size attribute which limits the amount of SFSB which can be contained in the cache. On the other hand, the clustered cache is backed by infinispan's cluster-passivation-store. (See *Chapter 8* for more information about Infinispan Cache).

Configuring the message driven beans

Message-driven beans (**MDBs**) are stateless, server-side, transaction-aware components for processing asynchronous JMS messages.

 One of the most important aspects of MDBs is that they can consume and process messages concurrently.

This capability provides a significant advantage over traditional JMS clients, which must be custom-built to manage resources, transactions, and security in a multithreaded environment.

Just as the session beans have well-defined life cycles, so does the MDB bean. The MDB instance's life cycle is pretty much the same as the stateless bean. In fact, it's divided in two states: **Does not Exist** and **Method ready Pool**.

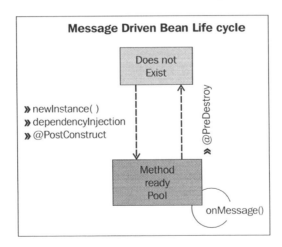

When a message is received, the EJB container checks to see if any MDB instance is available in the pool. If a bean is available in the free pool, JBoss uses that instance. After an MDB instance's `onMessage()` method returns, the request is complete, and the instance it is placed back in the free pool. This results in the best response time, as the request is served without waiting for a new instance to be created.

If no bean instances are handy, the container checks if there is room for more MDB in the pool by comparing the MDB's MaxSize attribute with the pool size.

If MaxSize still has not been reached, a new MDB is initialized. The creation sequence, as pointed out in the image, is just the same as stateless bean. Failure to create a new instance, on the other hand, will imply that the request will be blocked until an active MDB completes. If the request cannot acquire an instance from the pool within the instance-acquisition-timeout, an exception is thrown

The configuration of the MDB pool is exactly the same as for the SLSB, so we will just include it here without further explanations:

```
<subsystem xmlns="urn:jboss:domain:ejb3:1.2">
  <mdb>
    <resource-adapter-ref resource-adapter-name="hornetq-ra"/>
    <bean-instance-pool-ref pool-name="mdb-strict-max-pool"/>
  </mdb>
  <pools>
    <bean-instance-pools>
      <strict-max-pool name="mdb-strict-max-pool" max-pool-size="20"
        instance-acquisition-timeout="5"
        instance-acquisition-timeout-unit="MINUTES"/>
    </bean-instance-pools>
  </pools>
</subsystem>
```

Configuring the Timer service

Applications with business processes, which are dependent on periodic notifications, can use the EJB 3 Timer service that provides a way to allow methods to be invoked at specific times or time intervals.

The EJB Timer service can be attached to any EJB 3 type, except for Stateful session beans and requires as little as setting a method marked with the @javax.ejb. Timeout annotation, which will be triggered by the container when the time interval expires.

The following example shows how to implement a very simple timer, which will be set on the client side by invoking the scheduleTimer(long milliseconds)

```
import java.util.Date;
import javax.annotation.Resource;
import javax.ejb.*;
@Stateless

// Remote interface TimerSample omitted for brevity
public class TimerSampleBean implements TimerSample{
```

```
  private @Resource SessionContext ctx;

  public void scheduleTimer(long milliseconds){
    ctx.getTimerService().createTimer(new Date(new Date().getTime() +
      milliseconds), "Hello World");
  }

@Timeout
  public void timeoutHandler(Timer timer){
    System.out.println("* Received Timer event: " + timer.getInfo());
    timer.cancel();
  }
}
```

As far as it concerns the configuration, you can define the `data-store` path, that is temporary file system path where planned executions are stored and the amount of threads to reserve to the timer service with the `thread-pool-name` attribute, which needs to reference a `thread-pool` element:

```
<subsystem xmlns="urn:jboss:domain:ejb3:1.2">
  <timer-service thread-pool-name="default">
    <data-store path="timer-service-data" relative-
      to="jboss.server.data.dir"/>
  </timer-service>
  <thread-pools>
    <thread-pool name="default" max-threads="10" keepalive-
      time="100"/>
  </thread-pools>
</subsystem>
```

Configuring the messaging system

Message oriented middleware has been an integral part of the application server, since the first releases of the application server. Messaging systems allow you to loosely couple heterogeneous systems together, whilst typically providing reliability, transactions, and many other features.

 In the current release of the application server (7.0.2), the messaging subsystem is included in a separate configuration file named `standalone-preview.xml`. Starting from the release 7.1.0 of the application server, the messaging sub-system will be included in the configuration file named `standalone-full.xml`.

Messaging systems normally support two main styles of asynchronous messaging: **Queue messaging** (also known as point-to-point messaging) and **Publish-Subscribe messaging**.

In the point-to-point model, a sender posts messages to a particular queue and a receiver reads messages from the queue. Here, the sender knows the destination of the message and posts the message directly to the receiver's queue.

On the other hand, the publish/subscribe model supports publishing messages to a particular message topic. Subscribers may register interest in receiving messages on a particular message topic. In this model, neither the publisher nor the subscriber know about each other.

The following table shows the characteristics of the two different paradigms:

Point-to-point messaging	Publish/Subscribe
Only one consumer gets the message.	Multiple consumers (or none) will receive the message.
The producer does not have to be running at the time the consumer consumes the message, nor does the consumer need to be running at the time the message is sent. Every message successfully processed is acknowledged by the consumer.	The publisher has to create a message topic for clients to subscribe. The subscriber has to remain continuously active to receive messages, unless it has established a durable subscription. In that case, messages published while the subscriber is not connected will be redistributed whenever it reconnects.

JBoss AS has used different JMS implementations across its releases. Since release 6.0, the default JMS provider is HornetQ (`http://www.jboss.org/hornetq`), which provides a multi-protocol, embeddable, very high performance, clustered, asynchronous messaging system.

 At its core, HornetQ is designed simply as set of **Plain Old Java Objects (POJOs)**, with few dependencies on external jars. In fact, the only one jar dependency is the Netty library which leverages the Java **New Input-Output (NIO)** API for building high-performance network applications.

Because of its easily-adaptable architecture, HornetQ can be embedded in your own project, or instantiated in any dependency injection framework, such as JBoss Microcontainer, Spring, or Google Guice.

In this book, we will cover the scenario where HornetQ is integrated into JBoss AS subsystem as a module. The following image shows how the HornetQ server fits in the overall picture:

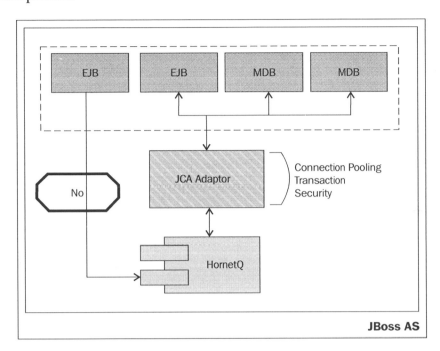

As you can see, a key part of the HornetQ integration is the **JCA Adaptor** that handles the communication between the application server and the HornetQ Server.

Why we cannot simply connect your resources (say your EJB) to HornetQ server?

This is theoretically possible, however, it violates Java EE specifications and will cause the loss of many benefits. As a matter of fact, the application server's JCA layer provides extra functionality, such as connection pooling and automatic transaction enlistment, which are desirable when using messaging, say, from inside an EJB. For a description of JCA Thread pooling configuration, refer to the section of this chapter named *Bounded Thread pool*.

Configuring the transport

Configuring the transport of JMS Message is a key part of the messaging system tuning. Out of the box, HornetQ currently uses Netty as its high-performance low-level network library. Netty is a NIO client server framework, which enables quick and easy development of network applications, such as **protocol servers** and **clients**. It greatly simplifies and streamlines network programming, such as TCP and UDP socket server.

One of the most important concepts in HornetQ transports is the definition of acceptors and connectors.

An **acceptor** defines which type of connection is accepted by the HornetQ server. On the other hand a **connector** defines how to connect to a HornetQ server. The connector is used by a HornetQ client.

HornetQ defines two types of acceptor/connector:

- **invm**: This type can be used when both HornetQ client and server run in the same **Virtual Machine (invm for Intra Virtual Machine)**

- **netty**: This type must be used when HornetQ client and server run in different virtual machines (this connector type uses the netty project to handle the IO)

    To communicate, a HornetQ client must use a connector compatible with the server's acceptor. A compatible client-server communication requires that it is carried on using the same type of acceptor/connector, as shown by the following image:

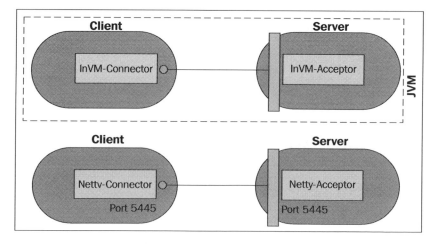

So, for example, it's not possible to connect an **InVM** client connector to a Netty server acceptor. On the other hand, it's possible to connect a Netty client connector to a Netty server acceptor, provided they are configured to run on the same host and port.

JBoss AS 7 comes with a preconfigured acceptor/connector pair, which is part of the JBoss messaging subsystem. We include them here:

```
<acceptors>
  <in-vm-acceptor name="in-vm" server-id="0"/>
  <netty-acceptor name="netty" socket-binding="messaging"/>
  <netty-acceptor name="netty-throughput" socket-binding="messaging-
    throughput">
    <param key="batch-delay" value="50"/>
    <param key="direct-deliver" value="false"/>
  </netty-acceptor>
</acceptors>
<connectors>
  <in-vm-connector name-"in-vm" server id="0"/>
  <netty-connector name="netty" socket-binding="messaging"/>
  <netty-connector name="netty-throughput" socket-binding="messaging-
    throughput">
    <param key="batch-delay" value="50"/>
  </netty-connector>
</connectors>
```

As you can see, besides the `in-vm` acceptor/connector pair, each section defines two kinds of acceptors/connectors: one which relies on Netty defaults, named `netty` and another one (`netty-throughput`), which is specialized for higher messaging throughputs.

You can further tune Netty TCP transport with a complete knowledge of the single parameters, which can be added to the acceptor/connector section. Here's a comprehensive list of all parameters and their meaning:

Parameter	Description
use-nio	If this is `true`, then Java non-blocking NIO will be used. If set to `false`, then old blocking Java IO will be used. Default is `true`.
host	This specifies the host name or IP address to connect to (when configuring a connector) or to listen on (when configuring an acceptor). The default value for this property is `localhost`. Multiple hosts or IP addresses can be specified by separating them with commas.
port	This specifies the port to connect to (when configuring a connector) or to listen on (when configuring an acceptor). The default value for this property is `5445`.
tcp-no-delay	If this is `true`, then Nagle's algorithm will be disabled. The default value for this property is `true`.
tcp-send-buffer-size	This parameter determines the size of the TCP send buffer in bytes. The default value for this property is `32768` bytes.
tcp-receive-buffer-size	This parameter determines the size of the TCP receive buffer in bytes. The default value for this property is `32768` bytes.
batch-delay	This parameter lets you configure HornetQ, so that messages are batched up writes for a maximum of batch-delay milliseconds, before sending them to the transport. This can increase overall throughput for very small messages. The default value for this property is `0` ms.
direct-deliver	This parameter lets you configure if message delivery is done using the same thread as the one that carried the message. Setting this to `true` (default), reduces the thread context switch's latency at the expense of message throughput. If your goal is a higher throughput, set this parameter to `false`.
nio-remoting-threads	When using NIO, HornetQ will, by default, use a number of threads equal to three times the number of core processors for processing incoming packets. If you want to override this value, you can set the number of threads, by specifying this parameter. The default value for this parameter is `-1`, which means use the value from `Runtime.getRuntime().availableProcessors() * 3`.

One frequent source of confusion among HornetQ users is why connectors are included in the server configuration if the server is in charge to accept connections and deliver messages. There are two main reasons for this:

1. Sometimes the server acts as a client itself when it connects to another server, for example, when one server is bridged to another, or when a server takes part in a cluster. In these cases, the server needs to know how to connect to other servers. That's defined by connectors.

2. If you're using JMS and the server-side JMS services to instantiate JMS ConnectionFactory instances and bind them in JNDI, then when creating the HornetQConnectionFactory it needs to know what server that connection factory will create connections to.

Configuring connection factories

The definition of connection-factory instances is included in the default server configuration:

```
<connection-factory name="InVmConnectionFactory">
  <connectors>
    <connector-ref connector-name="in-vm" backup-connector-
      name="netty"/>
  </connectors>
  <entries>
    <entry name="java:/ConnectionFactory"/>
  </entries>
</connection-factory>
<connection-factory name="RemoteConnectionFactory">
  <connectors>
    <connector-ref connector-name="netty"
      backup-connector-name="in-vm"/>
  </connectors>
  <entries>
    <entry name="RemoteConnectionFactory"/>
  </entries>
</connection-factory>
```

A JMS ConnectionFactory object is used by the client to make connections to the server. You can find two Connection factory definitions:

1. InVmConnectionFactory: This connection factory is bound under the entry java:/ConnectionFactory, and is used when server and client are part of the same process (that is, they are running in the same JVM).

2. `RemoteConnectionFactory`: This connection factory, as the name implies, can be used when JMS connections are provided by a remote server, using Netty as connector.

Configuring JMS destinations

Along with the definition of connection factories in the JMS subsystem, you can find the JMS destinations (**Queues** and Topics), which are part of the server distribution:

```
<jms-queue name="testQueue">
  <entry name="queue/test"/>
</jms-queue>
<jms-topic name="testTopic">
  <entry name="topic/test"/>
</jms-topic>
```

This `name` attribute of `queue` defines the name of the `queue`. At JMS level, the actual name of the `queue` follows a naming convention, so it will be `jms.queue.testQueue`.

The `entry` element configures the name that will be used to bind the queue to JNDI. This is a mandatory element and the `queue` can contain multiple of these to bind the same `queue` to different names.

So, for example, here's how you would configure a `MessageDrivenBean` component to consume messages from the `"queue/test"` Queue:

```
@MessageDriven(name = "MessageMDBSample", activationConfig = {
  @ActivationConfigProperty(propertyName = "destinationType",
    propertyValue = "javax.jms.Queue"),
  @ActivationConfigProperty(propertyName = "destination",
    propertyValue = " queue/test"),
  @ActivationConfigProperty(propertyName = "acknowledgeMode",
    propertyValue = "Auto-acknowledge") })
public class SampleMDBean implements MessageListener {
  @Resource
  private MessageDrivenContext context;
}
```

Why it's useful to know the actual destination name?

Apparently it seems not important at all to know the server's destination name (in the example `jms.queue.testQueue`). Rather, we would be concerned about the JNDI entry where the destination is bound. However, the actual destination name plays an important role if you want to define some properties across a set of destinations. See the next section *Customizing destinations with address settings.*

Queues and topics definitions can optionally include some non-mandatory elements, such as `selector` and `durable`:

```
<jms-queue name="selectorQueue">
    <entry name="/queue/selectorQueue"/>
    <selector>name='john'</selector>
    <durable>true</durable>
</jms-queue>
```

The `selector` element defines what JMS message selector the pre-defined `queue` will have. Only messages that match the `selector` will be added to the `queue`. This is an optional element with a default value of `null` when omitted.

The `durable` element specifies whether the `queue` will be persisted. This again is optional and defaults to `true`, if omitted.

Customizing destinations with address settings

If you want to provide some custom settings for JMS destinations, you can use the `address-setting` block, which can be applied both to a single destination and to a set of them. The default configuration applies a set of minimal attributes to all destinations:

```
<address-settings>
  <!--default for catch all-->
  <address-setting match="#">
    <dead-letter-address>jms.queue.DLQ</dead-letter-address>
    <expiry-address>jms.queue.ExpiryQueue</expiry-address>
    <redelivery-delay>0</redelivery-delay>
    <max-size-bytes>10485760</max-size-bytes>
    <message-counter-history-day-limit>10</message-counter-history-
      day-limit>
    <address-full-policy>BLOCK</address-full-policy>
  </address-setting>
</address-settings>
```

Here is a brief description of the addresses settings:

Address-setting's `match` attribute defines a filter for the destinations. When using the wildcard "#", the properties will be valid across all destinations. Other examples:

```
<address-setting match="jms.queue.#">
```

The settings would apply to all queues defined in the `destination` section.

```
<address-setting match="jms.queue.testQueue ">
```

The settings would apply to the queue named `jms.queue.testQueue`.

A short description of the destination's properties follows here:

Property	Description
`dead-letter-address`	Specifies the destination for messages that could not be delivered.
`expiry-address`	Defines where to send a message that has expired.
`redelivery-delay`	Defines how long to wait before attempting re-delivery of a cancelled message.
`max-size-bytes`	The maximum size of the message in bytes ,before entering the `page` mode.
`page-size-bytes`	The size of each page file used on the paging system.
`max-delivery-attempts`	Defines how many time a cancelled message can be re-delivered, before sending to the `dead-letter-address`.
`message-counter-history-day-limit`	Specifies how many days the message counter history will be kept.
`address-full-policy`	It will be used when a destination max size is reached. When set to PAGE, further messages will be paged to disk. If the value is DROP, further messages will be silently dropped. When BLOCK is used, client messages producers will block when they try to send further messages.

HornetQ persistence configuration

The last piece of information we need to cover is about message persistence. HornetQ has its own optimized persistence engine, which can be further tuned when you know all about its building blocks.

The secret of HornetQ's high-data persistence consists in appending data to the journal files, instead of using the costly random access operations which requires a higher degree of disk-head movement

Journal files are pre-created and filled with padding characters at runtime. By pre-creating files, as one is filled, the journal can immediately resume with the next one without pausing to create it.

The following is the default journal configuration, which ships with JMS subsystem:

```
<journal-file-size>102400</journal-file-size>
<journal-min-files>2</journal-min-files>
<journal-type>NIO</journal-type>
<persistence-enabled>false</persistence-enabled>
```

The default `journal-file-size` (expressed in bytes) is `100` KB. The minimum number of files the journal will maintain is indicated by the property `journal-min-files`, which states that at least two files will be maintained.

The property `journal-type` indicates the type of input/output libraries used for data persistence. Valid values are `NIO` or `ASYNCIO`.

Choosing `NIO` sets the Java NIO journal. Choosing `AIO` sets the Linux asynchronous IO journal. If you choose `AIO` but are not running Linux or you do not have `libaio` installed, then HornetQ will detect this and automatically fall back to using `NIO`.

The property `persistence-enabled` when set to `false`, will disable message persistence. That means no bindings data, message data, large message data, duplicate ID caches, or paging data will be persisted. Disabling data persistence will give to your applications a remarkable performance boost, however, the other side of it is your data messaging will inevitably lose reliability.

For the sake of completeness, we include some additional properties that can be included if you want to customize the messages/paging and journal storage directories:

```
<bindings-directory relative-to="jboss.server.data.dir"
  path="hornetq/bindings" />

<large-messages-directory relative-to="jboss.server.data.dir"
  path="hornetq/largemessages" />

<paging-directory relative-to="jboss.server.data.dir"
  path="hornetq/paging" />

<journal-directory relative-to="jboss.server.data.dir"
  path="hornetq/journal" />
```

For the best performance, we recommend the journal be located on its own physical volume in order to minimize disk-head movement. If the journal is on a volume that is shared with other processes, which might be writing other files (for example, bindings journal, database, or transaction coordinator), then the disk-head may be well moving rapidly between these files as it writes them, thus drastically reducing performance.

Configuring transactions

A transaction can be defined as a group of operations that must be performed as a unit and can involve persisting data objects, sending a message, and so on.

When the operations in a transaction are performed across databases or other resources that reside on separate computers or processes, this is known as a distributed transaction. Such enterprise-wide transactions require special coordination between the resources involved and can be extremely difficult to program reliably. This is where **Java Transaction API (JTA)** comes in, providing the interface that resources can implement and to which they can bind, in order to participate in a distributed transaction.

The EJB container is a transaction manager that supports JTA and so can participate in distributed transactions involving other EJB containers, as well as third-party JTA resources, such as many database management systems.

Within JBoss AS 7 transactions are configured in their own subsystem. The transactions subsystem consists mainly of four elements:

- Core environment
- Recovery-environment
- Coordinator-environment
- Object-store

The core environment includes the `TransactionManager` interface, which allows the application server to control the transaction boundaries on behalf of the resource being managed.

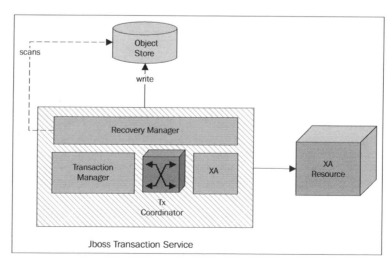

A transaction coordinator, in turn, manages communication with transactional objects and resources that participate in transactions.

The recovery subsystem of JBossTS ensures that results of a transaction are applied consistently to all resources affected by the transaction, even if any of the application processes or the machine hosting them crashes or loses network connectivity.

Within the transaction service, JBoss transaction service uses an `ObjectStore` to persistently record the outcomes of transactions, for failure recovery. As a matter of fact, the `RecoveryManager` scans the `ObjectStore` and other locations of information, looking for transactions and resources that require, or may require, recovery.

The core and recovery environment can be customized by changing their socket-binding properties, which are referenced in the socket-binding-group configuration section.

You might find it more useful to define custom properties in the coordinator-environment section, which might include the default-timeout and logging statistics. Here's a sample custom transaction configuration:

```
<subsystem xmlns="urn:jboss:domain:transactions:1.0">
  <core-environment>
    <process-id>
      <uuid/>
    </process-id>
  </core-environment>
  <recovery-environment socket-binding="txn-recovery-environment"
    status-socket-binding="txn-status-manager"/>
  <coordinator-environment default-timeout="300" enable-
  statistics="true" />
  <object-store/>
</subsystem>
```

`default-timeout` specifies the default transaction timeout to be used for new transactions, which is specified as an integer in seconds.

`enable-statistics` determines whether or not the transaction service should gather statistical information. The default is to not gather this information.

How does the transaction timeout impact your applications?

The transaction timeout defines the timeout for all JTA transaction enlisted and thus severely affects your application behavior. A typical JTA transaction might be started by your EJBs or by a JMS Session. So, if the duration of these transactions exceeds the specified timeout setting, the transaction service will roll-back the transactions automatically.

Summary

In this chapter, we have continued the analysis of the application server configuration by looking at Java Enterprise Services.

We have first learnt how to configure datasources, which can be used to add database connectivity to your applications. The new server release departed from the standard approach, which consisted in dropping -ds.xml files in the deployment folder. Installing a datasource with the AS 7 requires two simple steps: installing the JDBC driver and adding the datasource into the server configuration.

We have then looked at the Enterprise Java Bean subsystem, by which you can configure and tune your EJB container. We have gone through the basic EJB components configuration (SLSB, SFSB, and MDB), and then, we have looked at the EJB Timer service configuration that can be used to provide time-based services to your applications.

Next, we have described the configuration of the message oriented middleware, which allows you to loosely couple heterogeneous systems together, whilst typically providing reliability, transactions, and many other features.

Finally, we have completed our journey into enterprise services, by looking at the transaction subsystem configuration, which can be used to collect transaction logs and to define the timeout for all JTA transaction enlisted.

In the next chapter, we will discuss about the Web container configuration, providing a complete example that uses a mix of enterprise technologies, keeping focused on the structure and the packaging of the application.

4
JBoss Web Server Configuration

In this chapter, we will complete the standalone server configuration overview by looking at the Web server configuration. JBoss AS ships with an enterprise-ready Web server, designed for medium and large applications, based on the Jakarta Tomcat.

At first, we will learn how to configure static and dynamic resources on JBoss Web server. We will then explore the structure of a web application by creating, packaging, and deploying a sample AS 7 project. Our sample application will be further enhanced with some other Java EE components including data persistence (JPA), which will ultimately give you the taste of a complete Java EE 6 application.

Configuring the Web container

This section covers the configuration of the Web container as a subsystem of the application server. Historically, the JBoss AS has always been bound to the popular Apache Tomcat engine for rendering web applications.

The new release of JBoss Web is actually based on a fork of Apache Tomcat 7.0, which implements the Servlet 3.0, the JavaServer Pages 2.2 specifications from the Java Community Process, and includes a Java Server Faces 2.1 compliant implementation.

On the top of the Web container, additional frameworks can be run, such as the Web service engine, which is based on the Apache CXF framework and helps you build and develop services using frontend programming APIs, such as JAX-WS and JAX-RS.

Where is the Web server configuration?

A standard Tomcat Web server uses a file named `server.xml` to define the configuration of its services. As we have anticipated at the beginning of this book, the AS 7 configuration is centralized into a single file named `standalone.xml` (or `domain.xml` if you are running a domain), so the Web server configuration is now also contained in this file. Here's an extract from the "web" subsystem:

```
<subsystem xmlns="urn:jboss:domain:web:1.1" default-virtual-
server="default-host">
 <connector name="http" protocol="HTTP/1.1" scheme="http"
   socket-binding="http"/>
 <virtual-server name="default-host" enable-welcome-root="true">
  <alias name="localhost"/>
  <alias name="example.com"/>
 </virtual-server>
</subsystem>
. . . . . . . .
<socket-binding-group name="standard-sockets" default-
  interface="public">
        <socket-binding name="http" port="8080"/>
        <socket-binding name="https" port="8443"/>
. . . . . . . .
</socket-binding-group>
```

As you can see, the default configuration is pretty short as it relies largely on default values. The web subsystem defines a virtual server named "default-host" with a set of aliases (like "localhost") contained in it. Virtual hosts allow you to group web applications according to the various DNS names by which the machine running JBoss is known.

The most interesting settings are about the Web server connector and its socket-binding interface. The socket-binding element in turn references the socket-binding group, located at the bottom of the configuration file.

Configuring the Web server connectors

A connector is basically a Java object, which provides an interface to Web server clients. The default configuration provides just a quintessential connector configuration, leaving the remaining attributes to default values. That could be just fine for simple applications. However, if you want to configure applications that require a minimum of complexity, you should configure by yourself the `connector` attributes with the most appropriate values.

The following is a connector configuration that shows off all the available `connector` attributes:

```
<subsystem xmlns="urn:jboss:domain:web:1.1">
  <connector enable-lookups="false" enabled="true"
    executor="http-executor"
    max-connections="200"
    max-post-size="2048" max-save-post-size="4096"
    name="http" protocol="HTTP/1.1"
    proxy-name="proxy" proxy-port="8081"
    redirect-port="8443" scheme="http"
    secure="false" socket-binding="http" />
</subsystem>
```

One important aspect that refers to the Web server Thread Pool is the `executor` attribute, which references a Thread Pool definition that will be used to handle client requests for this connector:

```
<subsystem xmlns="urn:jboss:domain:threads:1.0">
  <bounded-queue-thread-pool
    name="http-executor"
    blocking="true">
  <core-threads count="10" per-cpu="20"/>
  <queue-length count="10" per-cpu="20"/>
  <max-threads count="10" per-cpu="20"/>
  <keepalive-time time="10" unit="seconds"/>
  </bounded-queue-thread-pool>
</subsystem>
```

So, when using this configuration, the `http connector` will use a bounded Thread Pool configuration to serve client requests (Please refer to *Chapter 2, Configuring the Application Server* for more details about the Thread Pool configuration.)

All the other `connector` settings refer to the equivalent properties used by Tomcat/earlier JBoss Web server, so we include them next just for your reference:

Parameter	Description
enable-lookups	Set to `true`, if you want calls to `request.getRemoteHost()` to perform DNS lookups, in order to return the actual hostname of the remote client. Set to `false` to skip the DNS lookup and return the IP address in `String` form instead (thereby improving performance).
enabled	Determines if the connector is enabled (default) or not.
executor	The executor represents a Thread Pool that can be shared between components in the JBoss Web server.

Parameter	Description
max-connections	The maximum number of request processing Threads to be created by this connector, which therefore determines the maximum number of simultaneous requests that can be handled.
max-post-size	Sets a limit on the maximum size of HTTP POST requests it accepts. By default, it's 2 MB.
max-save-post-size	Maximum size of a POST that will be saved by the container during authentication, which is 4 KB by default.
name	The name of the connector.
protocol	This attribute value must be HTTP/1.1 to use the HTTP handler, which is the default. When set to AJP/1.3, the **Apache JServ Protocol (AJP)** will be used.
proxy-name	The server name to which we require our requests to this connector were proxied.
proxy-port	The server port to which we require our requests to this connector were proxied.
redirect-port	If this connector is supporting non-SSL requests and a request is received for which a matching <security-constraint> requires SSL transport, Catalina will automatically redirect the request to the port number specified here.
scheme	Set this attribute to the name of the protocol you wish to have returned by calls to request.getScheme(). For example, you would set this attribute to https for an SSL connector. The default value is http.
secure	Set this attribute to true if you wish to have calls to request.isSecure() to return true for requests received by this connector (you would want this on an SSL connector). The default value is false.
socket-binding	The corresponding socket-binding interface for the connector.

The protocol parameter deserves a bit more of explanation. As a matter of fact, the embedded JBoss Web server is able to listen for incoming connections, using either the standard HTTP Protocol or the Apache JServ Protocol (AJP).

In *Chapter 9, Load Balancing Web Applications*, we will show what the available options are to cofigure the Apache – JBoss connectivity. For the moment, let's see how you can upgrade the default HTTP connector using the **Apache Portable Runtime Connector (APR)**.

Configuring the HTTP connector

Out of the box, JBoss Web server uses the Java-based HTTP/1.1 (Coyote) connector for parsing HTTP requests and passes the request to the Web server engine.

The Java-based Coyote connector is a mature and extremely stable component and should be the choice for most situations, especially if you are just beginning to use JBoss AS.

On highly loaded systems, however, you can opt for the newer APR HTTP connector, which potentially offers the highest level of performance improvement, by leveraging proven operating system–level optimization on it.

The native APR connector is not a complete connector in the strictest sense. It actually makes use of the standard Java-based connector for most of its operations. However, when the native code APR connector is enabled, the Java code will switch to native implementation for several performance-sensitive and scalability-sensitive operations.

The APR connector optimizes performance and enhances scalability through three main mechanisms:

- Use of a `sendfile` kernel mode call to send large static files directly from the buffer cache
- Use of a single native code keep alive poller, to implement connection keep alive for a large number of connections

Installing the APR connector

JBoss AS is a pure Java application server and so the APR connector does not ship with the standard distribution. When you start the application server, you might have noticed the following log message:

```
15:50:39,187 INFO  [org.apache.catalina.core.AprLifecycleListener] (MSC
    service Thread 1-2) The Apache Tomcat Native library, which allows
    optimal performance in production environments, was not found on the
    java.library.path
```

As a matter of fact, the `AprLifecycleListener` tries to find the APR libraries at startup. Since we still haven't added them to the server installation, the Web server will fall back to the standard HTTP/1.1 connector.

Installing the APR connector is just a matter of following a few simple steps:

1. First, download the JBoss Native connector (part of the JBoss Web project) from: `http://www.jboss.org/jbossweb/downloads/jboss-native-2-0-9`, taking care to choose the right native-built libraries for your operating system.

JBoss Web Native Connectors – Current packages

Version 2.0.9

Name	Description	Size	Release date	License	Download
source tarball	jboss-native 2.0.9 sources	7.6M	2010-03-29	LGPL	jboss-native- Downloads: **362**
source zip	jboss-native 2.0.9 sources	11M	2010-03-29	LGPL	jboss-native- Downloads: **702**
binaries 2.0.9-hpux parsic2	jboss-native 2.0.9 tar bundles	2.8M	2010-03-29	LGPL	jboss-native- Downloads: **21**
binaries 2.0.9-linux2 i64	jboss-native 2.0.9 tar bundles	2.4M	2010-03-29	LGPL	jboss-native- Downloads: **131**
binaries 2.0.9-linux2 x64	jboss-native 2.0.9 tar bundles	1.8M	2010-03-29	LGPL	jboss-native- Downloads: **697**
binaries 2.0.9-linux2	jboss-native 2.0.9 tar bundles	1.7M	2010-03-29	LGPL	jboss-native- Downloads: **509**
binaries 2.0.9-macosx	jboss-native 2.0.9 tar bundles	1.2M	2010-03-29	LGPL	jboss-native- Downloads: **83**
binaries 2.0.9-solaris10 sparc32	jboss-native 2.0.9 tar bundles	1.9M	2010-03-29	LGPL	jboss-native- Downloads: **44**
binaries 2.0.9-solaris9 sparc32	jboss-native 2.0.9 tar bundles	1.9M	2010-03-29	LGPL	jboss-native- Downloads: **9**
binaries 2.0.9-solaris10 x86	jboss-native 2.0.9 tar bundles	1.7M	2010-03-29	LGPL	jboss-native- Downloads: **56**
binaries 2.0.9-windows (i64)	jboss-native 2.0.9 zip bundles	2.4M	2010-03-29	LGPL	jboss-native- Downloads: **2375**

2. Once downloaded, unzip the JBoss Native into the `home` folder of your JBoss AS distribution.

As you can see, the archive contains into the native folder some operating system libraries, which will be used to enhance the capabilities of the HTTP connector. Here, for example, is the library that will be used for a Windows machine:

```
jboss-native-2.0.9-windows-x86-ssl.zip
├───bin
│   │   jbosssvc.exe
│   │   jbossweb.exe
│   │   jbosswebw.exe
│   │   service.bat
│   │
│   └───native
│           openssl.exe
│           tcnative-1.dll
│
└───licenses
```

Now, since the APR is a native library, you need to make sure that it's available in the `java.library.path` environment variable. There are already a few places where the JVM will look for native libraries, such as the `JAVA_HOME/bin` folder or (on Windows machine) the `c:\Windows32\system32`. You can either place the native library there or add its path into the startup script of the application server:

```
set "JAVA_OPTS=%JAVA_OPTS% -Djava.library.path=C:\JBoss-as-
    7.0.2.Final\bin\native"
```

3. Now, restart JBoss AS, which will now detect the presence of the native libraries and leverage them:

    standalone.bat or standalone.sh

    You will notice certain console output that indicates the presence of the APR:

```
on Version 3.0.0.Beta3
09:02:48,828 INFO  [org.jboss.as.ee] (Controller Boot Thread) Activating EE subs
ystem
09:02:49,015 INFO  [org.apache.catalina.core.AprLifecycleListener] (MSC service
thread 1-3) An older version 1.1.20 of the Apache Tomcat Native library is insta
lled, while Tomcat recommends version greater then 1.1.21
09:02:49,093 INFO  [org.jboss.as.remoting] (MSC service thread 1-1) Listening on
/127.0.0.1:9999
09:02:49,328 INFO  [org.jboss.as.jmx.JMXConnectorService] (MSC service thread 1-
4) Starting remote JMX connector
09:02:50,015 INFO  [org.jboss.as.connector] (MSC service thread 1-1) Starting JC
A Subsystem (JBoss IronJacamar 1.0.3.Final)
09:02:50,515 INFO  [org.jboss.as.connector.subsystems.datasources] (MSC service
thread 1-2) Bound data source [java:/WFODS]
09:02:50,531 INFO  [org.jboss.as.connector.subsystems.datasources] (MSC service
thread 1-4) Bound data source [java:jboss/datasources/ExampleDS]
09:02:50,921 INFO  [org.apache.coyote.http11.Http11AprProtocol] (MSC service thr
ead 1-3) Starting Coyote HTTP/1.1 on http--127.0.0.1-8080
09:02:51,031 INFO  [org.jboss.as.deployment] (MSC service thread 1-3) Started Fi
leSystemDeploymentService for directory D:\jboss-as-7.0.2.Final\standalone\deplo
yments
09:02:51,093 INFO  [org.jboss.as] (Controller Boot Thread) JBoss AS 7.0.2.Final
"Arc" started in 6953ms - Started 98 of 153 services (55 services are passive or
on-demand)
```

Configuring the Web server resources

Now that we have covered the standard Web server configuration, we will look at the additional configuration options that are available, but not explicitly shown in the `standalone.xml` configuration file. The Web server configuration section is divided into two broad areas:

- **Static resources configuration**: This includes resources, such as HTML pages and images

- **JSP configuration**: This is used for pages that are dynamically generated by the Web container

We will deal with the two options in the following two sections.

Configuring static resources

Static resources include that part of the Web application (notably HTML pages and images) that do not require processing by the Web container, but just need to be rendered to the end user. For large applications requiring the highest throughput, we suggest you configure Apache as dispatcher for static resources. This will be explained in detail in *Chapter 9, Load Balancing Web Applications*, which discusses in depth load balancing applications.

For smaller projects, using JBoss for this purpose might be just as good, so we have included a sample static resources configuration which is based on the default values:

```
<subsystem xmlns="urn:jboss:domain:web:1.1" default-virtual-
server="default-host">
  <configuration>
   <static-resources listings="false" sendfile="49152"
   file-encoding="utf-8" read-only="true" webdav="false" max-depth=
   "3" disabled="false"/>
  </configuration>
  . . . . . .
</subsystem>
```

And here is a table reinforcing the meaning of the single properties:

Property	Meaning
disabled	Setting to `true` disables static resources handling by connectors.
file-encoding	File encoding to be used when reading static resources. Defaults to platform file encoding.
listings	When set to `true`, and no welcome file is present, a directory listing is shown.
max-depth	Defines the `max-depth` for a WebDAV request. See `webdav` parameter.

Property	Meaning
read-only	When set to `true`, HTTP commands, such as PUT and DELETE, are rejected.
sendfile	When `sendfile` is enabled, set the `sendfile` buffer size. Default is `49152`. Higher values will cause `sendfile` to increase its buffer instead of sending large response using blocking writes. This may or may not increase the performance of your data transfer, depending on your network configurations.
webdav	This parameter lets you configure your JBoss AS as a WebDAV server (allows the users to easily upload/download documents to/from your web application, such as a Share Drive. Read more here: `http://wiki.apache.org/tomcat/Tomcat/WebDav`).

Configuring dynamic resources

Besides the configuration of static resources, you will more likely be interested in tuning the configuration of dynamic resources, such as JSP pages that are handled by JBoss Web server. By default, there's no `jsp-configuration` element. If you want to include it, you need to add it as a child element of the configuration section, just like for the static resources. Here's a `jsp-configuration` that relies on default values:

```
<configuration>
  <jsp-configuration check-interval="1"
  development="false"
  disabled="false"
  display-source-fragment="true"
  dump-smap="false"
  error-on-use-bean-invalid-class-attribute="false"
  generate-strings-as-char-arrays="false"
  java-encoding="UTF8"
  keep-generated="true"
  mapped-file="true"
  modification-test-interval="4"
  recompile-on-fail="false"
  scratch-dir=""
  smap="true"
  source-vm="1.5"
  tag-pooling="true"
  target-vm="1.5"
  trim-spaces="false"
  x-powered-by="true"/>
</configuration>
```

Most of the `configuration` section is targeted at providing additional information to developers and some minor optimization to applications running in production. You should be aware of the `development` attribute, which determines if your dynamic pages (such as JSPs) will be ultimately checked for recompilation using the `check-interval` time (in seconds). So, when developing your applications, you should generally set this element to `true`, and to `false` when running in production.

The full description of the `jsp-configuration` section element follows here:

Property	Meaning
`check-interval`	If `development` is enabled, this setting decides how frequently the compiles are triggered. This defaults to `300` seconds.
`development`	Setting this to `false` disables JBoss AS from checking the JSP pages for modification.
`disabled`	If set to `true`, this parameter disables the JSP configuration settings.
`display-source-fragment`	If this parameter is set to `true`, a source fragment is included when displaying exception messages.
`dump-smap`	If this parameter is set to `true`, the SMAP info (source files are mapped to class files -JSR 45) will be logged to a file.
`error-on-use-bean-invalid-class-attribute`	When set to `true`, the Jasper compiler performs a stricter check on JSP by issuing a compilation error if there's an error in the `useBean` action.
`generate-strings-as-char-arrays`	This is a minor performance optimization, which causes the compiler to generate slightly more efficient char arrays when set to `true`.
`java-encoding`	Sets the Java platform encoding to generate the JSP page servlet. Default is `UTF8`.
`keep-generated`	When set to `true` (default), the generated source files for JSP files are not deleted.
`mapped-file`	When set to `true`, JBoss Web server generates static content with one print statement per-input-line, to ease debugging.
`modification-test-interval`	This sets the frequency for checking the modification of JSP files. This defaults to `4` seconds, and setting it to `0` causes the JSP to be checked on every access. Needs the development element to be `true` to work.
`recompile-on-fail`	When set to `true`, the Web server ignores the `modificationTestInterval` if there's a compilation error. Used in `development` mode only and is disabled by default, as compilation may be expensive and could lead to excessive resource usage.

Property	Meaning
scratch-dir	If set, this parameter determines the scratch directory that we should use when compiling JSP pages.
smap	If this parameter is set to true, the generation of SMAP info for JSR45 debugging is enabled. Otherwise it's suppressed.
source-vm	Selects which JDK versions the source files are compatible with (default value: 1.5).
tag-pooling	The enablePooling attribute specifies if pooling of Tag library classes is to be enabled (true) or not (false). This parameter defaults to true.
target-vm	Selects which JDK version the generated files are compatible with (default value: 1.5).
trim-spaces	To remove useless white space bytes from the response, set this to true.
x-powered-by	When set to true, it adds the x-powered-by text in the response.

Creating and deploying a web application

As you can see, the application server provides a straightforward way to configure the Web container. In order to run a web application, you need to learn how to organize its specific configuration files and which libraries are needed to render the web application.

JBoss AS 7 is a Java EE 6-compatible application server and thus, it can be used to deploy a wide range of web applications. Today, one of the most common approaches to building your application is using the Java Server Faces technology, which is an evolution of JSP technology.

Currently, JBoss AS 7 supports the JSF release 2.1 using the Mojarra implementation, although there are plans for supporting MyFaces implementation too.

 The purpose of this example is to teach the reader how to create, configure, and deploy a Java EE 6 application on JBoss AS 7. If you want to learn the best practices for developing a Java EE 6 application on AS 7, you should check out the quick-start examples that are available along with the server distribution.

Creating a new Dynamic Web Project

There are several options for creating a JSF project using Eclipse Enterprise. The most basic option will be creating a new **Dynamic Web Project** from the menu.

Let's call this project `as7project` and use as target runtime the JBoss AS 7 runtime, which we installed at the beginning of the book.

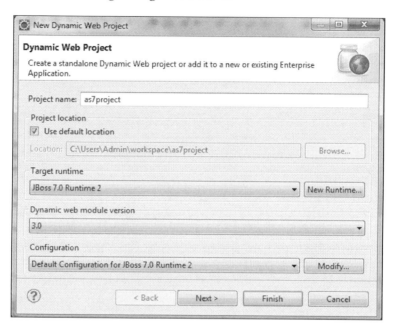

Configuring JSF 2.1 support for a web application requires very little effort. As a matter of fact, you can do it in two single steps: first, declare in your web application configuration file (`web.xml`) your `FacesServlet` and what kind of URL patterns will be directed to it.

 The `FacesServlet` is a servlet that manages the request processing lifecycle for web applications that are utilizing JavaServer Faces to construct the user interface.

Here's the `web.xml` file that needs to be placed in the `WEB-INF` folder of your application:

```
<web-app xmlns="http://java.sun.com/xml/ns/javaee"
    xmlns:xsi="http://www.w3.org/2001/XMLSchema-instance"
    xsi:schemaLocation="http://java.sun.com/xml/ns/javaee
    http://java.sun.com/xml/ns/javaee/web-app_3_0.xsd"
    version="3.0">
```

```xml
<display-name>WebExample</display-name>

<welcome-file-list>
  <welcome-file>index.html</welcome-file>
  <welcome-file>index.htm</welcome-file>
  <welcome-file>index.jsp</welcome-file>
  <welcome-file>default.html</welcome-file>
  <welcome-file>default.htm</welcome-file>
  <welcome-file>default.jsp</welcome-file>
</welcome-file-list>

<servlet>
  <servlet-name>Faces Servlet</servlet-name>
  <servlet-class>javax.faces.webapp.FacesServlet</servlet-class>
  <load-on-startup>1</load-on-startup>
</servlet>

<servlet-mapping>
  <servlet-name>Faces Servlet</servlet-name>
  <url-pattern>*.xhtml</url-pattern>
</servlet-mapping>


</web-app>
```

Next, you need to create a minimal JSF configuration file, named `faces-config.xml`, which will be placed in the `WEB-INF` folder of your application. This file declares the JSF release that we are going to use, in our case 2.1.

```xml
<?xml version="1.0" encoding="UTF-8"?>

<faces-config
  xmlns="http://java.sun.com/xml/ns/javaee"
  xmlns:xsi="http://www.w3.org/2001/XMLSchema-instance"
  xsi:schemaLocation="http://java.sun.com/xml/ns/javaee
  http://java.sun.com/xml/ns/javaee/web-facesconfig_2_1.xsd"
  version="2.1">
</faces-config>
```

Please note that Eclipse is actually able to install these files for you by activating the **Java Server Faces Facets**. Right-click on your project and select **Project Properties**. From there, you will find under the **Project Facets** option a set of configuration options that can be automatically added to your project. In our case, Eclipse will exactly do the file configuration that we did manually.

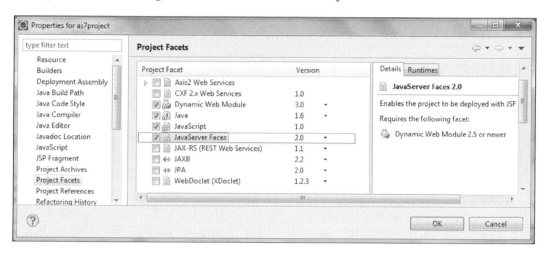

Adding JSF components

For the purpose of learning the packaging of a Java EE 6 application, we will show how to combine some JSF components, such as Managed Beans and JSF views, with some Enterprise components, such as the EJB singleton, which we formerly introduced in *Chapter 3, Configuring Enterprise Services*.

In this example, we will create a simple caching system that uses an EJB singleton to handle the cache in memory. Later, we will show how to introduce data persistence to keep our cache on a storage.

1. Let's start by adding a page named `home.xhtml` to your Dynamic Web Project:

```
<!DOCTYPE html PUBLIC "-//W3C//DTD XHTML 1.0 Transitional//EN"
    "http://www.w3.org/TR/xhtml1/DTD/xhtml1-transitional.dtd">
<html xmlns="http://www.w3.org/1999/xhtml"
    xmlns:ui="http://java.sun.com/jsf/facelets"
    xmlns:h="http://java.sun.com/jsf/html"
    xmlns:f="http://java.sun.com/jsf/core"
    xmlns:c="http://java.sun.com/jsp/jstl/core">

    <h:head>
        <style type="text/css">
            <!-- omitted for the sake of brevity -->
```

```
      </style>
  </h:head>

  <h:body>
    <h2>JSF 2 example on JBoss 7</h2>

    <h:form id="jsfexample">
      <h:panelGrid columns="2" styleClass="default">
      <h:outputText value="Enter key:" />
      <h:inputText value="#{manager.key}" />
      <h:outputText value="Enter value:" />
      <h:inputText value="#{manager.value}" />
      <h:commandButton actionListener="#{manager.save}"
        styleClass="buttons" value="Save key/value" />
      <h:commandButton actionListener="#{manager.clear}"
        styleClass="buttons" value="Clear cache" />
      <h:messages />
      </h:panelGrid>

      <h:dataTable value="#{manager.cacheList}" var="item"
        styleClass="table" headerClass="table-header"
        rowClasses="table-odd-row,table-even-row">

        <h:column>
          <f:facet name="header">Key</f:facet>
          <h:outputText value="#{item.key}" />
        </h:column>

        <h:column>
          <f:facet name="header">Value</f:facet>
          <h:outputText value="#{item.value}" />
        </h:column>

      </h:dataTable>

    </h:form>
  </h:body>
</html>
```

This page references a **Managed Bean** named "**manager**", which is used to store and retrieve key/value pairs. Managed Beans are simple Java classes, which are used as models for UI components. In JSF 1.2, for a bean to become a managed bean, you had to register it in the JSF configuration file (`faces-config.xml`). One of the biggest annoyances was that as the number of beans grew, the JSF configuration file grew as well, and it was difficult to keep track of all names and changes in three different files that were all "connected" (JSF configuration file, the JSF view, and the bean itself).

Luckily, JSF 2 has introduced annotations to register Managed Beans. With annotations, the bean and its registration are in the same place (Java class), so it becomes much easier to manage.

2. Now, let's see how to code the `PropertyManager` Managed Bean:

```
package com.packtpub.chapter4.bean;

import java.util.ArrayList;
import java.util.List;
import javax.ejb.EJB;
import javax.faces.application.FacesMessage;
import javax.faces.bean.ManagedBean;
import javax.faces.context.FacesContext;
import javax.faces.event.ActionEvent;
import com.packtpub.chapter4.ejb.SingletonBean;

@ManagedBean(name="manager")
public class PropertyManager {
  @EJB
  SingletonBean ejb;
  ArrayList  cacheList  = new ArrayList ();

  private String key;
  private String value;
  // key/value GETTERS /SETTERS omitted for brevity

  public void save(ActionEvent e) {
    ejb.put(key, value);
  }

  public void clear(ActionEvent e) {
    System.out.println("Called clear");
    ejb.delete();
  }

  public List getCacheList() {
    return ejb.getCache();
  }

}
```

The most relevant part of this class is the @ManagedBean annotation that registers this class as a JSF Managed Bean. Next, the @EJB annotation that is used to inject the SingletonBean into the class.

Adding the EJB layer

The SingletonBean is an EJB, which is marked with the special @javax.ejb. Singleton annotation. A class with such annotation is guaranteed to be instantiated only once, thus it is the middleware equivalent of the J2SE singleton pattern. In the Java EE context, they are primarily used to store application-wide shared data.

1. Create a new class named SingletonBean. The aim of this class will be to store key-value pairs in HashMap:

```
package com.packtpub.chapter4.ejb;

import java.util.ArrayList;
import java.util.List;
import javax.annotation.PostConstruct;
import javax.ejb.Singleton;
import com.packtpub.chapter4.entity.Property;

@Singleton
public class SingletonBean {
  private  List<Property> cache;

  @PostConstruct
  public void initCache(){
    this.cache = new ArrayList();
  }

  public void delete(){
    this.cache.clear();
  }

  public void put(String key,String value){
    Property p = new Property();
    p.setKey(key);
    p.setValue(value);
    this.cache.add(p);
  }

  public List<Property> getCache() {
    return cache;
  }

}
```

2. The last class we need to add is `Property`, which is a plain `JavaBean` class. The aim of this class will be to store key-value pairs in `HashMap`:

```
package com.packtpub.chapter4.entity;

public class Property {
  private String key;
  private String value;
  // GETTERS / SETTERS omitted for brevity
}
```

This class is intentionally placed in a package `com.packtpub.chapter4.entity`, since in the next section of this chapter, we will use this class as an **Entity** for storing data.

If you have completed all these steps correctly, you will end up with a project containing the following items:

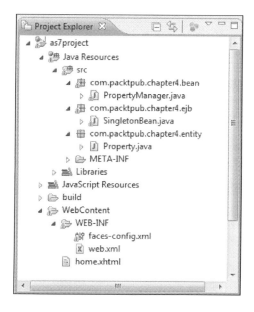

Choosing the web context of the application

By default, a Web application inherits the Web context name from the archive name, which is deployed on the application server. So, in our example, if we deploy an archive named `as7project.war`, it will be accessible using the Web context name `as7project`, as shown by the following image:

The context name is, however, customizable, and the simplest way to achieve it (without changing the archive name) is by adding a `jboss-web.xml` file to the `WEB-INF` folder of your project:

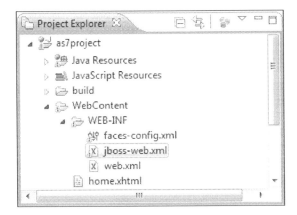

The content of this file will include the custom Web context, as specified by the context-root element:

```
<jboss-web>
  <context-root>customContext</context-root>
</jboss-web>
```

The file `jboss-web.xml` can also be used in other contexts. For example within it you can define a `Valve` component. A `Valve` element represents a high-level component that will be inserted into the request processing pipeline. There are many available `Valve` that can be used by checking in the Apache Tomcat guide: `http://tomcat.apache.org/tomcat-7.0-doc/config/valve.html`.

In the following example, we are adding to our web application a `RequestDumperValve`, which can be used to print out the request information:

```
<jboss-web>
  <valve>
    <class-name>
      org.apache.catalina.valves.RequestDumperValve
    </class-name>
  </valve>
</jboss-web>
```

Deploying the web application

Once you are happy with your settings, you can deploy and verify your application. If you are deploying your application from within Eclipse, just right-click on the JBoss Runtime Server and choose the **Add and Remove** option. Next, add the web project to the list of deployed projects.

You can actually deploy the application by right-clicking on the project and choosing **Full Publish**.

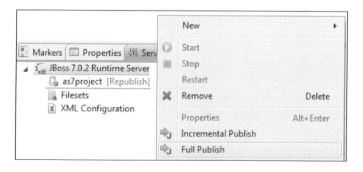

You will notice that once your application is deployed, Eclipse will move on the server the web application archive (`as7project.war`) along with a file named `as7project.war.dodeploy`. As you will learn in *Chapter 6, Deploying Applications on JBoss AS 7*, expanded archives, by default, require a marker file in JBoss AS 7 to trigger the deployment. Luckily, Eclipse is aware of it and does its job well.

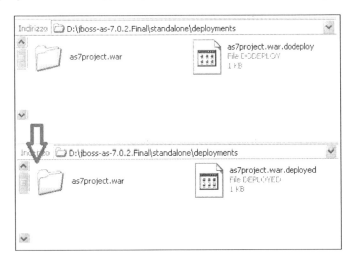

Upon successful deployment, the `as7project.war.dodeploy` will be replaced by a `as7project.war.deployed` marker file, which indicates that you have successfully deployed the web application. You can verify that your application works correctly by pointing to the `home.xhtml` page: `http://localhost:8080/as7project/home.xhtml`.

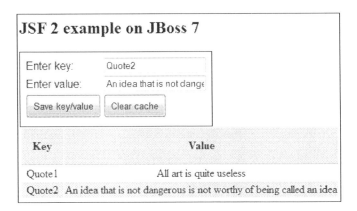

Deploying a web application to the root context

In this example, we have showed how to deploy the web application to a custom context using the `jboss-web.xml`. One particular case of Web context is the `root` context, which will be used by the Web server if you don't provide a specific one in your request. This typically resolves to `http://localhost:8080` and is used to provide some welcome context by the Web server. By default, JBoss AS 7 has a root context that is mapped in the `JBOSS_HOME/welcome-content` folder. You can, however, override it by deploying one of your applications to the `root` context. This requires two simple steps:

1. At first, set to `false` the `enable-welcome-root` parameter in the `virtual-server` section:

   ```
   <virtual-server name="default-host" enable-welcome-root="false">
   </virtual-server>
   ```

2. Then, in your application, add a `jboss-web.xml` file that contains the `root` context for your application:

   ```
   <jboss-web>
     <context-root>/</context-root>
   </jboss-web>
   ```

Adding a remote EJB client

A couple weeks before this book was printed, the new release 7.1.0 Beta of the application server was finally available for download. This release adds some enhancements, the most important one being the introduction of a new JBoss specific EJB client API, which can be used to perform remote invocations on the EJBs.

In order to test our application with a remote client, we need at first to provide a remote interface to the EJB:

```
package com.packtpub.chapter4.ejb;
import java.util.List;
import com.packtpub.chapter4.entity.Property;
public interface SingletonBeanRemote {
  public void delete();
  public void put(String key,String value);
  public List<Property> getCache();
  public List<Property>  queryCache();
}
```

The concrete implementation of this interface is the `SingletonBeanRemoteImpl` class, which has the same java method implementations as the `SingletonBean` class that we have shown in the earlier section:

```
@Singleton
@Remote(SingletonBeanRemote.class)
public class  SingletonBeanRemoteImpl implements SingletonBeanRemote
{
// Bean class unchanged
}
```

Here comes the most interesting part, which is the remote EJB client. EJB remote invocation happens through the **Remoting** framework, which uses **Simple Authentication and Security Layer (SASL)** for client-server authentication. In the current release of the application server, we need to explicitly set the Security provider, by adding into our test client the following specification:

```
static {
   Security.addProvider(new JBossSaslProvider());
}
```

This will grant an anonymous access to the remote server where EJBs located. The next tricky part is determining the JNDI name of the EJB, which needs to be looked up. The actual JNDI name of the EJB varies, depending on the type of EJB. The following table reinforces the two available syntax for both SLSBs and SFSBs:

EJB type	JNDI syntax
Stateless EJB	`ejb:<app-name>/<module-name>/<distinct-name>/<bean-name>!<fully-qualified-classname-of-the-remote-interface>`
Stateful EJB	`ejb:<app-name>/<module-name>/<distinct-name>/<bean-name>!<fully-qualified-classname-of-the-remote-interface>?stateful`

That's a pretty complex syntax. However, we will try to dissect every piece of it with another reference table:

Parameter	Description
`app-name`	This is the application name and is used in case the application has been deployed as an Enterprise archive. It typically corresponds to the Enterprise archive name without `.ear`. Since we have packed our application in a Web archive, this parameter will not be used.
`module-name`	This is the module within which the EJBs are contained. Since we have deployed the application in a file named `as7project.war`, it corresponds to `as7project`.

Parameter	Description
distinct-name	This is an optional name that can be assigned to distinguish between different EJB implementations. It's not used in our example.
bean-name	The EJB name, which by default is the class name of the bean implementation class. In our case, `SingletonBeanRemoteImpl`.
fully-qualified-classname-of-the-remote-interface	This obviously corresponds to the fully qualified class name of the interface for which you are doing the lookup. In our case, `com.packtpub.chapter4.ejb.SingletonBeanRemote`.

 Please notice that Stateful EJBs require an additional `?stateful` parameter to be added to the JNDI lookup name.

Now you should be pretty comfortable with the tedious JNDI namespacing and ready to understand the client code:

```
package com.packtpub.chapter4.client;
import javax.naming.*;
import java.security.Security;
import java.util.*;
import org.jboss.sasl.JBossSaslProvider;
import com.packtpub.chapter4.ejb.SingletonBeanRemote;
import com.packtpub.chapter4.ejb.SingletonBeanRemoteImpl;
import com.packtpub.chapter4.entity.Property;

public class RemoteEJBClient {
  static {
    Security.addProvider(new JBossSaslProvider());
  }

  public static void main(String[] args) throws Exception {
    testRemoteEJB();
  }
  private static void testRemoteEJB() throws NamingException {
    final SingletonBeanRemote ejb = lookupEJB();
    System.out.println("Got a remote Singleton EJB");
    // Adds an entry to the cache
    ejb.put("key", "value");
    // Retrieves the cache entries and prints them
    List <Property> list = ejb.getCache();
    System.out.println(list);
  }
  private static SingletonBeanRemote lookupEJB() throws
    NamingException {
```

```
final Hashtable jndiProperties = new Hashtable();
jndiProperties.put(Context.URL_PKG_PREFIXES,
  "org.jboss.ejb.client.naming");
final Context context = new InitialContext(jndiProperties);
    final String appName = "";
    final String moduleName = "as7project";
    final String distinctName = "";
    final String beanName = SingletonBeanRemoteImpl.
      class.getSimpleName();
    final String viewClassName = SingletonBeanRemote.class.getName();
    return (SingletonBeanRemote) context.lookup("ejb:" + appName +
      "/" + moduleName + "/" + distinctName + "/" + beanName + "!" +
      viewClassName);
  }
}
```

As you can see, the major complexity of the remote EJB client code is related to the JNDI lookup section. You might have noticed that in the highlighted section, we have initialized the JNDI Context with a property named Context.URL_PKG_PREFIXES to specify the list of packages prefixes to be used when loading URL context factories. In our case, we have set it to org.jboss.ejb.client.naming so that the JNDI API knows which classes are in charge to handle the ejb: namespace.

Finally, you might wonder how the client actually knows the server location where the remote EJB are hosted. This will be solved by the following client-side property file named jboss-ejb-client.properties that needs to be available to the client classpath:

```
remote.connectionprovider.create.options.org.xnio.Options.
  SSL_ENABLED=false
remote.connections=default
remote.connection.default.host=localhost
remote.connection.default.port = 4447
remote.connection.default.connect.options.org.xnio.Options.SASL_
POLICY_NOANONYMOUS=false
```

Within this file, you can specify a set of properties prefixed by remote. connectionprovider.create.options, which will be used during the remote connection. In our example, we have just set the org.xnio.Options.SSL_ENABLED to false, which means that a clear text transmission will be used to connect the client and the server.

The remote.connections is used to specify a set of one or more connections that map to an EJB receiver. In our case, there is single remote connection named default, which maps to the host localhost and the remoting port 4447.

Finally, we need to specify that a SASL anonymous connection will be used, otherwise without an authentication, our connection will be refused.

Configuring data persistence

After our short excursus on the EJB remote client API, we will further enhance our application adding a **Persistence Context** to it so that we are able to store the key-value pairs on a relational database instead of keeping them in memory. Again, we remind you that the purpose of it is not to teach the theory behind Data Persistence, but rather to show how to configure it within your applications.

As you probably know, a major enhancement in Java EE spec 3.x technology is the addition of the new Java Persistence API, which simplifies the Entity Persistence model. In the Java Persistence API, what used to be called Entity Beans in EJB 2.x are now simply called **Entities**.

The persistence subsystem is included by default into all server configurations:

```
<extension module="org.jboss.as.jpa"/>
<subsystem xmlns="urn:jboss:domain:jpa:1.0"></subsystem>
```

The `javax.persistence` API are not loaded by default in the application server. However, as soon as the application server will detect the main configuration file (named `persistence.xml`) or persistence annotations, the persistence API will be automatically linked to your application.

So, let's add the `JPA persistence.xml` configuration file to our project, which will reference the datasource used for mapping our entities to the database:

```
<?xml version="1.0" encoding="UTF-8"?>
<persistence version="2.0"
  xmlns="http://java.sun.com/xml/ns/persistence"
  xmlns:xsi="http://www.w3.org/2001/XMLSchema-instance"
  xsi:schemaLocation="http://java.sun.com/xml/ns/persistence
  http://java.sun.com/xml/ns/persistence/persistence_2_0.xsd">
  <persistence-unit
    name="persistenceUnit" transaction-type="JTA">
    <provider>org.hibernate.ejb.HibernatePersistence</provider>
      <jta-data-source>java:/MySqlDS</jta-data-source>
    <properties>
      <property name="hibernate.dialect"
        value="org.hibernate.dialect.MySQLDialect" />
    </properties>
  </persistence-unit>
</persistence>
```

The key attributes of this file are the persistence unit name, which will identify its unique name, and the `jta-data-source`, which must match with a valid datasource definition. In the earlier chapter, we have defined this datasource bound to a MySQL database.

The `persistence.xml` can specify either a JTA datasource or a non-JTA datasource. The JTA datasource is expected to be used within the EE environment (even when reading data without an active transaction).

Finally, the `properties` element can contain any configuration property for the underlying persistence provider. Since JBoss AS uses Hibernate as the EJB3 persistence provider, you can pass in any Hibernate options here.

Once created, this file needs to be placed in the META-INF folder of your source classes, as shown in the following screenshot:

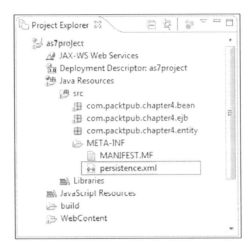

 The real path of persistence.xml file

Please note that the `Eclipse src/META-INF` virtual path will be translated at runtime into the `WEB-INF/classes/META-INF` of your web application.

Using a default datasource for the JPA subsystem

In this example, we are referencing the datasource from within the `persistence.xml`, thus following a "canonical" approach well-known to many developers.

You can, however, choose a default datasource for all your JPA applications, by adding the default-datasource element into the JPA subsystem:

```
<subsystem xmlns="urn:jboss:domain:jpa:1.0">
  <jpa default-datasource="java:/MySqlDS"/>
</subsystem>
```

This way, all JPA applications that haven't defined the `jta-data-source` element in `persistence.xml` will use the default-datasource configured in the main server configuration file.

Configuring entities

Once your persistence configuration is defined, the only change we need to do in our application is adding the `javax.persistence` annotations to our property `POJO`. This will make it suitable to map the database table with its same name, which will store the key/value pair entered by the user:

```
package com.packtpub.chapter4.entity;
import javax.persistence.*;

@Entity
public class Property {
  @Id
  @Column(name="key")
  private String key;
  @Column(name="value")
  private String value;
  // Getter & setters omitted for brevity
}
```

Our Session Bean needs to be changed as well. Taking inspiration from today's caching systems, we are letting our application persist data into the storage (database), but we are using the in-memory cache to retrieve data from it. When the application is re-started, the in-memory cache will be filled with data queried from the database. Nothing fancy, however; for our purpose it will be just fine.

```
package com.packtpub.chapter4.ejb;

import java.util.ArrayList;
import java.util.List;
import javax.annotation.PostConstruct;
import javax.ejb.Singleton;
import javax.persistence.*;
import com.packtpub.chapter4.entity.Property;

@Singleton
public class  SingletonBean    {
  private  List<Property> cache;
  @PersistenceContext(unitName = "persistenceUnit")
  private EntityManager em;

  @PostConstruct
  public void initCache(){
    this.cache = queryCache();
```

```
      if (cache == null) cache = new ArrayList<Property>();
    }

    public void delete(){
      Query query = em.createQuery("delete FROM
        com.packtpub.chapter4.entity.Property");
      query.executeUpdate();
      this.cache.clear();
    }

    public void put(String key,String value){
      Property p = new Property();
      p.setKey(key);
      p.setValue(value);
      em.persist(p);
      this.cache.add(p);
    }

    public List<Property> getCache() {
      return cache;
    }

    public List<Property>  queryCache(){
      Query query = em.createQuery("FROM
        com.packtpub.chapter4.entity.Property");
      List <Property> list =  query.getResultList();
      return list;
    }
}
```

We have highlighted the sections of the code that have been modified to use data persistence. The most relevant section is the `@javax.persistence.PersistenceContext` annotation, which references a JPA context defined into `persistence.xml`.

Once deployed, this application should persist data in your MySQL database:

Configuring persistence in other application archives

In this example, we have created a Java EE 6 application made up of web components and EJBs using a single web application archive. That's absolutely possible, since Java EE 6 enables mixing-and-matching front-end components and server-side components in a single web archive.

You can, however, consider deploying an application where the Web layer is separated from the business service layer. For example, supposing you were to deploy your EJBs and entities in a separated JAR file, then the right place for the persistence.xml file would be beneath the META-INF folder of your JAR archive:

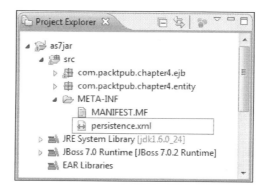

Technically speaking, if you have multiple JAR files in your application, you can deploy the persistence.xml file in a single archive and refer to the persistence unit using the notation jarName#unitName. For example, this application persistence unit could be referenced from another JAR using the following annotation:

```
@PersistenceContext(unitName="as7.jar#unitName")
```

Switching to a different provider

By default, AS7 uses Hibernate 4.0 as a persistence provider. The Hibernate JARs are included under the modules folder in the `org.hibernate` path. If, however, your application requires a different version of Hibernate, such as 3.5 or greater, you can still bundle the JARs into your application.

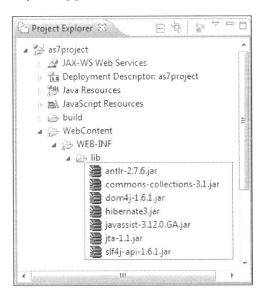

Besides this, you need to set the `jboss.as.jpa.providerModule` property to `hibernate3-bundled` in your `persistence.xml` configuration file. So, the JPA deployer will detect the presence of a different version of the persistence provider and activate that version:

```
<properties>
  <property name="jboss.as.jpa.providerModule" value="hibernate3-
    bundled" />
</properties>
```

Summary

In this chapter, we have described the Web subsystem configuration, which is now completely embedded into the JBoss AS configuration file. JBoss AS 7 uses a forked version of Tomcat Web server, which is still based around the concept of the connector as a Java object that provides an interface to Web server clients.

The Web server configuration is broken into:

- **static-resources configuration**: This comes into play when JBoss AS is used to serve static resources, such as HTML pages and images
- **jsp-configuration**: This is used to configure and fine-tune the dynamic pages creation

We have then gone through an example that showed off how to package and deploy a Java EE 6 Web module on the application server.

In the next part of this chapter, we have discussed the JPA subsystem by adding data persistence to our initial example. We have stressed the correct location of the `persistence.xml` file, which is required to be placed in the `WEB-INF/classes/META-INF` of your web application or in the `META-INF` folder of your JAR.

Having completed the application server standalone configuration, we will now move on in the next chapter to the domain configuration, which is one of the most appetizing new features of this release.

5
Configuring a JBoss
AS Domain

This chapter ends up the configuration of the application server by including the domain configuration. Shaping a server domain is a key section for administrators who want to coordinate efficiently a set of application servers, and we will describe here all the steps for creating and configuring a domain of JBoss AS instances.

As we will see, the configuration of single modules or subsystems does not vary from standalone to domain configuration; rather, what we need to learn is the domain controller and host controller configurations, which are responsible for handling and coordinating the lifecycle of application server instances.

So, these are the topics we are going to cover in this chapter:

- Introduction to JBoss AS domain
- How to configure the domain components
- What is the criteria for choosing a domain or a standalone

Introducing the JBoss AS domain

The concept of domain may be, initially, perceived as a little difficult to understand. The reason for this is that in Java EE paradigm, one is used to dealing with servers rather than domains. This is especially true with developers.

Basically, a domain is an administrative unit. It's a perimeter within which all JBoss AS servers are managed by a domain controller.

It's important to understand that the concept of domain does not interfere with the capabilities delivered by the managed servers. For example, you might set up a domain of application server nodes running in a cluster, providing load balancing, and high availability. But, you might as well provide the same services with a set of standalone application servers.

What differentiates these two scenarios is that when running in a domain, you can manage efficiently your set of servers from a single, centralized unit. On the other hand, managing a set of standalone instances often requires sophisticated multi-server management capabilities, which are not always affordable by companies.

From the process point of view, a domain is made up of four elements:

1. **Domain controller**: The domain controller is the management control point of your domain. An AS instance running in domain mode will have at most one process instance acting as a domain controller. The domain controller holds a centralized configuration, which is shared by the node instances belonging to the domain.

2. **Host controller**: It's a process that is responsible for coordinating with a domain controller the lifecycle of server processes and the distribution of deployments, from the domain controller to the server instances.

3. **Process controller**: It's a very lightweight process whose primary function is to spawn server processes and host controller processes, and manage their input/output streams. This also allows the host controller to be patched and restarted without impacting the associated servers.

4. **Application server nodes**: These are regular Java processes that map to instances of the application server. Each server node, in turn, belongs to a domain group. Domain groups are explained in detail when we discuss the domain configuration file.

In order to understand how to configure these components, we will first look at the basic domain configuration, which is built-in with the application server.

Understanding the default domain configuration

Out of the box, the domain configuration includes a basic configuration made up of the following elements:

- One process controller that starts the other JVM processes.

- One host controller that acts as domain controller.
- Three server nodes. The first two are part of the main server group, and the third one (inactive) is part of the other server group.

The following image reinforces these concepts:

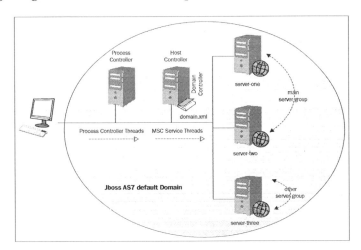

If you want to see this configuration from the JVM point of view, then you can use the `VisualVM` utility to have a look at the low-level details of your domain. As depicted by the following screenshot, four JVM processes are spawned. At first, the process controller is started, which in turn launches the host controller process and the two server nodes.

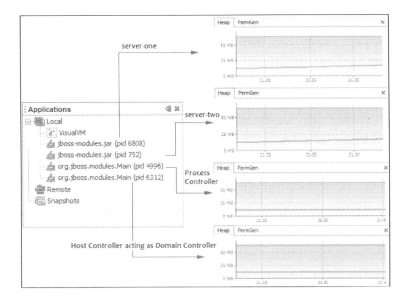

VisualVM is a Java Virtual Machine monitoring tool, which is included in the default J2SE distribution. You can find it in your JAVA_HOME/bin folder. Simply launch either `jvisualvm.exe` (Windows) or `jvisualvm` (Linux), depending on your operating system.

What is relevant to see from this screenshot is that with the basic domain setup, the host controller is also acting as domain controller; that is, it will hold the centralized configuration of the domain. This means that the host controller and domain controller will share the same JVM process. You can have proof of it by checking which is the operating system's process ID that is bound to port `9999` (one port used by the domain controller).

On a Windows machine you would execute:

```
C:\Users\Admin>netstat -ao | find "9999"
TCP     127.0.0.1:9999          CP11-010:0      LISTENING       6312
```

Looking up to the `VisualVM` process table, you can see that this process ID (`6312`) matches with the `org.jboss.as.host-controller` process.

Having completed a basic introduction to the application server domain, we will now cover all the details concerning its configuration.

Starting up and stopping a domain

Starting up a JBoss AS domain is simply a matter of launching the `JBoss_HOME\bin\domain.bat` or `JBoss_HOME\bin\domain.sh` script file, which is part of the server distribution. In a matter of seconds, your domain will be up and running:

```
C:\windows\system32\cmd.exe

SC service thread 1-3) Starting remote JMX connector
[Server:server-two] 21:09:18,570 INFO  [org.jboss.as.connector.subsystems.dataso
urces] (Controller Boot Thread) JBAS010403: Deploying JDBC-compliant driver clas
s org.h2.Driver (version 1.2)
[Server:server-two] 21:09:18,959 INFO  [org.jboss.as.logging] (MSC service threa
d 1-1) Removing bootstrap log handlers
[Server:server-two] 21:09:18,971 INFO  [org.jboss.as.connector.subsystems.dataso
urces] (MSC service thread 1-4) JBAS010400: Bound data source [java:jboss/dataso
urces/ExampleDS]
[Host Controller] 21:09:19,175 INFO  [org.jboss.as.host.controller.mgmt] (pool-3
-thread-1) Server [Server:server-two] registered using connection [org.jboss.as.
protocol.mgmt.ManagementChannel@fd50fd2]
[Host Controller] 21:09:19,176 INFO  [org.jboss.host.controller] (pool-3-thread-
1) Registering server server-two
[Server:server-one] 21:09:21,025 INFO  [org.jboss.as.ee] (Controller Boot Thread
) Activating EE subsystem
[Server:server-two] 21:09:21,026 INFO  [org.jboss.as.ee] (Controller Boot Thread
) Activating EE subsystem
[Server:server-one] 21:09:21,080 INFO  [org.jboss.as] (Controller Boot Thread) J
Boss AS 7.1.0.Alpha1 "Ahoy!" started in 7510ms - Started 88 of 139 services (51
services are passive or on-demand)
[Server:server-two] 21:09:21,082 INFO  [org.jboss.as] (Controller Boot Thread) J
Boss AS 7.1.0.Alpha1 "Ahoy!" started in 6333ms - Started 88 of 139 services (51
services are passive or on-demand)
```

In order to stop the application server domain, you can use the command-line client and issue the `shutdown` command on the host controller:

Unix/Linux users will issue:

```
./jboss-admin.sh --connect command=/host=master:shutdown
```

Windows users will issue:

```
jboss-admin.bat --connect command=/host=master:shutdown
```

 The default host name is `master` and it's defined in the file `host.xml`, which is located in the `JBOSS_HOME\domain\configuration` folder. We will learn more about it in the next section.

Once the domain has started, some logfiles will be created. The host controller activity will be traced at `JBOSS_HOME\domain\log\host-controller`, while the process controller logs are located in the folder `JBOSS_HOME\domain\log\process-controller`.

Configuring the domain

As we said, one of the main advantages of setting up a JBoss AS domain is to control and manage the server configurations and deployments from a single centralized point. The domain configuration consists mainly of two files, which are placed by default in the `JBOSS_HOME\domain\configuration` folder:

1. The `domain.xml` file describes the capabilities of your domain servers and defines the server groups that are part of the domain.
2. The `host.xml` file is present on each host where the domain is installed and specifies the elements that are specific to the servers running on the host.

Overriding the default configuration files

At any time, it's possible to change the default configuration filenames and their path. By adding the following parameter to your domain shell, Windows users can define the new domain and host filename:

domain.bat --domain-config=custom_domain.xml

domain.bat --host-config=custom_host.xml

The equivalent for Linux users will be:

./domain.sh --domain-config=custom_domain.xml

./domain.sh --host-config=custom_host.xml

Note also that if you don't provide any path, it's assumed to be relative to the jboss.server.config.dir directory. Otherwise, it's intended to be an absolute path.

Configuring the domain.xml file

The domain.xml contains the domain subsystems' configuration that is shared by all servers in the domain. The content of the file follows the same structure of the standalone file, with an obvious and important difference. A domain can have several profiles defined in it. By default, two profiles are defined: a **default profile** and a **ha profile**, with the latter one to be used for clustered domains. You might, however, define your custom profile within it, such as a web profile or a messaging profile:

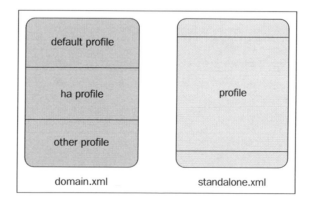

Changing from one profile to another is the recommended way to expand or narrow the capabilities of the servers running in your domain.

Each AS domain can be further split into server groups, each one bound to a different profile. The concept of server groups can be seen as a set of servers managed as a single unit by the domain. You can actually use server groups for fine-grained configuration of nodes, for example, each server group is able to define its own settings, such as customized JVM settings, socket bindings interfaces, or deployed applications.

The following image illustrates some common attributes, which can be applied to a server group:

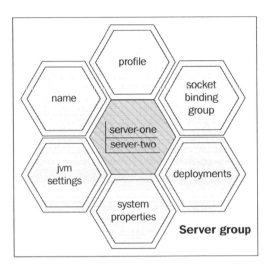

For example, here's a richer server group definition bound to the `default` profile that provides to the servers which are part of it a deployed web application named `sample.war`, a customized JVM configuration, some system properties (which are loaded at boot time), and binds its services to the `standard-sockets` definition:

```
<server-group name="custom-server-group" profile="default">
  <deployments>
    <deployment name="sample.war_v1" runtime-name="sample.war"
      hash="ABCDEFG1234567890ABC"/>
  </deployments>
  <jvm name="default">
    <heap size="512m" max-size="1g"/>
  </jvm>
  <socket-binding-group ref="standard-sockets"/>
  <system-properties>
    <property name="foo" value="bar" boot-time="true"/>
    <property name="key" value="value" boot-time="true"/>
  </system-properties>
</server-group>
```

Configuring the host.xml file

The other domain configuration file is named `host.xml`, which is well-placed in the `JBOSS_HOME\domain\configuration` folder. This file basically defines and configures the server nodes that are running on a host as part of a domain.

The term **host** here means a physical structure that is the portion of the domain which is contained in your AS distribution. Confused? Looking at the following image will make things clearer.

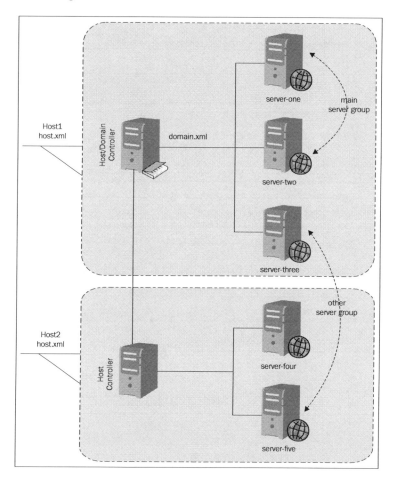

As you can see, a domain can contain several hosts (**host1, host2**) and also several groups (**main server group, other server group**). However, while a **server group** is simply a logical association of server nodes that can be located anywhere, a **host** refers to a set of nodes that are part of the same server distribution.

The term host can exactly match with the common meaning of **machine**, if you install one server distribution per machine. That's not always true: as a matter of fact, you can also install several AS distributions on the same machine; thus you will have multiple hosts on the same machine.

Having completed our definition of hosts, we will look into the host configuration file, which allows you to shape the following set of core domain elements:

- The management interfaces used to control the domain
- The domain controller definition
- The network interfaces where services are bound
- The defined JVMs configurations
- The servers that are part of the domain

In the next section, we will see each element of this file in detail and learn how to configure it appropriately.

Configuring the management interfaces

The management interface includes the definition of the native **Command Line Interface (CLI)** and `http` interface that are used to manage to the domain:

```
<management-interfaces>
            <native-interface security-realm="ManagementRealm">
                <socket interface="management" port="9999"/>
            </native-interface>
            <http-interface security-realm="ManagementRealm">
                <socket interface="management" port="9990"/>
            </http-interface>
</management-interfaces>
```

With the default configuration, both services will be bound to the `management` network interfaces. What distinguishes them is the `native` management interface, which is used by the CLI that will, by default, listen on port `9999`, while the `http` administrative interface will listen on port `9990`.

Configuring the network interfaces

We have just mentioned `network` interfaces. As you can guess from its name, a **network interface** refers to one or a set of network addresses. By default, the server contains two network interfaces definitions, which are named **management** and **public** respectively, and both of them are bound to the loopback address (`127.0.0.1`).

By changing the `inet-address` value of your network interface, you can configure the listening addresses of your application server. For example, if we want to bind the `management` interfaces to the loopback address (`127.0.0.1`) and the `public` interface to the address `192.168.1.1`, you can simply use this configuration:

```
 <interfaces>
<interface name="management">
    <inet-address value="127.0.0.1"/>
  </interface>
<interface name="public">
    <inet-address value="192.168.1.1"/>
  </interface>
 </interfaces>
```

What this means in practice is that the `management` interfaces (the `http` admin console and the CLI) will be bound to the loopback address, while application-related services (bound to the public interface) will be bound to the IP address `192.168.1.1`.

```
<socket-binding-group name="standard-sockets"
default-interface="public">
  <socket-binding name="http" port="8080"/>
  <socket-binding name="https" port="8443"/>
  . . . . .
</socket-binding-group>
```

Configuring the domain controller

By default, the domain controller is located on the same machine where you started your domain:

```
<domain-controller>
  <local/>
</domain-controller>
```

You can, however, configure your host to use a domain controller located on a remote host, in the following way:

```
<domain-controller>
  <remote host="192.168.100.1" port="9999"/>
</domain-controller>
```

Configuring the domain controller on a remote host means that the local configuration (`domain.xml`) will not be used and that all server nodes will use the centralized configuration, stored in the remote host.

Configuring the JVM

One of the key aspects of the domain configuration is the definition of the JVMs that are a part of the domain. The JVMs' elements are defined into the host.xml file, where you can specify their settings and associate them with a name:

```
<jvms>
  <jvm name="default">
    <heap size="64m" max-size="512m"/>
  </jvm>
</jvms>
```

This JVM definition can then be used (and possibly overridden) as part of your server group configuration. For example, the server group other-server-group (domain.xml) will use the default JVM for all server nodes, re-defining the heap max-size setting:

```
<server-group name="other-server-group" profile="default">
  <jvm name="default">
    <heap max-size="512m"/>
  </jvm>
  <socket-binding-group ref="standard-sockets"/>
</server-group>
```

The defined JVMs can be also associated with a single server, thus overriding the server group definition. For example, here server-one (defined in host.xml) inherits the default JVM configuration, setting a custom min (512 MB) and max heap size (1 GB):

```
<server name="server-one" group="main-server-group" auto-
  start="true">
  <jvm name="default">
    <heap size="512m" max-size="1G"/>
  </jvm>
</server>
```

Adding JVM options to a server definition

If you want to further specialize your JVM configuration, for example, by adding non-standard options to the virtual machine, you can use the jvm-options element. In this sample, we are adding to the default JVM options the concurrent low-pause garbage collector:

```
<jvm name="default">
  <heap size="64m" max-size="128m"/>
  <jvm-options>
    <jvm-option value="-XX:+UseConcMarkSweepGC"/>
  </jvm-options>
</jvm>
```

Order of precedence between elements

In the earlier section, we showed how to use the `default` JVM definition in different configuration files. As a matter of fact, the Java Virtual Machine definition is a typical example of overlapping between configuration files, which means that the JVM can be defined either at:

- **Host level**: In this case, the configuration will apply to all servers that are defined in `host.xml`
- **Server group level**: In this case, the configuration applies to all servers that are part of the group
- **Server level**: In the last case, the configuration is used just for the single host

So far, so good. However, what happens if we define an element with the same name at multiple levels? As a matter of fact, the application server resolves overlapping by letting most specific elements override their parent configuration. In other words, if you define a generic JVM at host level, it will be overridden by the same JVM at server-group level.

```
<!-- host.xml -->
<jvms>
  <jvm name="default">
    <heap size="64m" max-size="256m"/>
  </jvm>
</jvms>

<!-- domain.xml -->

<!-- Here the "default" JVM will be overridden by the server group JVM
definition -->

<server-group name="other-server-group" profile="default">
  <jvm name="default">
    <heap size="64m" max-size="512m"/>
  </jvm>
  <socket-binding-group ref="standard-sockets"/>
</server-group>
```

If you also define it at the server level, then that will be the final choice for that server.

```
<!-- Here, the server definition overrides any other host/group
   definition -->
<server name="server-one" group="main-server-group">
  <jvm name="default">
    <heap size="256m" max-size="768m"/>
  </jvm>
</server>
```

The following image describes the elements that can be defined (and possibly overridden) at different configuration levels:

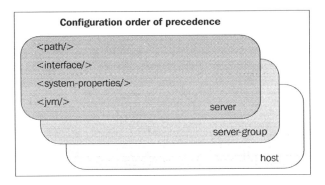

As you can see, this list also includes some elements, such as the <path> element, the <interface>, and the <system-properties> that we have discussed about in *Chapter 2, Configuring the Application Server*.

Configuring server nodes

The last element of the host configuration includes the list of server nodes that are part of the domain. Configuring a server requires, at minimum, the name of the server and the group to which the server belongs:

```
<!-- host.xml configuration file -->
<servers>
  <server name="server-one" group="main-server-group" />
</servers>
```

This server definition relies largely on default attributes for the application server nodes. You can, however, highly customize your servers by adding specific paths, socket binding interfaces, system properties, or JVMs.

```
<server auto-start="true" name="sample" group="sample-group" >
  <paths>
    <path name="example" path="example"
      relative-to="jboss.server.log.dir"/>
  </paths>
  <socket-binding-group port-offset="250" ref="standard-sockets"/>
  <system-properties>
    <property boot-time="true" name="envVar" value="12345"/>
  </system-properties>
  <jvm name="default">
    <heap size="256m" max-size="512m"/>
  </jvm>
</server>
```

If you want to know all the applicable attributes of the server nodes configuration, we suggest you have a look at the schema `jboss-as-config_1.1.xsd`, which can be located in the `JBOSS_HOME/docs/schema` folder of your server distribution.

Applying domain configuration

A common misconception between users who are approaching the concept of domain is that a domain is pretty much the equivalent of a cluster of nodes, so it could be used to achieve important features such as load balancing or high availability.

It's important to understand that a domain is not pertinent to the functionalities that your application will deliver—a domain is designed around the concept of server management. Thus you can use it both for clustered applications and for applications that are not intended to run in a cluster.

To understand it better, let's give an example: supposing your server topology consists of multiple servers and you have defined a datasource that will be used by your application. So, whether or not you use a cluster, you would need to configure your datasource across all your standalone servers configuration (this means adding the definition of the datasource in every `standalone.xml`).

In this case, the advantage of using a domain is evident: the datasource definition will be contained just in the domain controller that provides a central point through which users can keep configurations consistent and also the ability to roll out configuration changes to the servers in a coordinated fashion.

One other important aspect of domain is the ability to provide a more fine-grained configuration than clustering is able to. For example, you can define server groups, each one with its own custom configuration. In order to achieve the same thing with a clustered configuration, you have to manage each machine's standalone configuration and adapt it to your needs.

Domain and clustering are not, however, mutually exclusive scenarios, but often part of a larger picture; for example, using a domain can further enhance the efficiency of a cluster in advanced configurations where you need to manage starting and stopping multiple AS instances. At the same time, clustering provides typical load balancing and high availability features, which are not integrated into domain management.

On the other hand, there are situations where using a domain may not prove that useful. For example, it's possible that your system administrators have bought or developed their own sophisticated multi-server management tools, which can do more or less the same things that a domain configuration is able to perform. In this situation, it may be not desirable to switch-out what is already ad-hoc configured.

Another classic example where a domain is not needed is the development phase where you don't gain anything from a domain installation. Rather, it may add an unneeded additional complexity to your architecture.

Furthermore, the standalone mode is the only choice available in some scenarios, such as if you are running the application server in embedded mode and thus the choice of a domain is incompatible. For example, when using Arquillian project you can test your Enterprise projects using an embedded container, which is managed by the Arquillian using a standalone-based configuration.

In definitive, since the individual server configuration does not vary if you are running domain mode or standalone mode, you can easily consider developing your application in standalone mode and then switch to domain mode when you are rolling in production the application.

An example domain configuration

We will now provide a detailed example of a domain configuration. In this sample, we will include two separate host controller configurations, each one with a list of three nodes. You would need two separate installations of JBoss AS 7, which can be either executed on two different machines or on the same machine. When running on the same machine, it's practical to assign a virtual IP address to your machines so that you don't have any port conflict in your domain.

The following image shows our domain project:

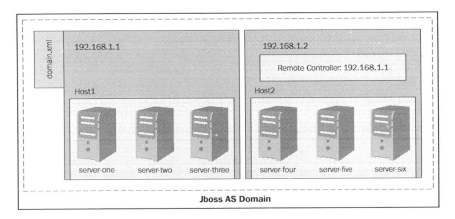

The first thing we need to do is bind the network interfaces to a valid `inet` address both for the public interfaces and for the management interfaces. So, assuming that the first domain installation will be bound to the `inet-address 192.168.1.1`, open the `host.xml` file and change it accordingly:

```
<interfaces>
        <interface name="management">
            <inet-address value="192.168.1.1"/>
        </interface>
        <interface name="public">
          <inet-address value="192.168.1.1"/>
        </interface>
</interfaces>
```

In the second domain installation, change the `inet-address` to `192.168.1.2` in `host.xml`:

```
<interfaces>
        <interface name="management">
          <inet-address value="192.168.1.2"/>
        </interface>
        <interface name="public">
          <inet-address value="192.168.1.2"/>
        </interface>
  </interfaces>
```

The next thing to do will be defining a unique host name for each installation. So, for the first `host.xml`, we will have:

```
<host name="host1"/>
```

While for the second one, simply use:

```
<host name="host2"/>
```

Next, the most important step will be choosing where the domain controller is located. As we have shown earlier in the image, the domain controller will be located in the first installation (`192.168.1.1`), so in the `host.xml` file you should contain the default:

```
<domain-controller>
  <local/>
</domain-controller>
```

Switching to the other installation, point to the domain controller that is running on the host `192.168.1.1`:

```
<domain-controller>
  <remote host="192.168.1.1" port="9999"/>
</domain-controller>
```

The domain configuration is complete. Now, first start up the installation containing the domain controller and then the second installation using the `domain.bat/domain.sh` script in both cases.

If everything was correctly configured, the domain controller will show evidence of the new host controller registered:

Now, let's have a look at the domain from the management console. The management interfaces are discussed in detail in the next chapter. However, we will peek at them shortly now, for the purpose of showing our domain example.

Point the browser to any of the management interfaces:

`http://192.168.1.1:9990/console/`

From the main screen, you can have a look at your domain configuration from different perspectives. By now, we are interested to have a look at host controllers that are part of the domain. So, in the top-right area of the screen, choose the **Runtime** tab, and then select the host you are interested in from the combo-box located on the left.

As you can see, you can find all servers that are running on the domain:

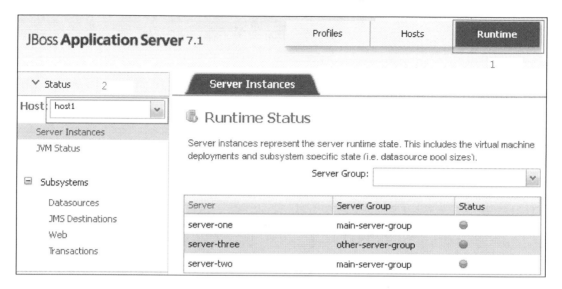

From there, you can not only check their status and group them by server-group, but also start and stop each node. For example, as per default, each distribution contains three nodes: two are activated at startup, while the third one will be started on demand.

Select the node and then, in the **Status** panel, you will be able to start/stop the single node:

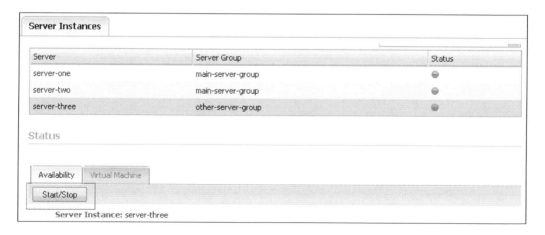

The same configuration could be observed on the **Host 2**, which pretty much contains the same number of nodes:

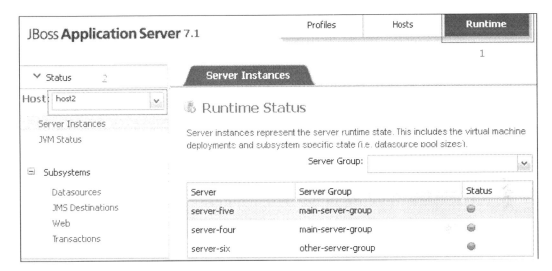

So, it should be clear that each **Host** section has its own list of nodes are part of the domain. What each **Host** depends on is, however, the **Profiles** section that contains the domain **Profile** used by your domain. As we said, one of the most evident advantages of a domain over individual installation is the ability to centralize the services configuration as well as deployed resources.

From within the Web console you can also install application or modules like datasources. In the next chapter we will discuss in depth about deploying and installing a module to a domain. The main difference from the standalone mode is that once the datasource is added to the domain controller (192.168.1.1), its definition will be part of the default profile, and every host that connects to the domain will inherit its configuration.

Changing the domain configuration at runtime

The configuration, which has been created before starting the domain, can actually be changed without restarting the domain. One example of this could be if you need to create, on the fly, a new server group and associate some servers and applications to it.

This is not an academic example. As a matter of fact, it can happen that some of your applications in production have some issues that need to be fixed. You might as well reproduce the issue on a development environment, but that's not always accurate, since development and production often use different database and class versions.

So, what might you do to quickly solve the issue? Create a new server group, for example, associate one or more servers to it, and deploy and test the application on it.

This can be done using the admin console (and also the CLI) in a matter of minutes. Bring back the admin console, and select the **Profiles** tab in the upper right area. From there choose the **Groups Configuration** in the left column of your GUI. This interface will let you Add server groups by clicking on the **Add** button:

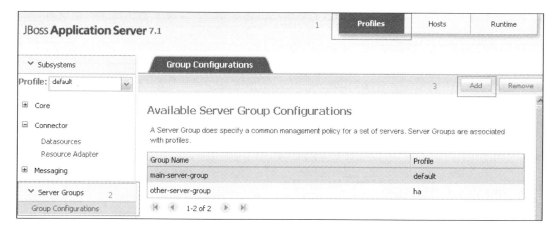

Then, choose a meaningful name for your group, for example, `Staging` will be just fine, and select a **Server Group** configuration on which the new group will be based:

Good. Now, it's time to associate one or more servers to the new group. Move to the **Hosts** section, and pickup any server from the **Server Configuration** menu, followed by the button **Add**.

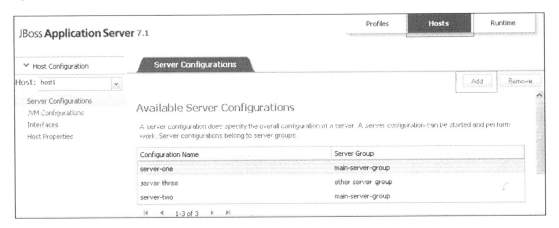

This will actually bring you to a dialog box, which will ask you the new server name and the associated server group. For example, add the Test Server and associate it to the **Staging** group, with a port offset of 750 (in practice, every service will be bound to a port of default port address + 750).

Once you have set up a new server group and one or more servers that are part of it, you can use it to deploy your applications. Deployment of applications can be done from the **Runtime** upper tab, which will activate the **Deployments** panel, in the lower-left side of the screen:

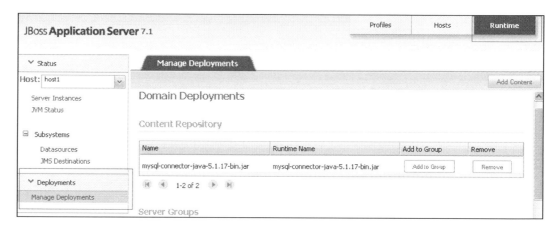

From there, you can add and remove deployments to your groups. Complete details about application deployment are included in the next chapter, which is all about deploying applications on JBoss AS 7.

Summary

In this chapter, we have gone through the JBoss domain set-up and configuration. By configuring a server domain, you will be able to manage your servers from a single centralized point, which is desirable when you have to administer a large set of server nodes.

Every domain is composed of four main elements:

- The **domain controller** that handles the domain configuration
- The **host controller** that coordinates the lifecycle of server processes and the distribution of deployments
- The **process controller** that handles the domain server processes and manages their I/O streams
- The **server** nodes where the applications are distributed

Every domain is made up of one or more server groups, which can promote a fine-grained configuration for a part of the domain. Each server group can define its own JVM attributes, the socket binding interfaces, and the system properties, which are loaded at startup, and finally deploy the applications running on the top of it.

Server groups are defined in the configuration file `domain.xml`, which also contains the enterprise services that are included in the domain.

The composition of server groups is contained in the file `host.xml`, which also contains the location of the domain controller, the default JVMs, and `network` and `management` interfaces.

6
Deploying Applications on JBoss AS 7

Deployment is the process of uploading resources or applications into the application server. In the software production cycle, it's the step that logically follows the development phase and can be performed either manually or in an automated fashion, using scripts.

In this chapter, we will explore both approaches using the set of tools that are part of the server distribution. We will also cover how to deploy resources on the applications server using the Eclipse development environment, which is the preferred choice of JBoss AS developers.

In the last part of this chapter, we provide details about the new JBoss AS **classloader** architecture. In short, our agenda for this chapter includes the following topics:

- Which resources can be deployed on the application server
- How to deploy applications on JBoss AS standalone
- How to deploy applications on JBoss AS domain
- Understanding the JBoss AS 7 classloading architecture

Deploying resources on the application server

There are basically three file types that we work with in Java Enterprise applications:

1. **JAR file**: This is the most basic package that can be used for both application and common resources.
2. **WAR file**: This archive is used for packaging web applications.
3. **EAR file**: This package acts as a container for Enterprise applications.

Besides these, JBoss AS is able to process the following archives, which provides additional functionalities to the application server:

*   **RAR file**: This is a resource adapter file, which is used to define a resource adapter component (the resource adapter subsystem is provided by IronJacamar project; for more information, look here: http://www.jboss.org/ironjacamar)
*   **SAR file**: This enables the deployment of Service Archives containing MBean Services, as supported by previous versions of the application server

In this chapter, we will discuss the first three kinds of archives, which constitute the typical packaging solution for Java Enterprise applications. Before discussing application deployment, let's see the single archives a bit more in detail.

The JAR archive

A **Java Archive (JAR)** file is used for organizing many files into one. The actual internal physical layout is much like a ZIP file, and as a matter of fact, it uses the same algorithm as the ZIP utility for compressing files.

A JAR is generally used to distribute Java classes and associated metadata. In Java EE applications, the JAR file often contains utility code, shared libraries, and EJBs.

The WAR archive

A **Web Application Archive (WAR)** file is essentially an archive used to encapsulate a web application. The web application usually includes a collection of **Java Server Pages (JSP)**, Servlets, Java classes, XHTML, and HTML files, plus other file types, depending on the technology used.

Since Java EE 6, a web application is now able to package EJBs in a WAR, using the same packaging guidelines that apply to web application classes. This means that you can place EJB classes under the WEB-INF/classes directory or as a JAR file within the WEB-INF/lib directory.

Because of this, it's expected that developers will use the WAR archive as the most common type of archive to distribute Java EE 6 applications.

The EAR archive

An **Enterprise Archive (EAR)** file represents an application archive, which acts as a container for a set of modules. An EAR file can contain any the following:

- One or more web modules packaged in WAR files
- One or more EJB modules packaged in JAR files
- One or more application client modules
- Additional JAR files required by the application
- JBoss specific archives such as Service Archives (.sar)

The advantage of using an Enterprise Archive file is two-fold: at first, it helps to distribute all applications components using a single archive, instead of distributing every single module. Second, and most important, is the fact that applications within an EAR archive will be loaded by a single classloader. Thus, by default, each module will have visibility on other modules packed in the archive.

The isolation level of applications modules contained in the EAR archive is controlled by the ear-subdeployments-isolated element of the main configuration file (standalone.xml/domain.xml).

```
<subsystem xmlns="urn:jboss:domain:ee:1.0" >
  <ear-subdeployments-isolated>false</ear-subdeployments-isolated>
</subsystem>
```

In the section of this chapter named *JBoss AS 7 classloading explained*, we will discuss in depth the application server classloading architecture, also showing how to override this configuration setting at application level.

Deploying applications on JBoss AS standalone

Deployment applications on JBoss AS has been traditionally a fairly simple task on JBoss AS, so our readers might argue why we have dedicated a full chapter to it. The answer is that deploying applications on AS 7 can be achieved using several different strategies. The first distinction, which we must account for, is about the automation of the deployment:

- **Automatic deployment**: This is triggered by the deployment scanner when a change happens in one deployed resource
- **Manual deployment**: This does not rely on the deployment scanner to trigger a deployment, but on a set of marker files to decide if the user needs to start/restart an application

Automatic application deployment

Automatic application deployment is a simple process that consists of dropping an application into the deployments folder, which is located in the path JBOSS_HOME\standalone\deployments.

By default, every application archive (WAR, JAR, EAR, and SAR) that is placed into this folder is automatically deployed on the server.

The service that scans for deployed resources is called the **deployment scanner,** and it is configured within the `standalone.xml` configuration file. You can find it by searching for the `deployment-scanner` domain.

```
<subsystem xmlns="urn:jboss:domain:deployment-scanner:1.0">
  <deployment-scanner name="default" path="deployments"
    scan-interval="5000" relative-to="jboss.server.base.dir"/>
</subsystem>
```

As you can see, by default the server scans in the deployments folder every `5000` ms. This service is, however, customizable in many ways. Let's see two main changes that we can operate on it.

Deploying applications on a custom folder

If you want to change the default deployment path, you need to operate on the `relative-to` and `path` properties. If you provide both properties, the `deployment` folder will be a sum of both properties. For example, supposing that you have defined the path `as7deployment`, you can later reference it as a relative path for your deployments:

```
<paths>
  <path name="as7deployments" path="C:/AS7" />
</paths>
<subsystem xmlns="urn:jboss:domain:deployment-scanner:1.0">
  <deployment-scanner name="default"
    path="deployments" relative-to="as7deployments"
    scan-enabled="true" scan-interval="5000"
  deployment-timeout="60"/>
</subsystem>
```

In this configuration, the deployment scanner will look for applications under the `C:/AS7/deployments` folder.

The same effect can be achieved by using an absolute path for your deployments, leaving out the `relative-to` property and by configuring the `path` element, as shown in this example:

```
<deployment-scanner scan-interval="5000"
  path="C:/AS7/deployments" />
```

Changing the behavior of the application scanner

As we said, by default every packaged archive that is deployed is automatically activated. Exploded applications, on the other hand, need one more step to be activated (see the section *Manual application deployment*).

We can, at any time, change the behavior of the deployment scanner. The properties that control the `auto-deploy` feature are `auto-deploy-zipped` and `auto-deploy-exploded`, respectively.

```
<deployment-scanner scan-interval="5000"
  relative-to="jboss.server.base.dir"
  path="deployments"
  auto-deploy-zipped="true" auto-deploy-exploded="false"/>
```

For example, you could set the `auto-deploy-exploded` to `true`, to achieve automatic redeployment of exploded archives as well:

```
<deployment-scanner scan-interval="5000"
  relative-to="jboss.server.base.dir"
  path="deployments"
  auto-deploy-zipped="true" auto-deploy-exploded="true"/>
```

Deploying an application using the CLI

Direct copy of the application archives is the favorite choice for many developers, as it can be performed automatically by the development environment. However, we would like to stress the advantage of using the CLI interface, which offers a wide choice of additional options when deploying and also provides the opportunity to deploy applications remotely.

All it takes to deploy an application archive is logging into the application server, either local or remote, and issuing the `deploy` shell command. When used without arguments, the `deploy` command provides the list of applications that are currently deployed:

```
[disconnected /] connect
Connected to standalone controller at localhost:9999
[localhost:9999 /] deploy
ExampleApp.war
```

If you feed to the shell a resource archive, such as `.war`, it will deploy it on the standalone server right away:

```
 [standalone@localhost:9999 /] deploy ../MyApp.war
'MyApp.war' deployed successfully.
```

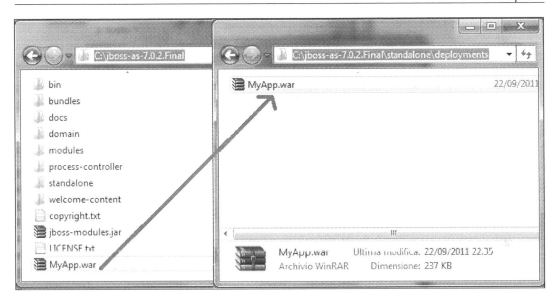

As you can see from the screenshot, the CLI uses the folder where your deployments were actually launched as their initial location by default JBOSS_HOME/bin). You can, however, use absolute paths when specifying the location of your archives; the CLI expansion facility (using the *Tab* key) makes this option fairly simple:

```
[standalone@localhost:9999 /] deploy c:\deployments\MyApp.war

'MyApp.war' deployed successfully.
```

As it is, the application is deployed and activated so that the user can access it. If you want to just perform the deployment of the application and defer to the activation at a later time, you have to add the --disabled switch:

```
[standalone@localhost:9999 /] deploy ../MyApp.war --disabled

'MyApp.war' deployed successfully.
```

In order to activate the application, simply issue another deploy command without the --disabled switch:

```
[standalone@localhost:9999 /] deploy --name=MyApp.war

'MyApp.war' deployed successfully.
```

 Noticed the optional --name switch that has been added? As a matter of fact, when using this switch you will be able to use the **tab completion** feature so that you can automatically find the inactive deployment unit.

Re-deploying the application requires an additional flag to the deploy command. Use the -f argument to force the application redeployment.

```
[localhost:9999 /] deploy -f ../MyApp.war
'MyApp.war' re-deployed successfully.
```

Un-deploying the application can be done through the undeploy command, which takes as argument the application deployed.

```
[localhost:9999 /] undeploy MyApp.war
'MyApp.war' undeployed successfully.
```

By checking the configuration file, you will notice that the deployment element for your application has been removed.

Deploying an application using the Web admin console

The previous steps can also be completed by using the other management interface, provided by the application server: the Web admin console. Start the console by launching your browser at the home address: http://localhost:9990/console.

 Since JBoss AS 7.1.0 you need to add at least one user to access the Web console. To add a new user execute the add-user.bat/add-user.sh script within the bin folder of your AS 7 installation and enter the requested information. See the chapter 10 for more details about it.

Server deployments are managed by the application server by selecting the "**Runtime**" (1) upper menu, and choosing the **Deployments | Manage Deployments** (2) label. If you want to add a new application to AS7, just click on the **Add Content** (3) button in the mid-right area of your console:

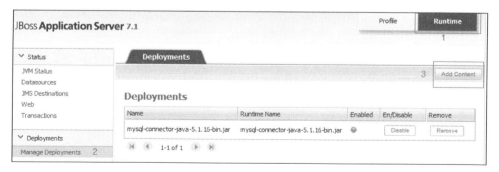

An intuitive wizard will guide you through the selection of the application to be added, including the runtime name that will be assigned to it:

The admin console, by default, deploys the application, but does not enable it for use. By clicking on the **Enable** button, the application is now finally available:

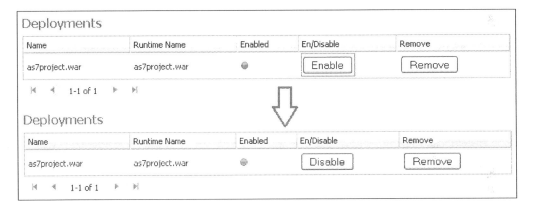

Deploying an application using the Eclipse environment

Eclipse is the most widely used application development environment for Java developers, and it's also the favorite IDE for JBoss developers, as the JBoss Tools project (http://www.jboss.org/tools) supports the Eclipse environment by providing a set of plugins for JBoss projects.

In the first chapter of this book, we have shown the installation steps for Eclipse Indigo, which is compatible with the JBoss Tools 3.3.0 M3 release. This release introduces a server adapter, which allows you to start/stop/debug and deploy applications on JBoss AS 7, using the standalone mode.

Deploying applications to JBoss AS 7 is fairly easy once you have your Eclipse plugin installed. Simply reach the **Server** tab and right-click on the project you want to deploy. Choose **Full Publish** to deploy your application:

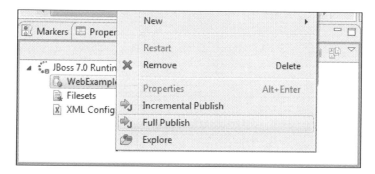

Choosing the packaging style for Eclipse deployments

If you have installed the JBoss Tools up-to-date release, you'll see that the **Server** tab offers more options than the traditional **Server** menu. By double-clicking on the JBoss 7.0 Runtime, you will have access to a tabbed menu, which contains two options: **Overview** and **Deployment**. The **Deployment** option is specific to JBoss tools and lets you choose the deployment location and the packaging style of deployment:

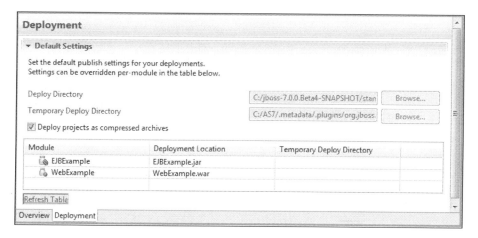

By checking the option **Deploy projects as compressed archives**, your application will be compressed and packaged.

If you choose to deploy your application as an exploded archive, Eclipse will add a `.dodeploy` marker file once the application copying has been completed. This will trigger immediate application deployment. See the next section for more information about marker files.

Manual application deployment

When using this approach, the deployment scanner will not directly deploy the applications that are placed in the deployments folder. Rather, it will use a set of marker files, which are used to trigger application re-deployment and capture the result of the operation.

You might wonder why marker files have been introduced in this release of the application server and chosen as the default server option for exploded deployments.

Actually, there are several reasons behind this choice, and all of them are related to the operating system's file system, API: as a matter of fact, exploded archives involve the moving/replacing of files in your file system, which should be performed atomically. By atomic operation, we mean that a file system operation needs to be performed as a single operation. Unfortunately, some operating systems such as Windows don't treat complex file system operations, such as a file moving, as an atomic operation.

As a proof of concept, most Windows users often experience deployment issues on earlier releases of JBoss AS, because, for example, the JVM refuses to release a file handle to `META-INF/application.xml` or an EJB descriptor file. That's because Windows uses a mandatory file lock, which means that it prevents any application from accessing the file. On the other hand, operating systems, such as UNIX, use an advisory file lock, which means that unless an application checks for a file lock, it will not be prevented from accessing the file. Additionally, one more reason why the deployment needs to be revised is the different structure of Java EE 6 applications, which does not mandate any more file descriptors, for example, the `web.xml`. Earlier releases of the application server used the file descriptors as a trigger to invoke the re-deployment of applications, so you could barely "touch" one of these files to start re-deployment. Without the need to provide file descriptors, it was necessary that a new solid approach for triggering deployments of applications be adopted, which could solve all these issues.

Finally, by using marker files, the application server is able to solve a common issue related to large deployment files. If you ever tried to deploy a large package unit (especially over a network), you might have experienced deployment errors, because the deployment scanner starts deploying before the copy operation is completed, resulting in partially-completed deployments.

Marker files provide the new default approach for JBoss AS 7 exploded deployments. They consist either in empty files, with a suffix, which are placed by the user, or in files that are added by the container to indicate the outcome of an operation.

The most relevant marker file is the `.dodeploy`, which triggers application re-deployment. As a matter of fact, when we add an explode the deployment and the `auto-deploy-exploded` attribute is false on the deployment scanner, the logs in the console warn us that the application is still not activated.

```
05:48:13,438 INFO  [org.jboss.as.deployment] (DeploymentScanner-threads -
1) Found MyApplication.war in deployment directory. To trigger deployment
create a file called MyApplication.war.dodeploy
```

Unix users can trigger deployment by simply using the `touch` command:

```
touch MyApplication.war.dodeploy
```

Windows users do not have an equivalent `touch` command. You have some viable alternatives: one of these is installing the `cygwin` shell, which provides a Linux look-and-feel environment for Windows.

If you don't feel worthy using `cygwin`, then you could simply use a DOS command to copy/replace the `.dodeploy` file in the `deployments` folder:

```
copy MyApplication.war.dodeploy %JBOSS_HOME%/standalone/deployments
```

If you feel more adventurous, you can use an advanced syntax of the `copy` command, which allows you to update the timestamp of an existing file:

```
copy /b MyApplication.war.dodeploy +,,
```

Once you have started the deployment process, the application server will reply with two possible outcomes. A deployed marker file (for example, `MyApplication.war.deployed`) will be placed by the deployment scanner service to indicate that the given content has been deployed into the runtime, and your logs should confirm the outcome:

```
05:49:23,211 INFO  [org.jboss.as.server.controller] (DeploymentScanner-
threads - 2) Deployed "MyApplication.war"I
```

> If you remove the file `.deployed`, the application will be un-deployed and an `.undeployed` marker file will be added to the deployments folder (for example, `MyApplication.war.undeployed`). If you try to remove the `.undeployed` file, the application will be again deployed. This is a useful shortcut for quickly un-deploying (or re-deploying) the application, without deleting it on the file system.

The other possible outcome is a deployment failure, which is indicated by a `.failed` marker. The content of the file will include some information about the cause of the failure; however, you are advised to check out the server logs for further information on the cause of the error.

 When using the `auto-deploy` mode, removing the `.failed` marker file will make the deployment eligible for deployment again.

Additionally, the user can place the `.skipdeploy` marker file (for example, `myapp.war.skipdeploy`), which disables `auto-deploy` of the content for as long as this marker file is present. When would you need to use this marker file? Mostly, if you are relying on automatic deployment, and you want to ensure that no deploy will be triggered when updates are still incomplete.

Let's see a sample script, which can be used to perform a safe re-deployment of a web application named `large.war`, when using the Linux operating system:

```
touch $JBOSS_HOME/standalone/deployments/large.war.skipdeploy
cp -r large.war/  $JBOSS_HOME /standalone/deployments
rm $JBOSS_HOME /standalone/deployments/large.war.skipdeploy
```

The Windows equivalent script is not exactly fit for the faint-hearted:

```
copy /b %JBOSS_HOME%\standalone\deployments\large.war.skipdeploy +,,
mkdir %JBOSS_HOME%\standalone\deployments\large.war
cd %JBOSS_HOME%\standalone\deployments\large.war
xcopy c:\application_home\large.war /e
del %JBOSS_HOME%\standalone\deployments\large.war.skipdeploy
```

Unfortunately, the standard DOS shell does not have an equivalent `cp -r` command to copy directories, but you have to move first in the destination directory, and then acquire with `xcopy` the directory content from the source folder, which in our case is `c:\application_home`.

Finally, the application server provides some additional temporary marker files, such as `.isdeploying`, `.isundeploying`, or `.pending`, which are placed by the deployment scanner to indicate the transition to a deployment or un-deployment of a resource. Full details of marker files are provided in the `README.txt` placed in the deployments folder of the server distribution.

Here's a short summary of the available marker files used by the application server:

Marker	Created by	Description
.dodeploy	User	Creating this file triggers application deployment. Touching this file causes application re-deployment.
.skipdeploy	User	Application auto-deployment is disabled as long as this file exists.
.deployed	JBoss AS	Application is deployed. Removing it causes un-deployment of the application.
.undeployed	JBoss AS	Application has been un-deployed. Removing it causes re-deployment of the application.
.failed	JBoss AS	Application deployment failed.
.isdeploying	JBoss AS	Application deployment in progress.
.isundeploying	JBoss AS	Application un-deployment in progress.
.pending	JBoss AS	One condition prevents application deployment (for example, file copying in progress).

Deploying applications on a JBoss AS domain

Deploying applications in a JBoss domain cannot be achieved with a single cut-and-paste operation like for standalone domains. As a matter of fact, there's no predefined deployments folder in the domain installation. The reason for this is because in the domain mode, there can be many servers belonging to different server groups, each one running different profiles. In that situation, a single deployments folder would raise the obvious question: which server groups will be using that folder? This requires some knowledge that the AS deployment scanner cannot have.

So, basically, a deployment on a JBoss AS domain can be performed using the following set of options:

- Using the Command Line interface
- Using the Admin Web interface

Here's a complete outline of both approaches:

Deploying to an AS domain using the CLI

Start by launching the CLI and connect to the domain controller:

```
[disconnected /] connect
Connected to domain controller at localhost:9999
```

When you are deploying an application using domain mode, you have to specify to which server group the deployment is associated. The CLI lets you choose between two options:

1. Deploy to all server groups.
2. Deploy to a single server group.

We discuss the options in two separate sections.

Deploy to all server groups

When choosing this option, the application will be deployed to all the available server groups. The `--all-server-groups` flag can be used for this purpose.

For example:

```
[domain@localhost:9999 /] deploy ../application.ear --all-server-groups
Successfully deployed application.ear
```

If, on the other hand, you want to un-deploy an application from all server groups belonging to a domain, you have to issue the `undeploy` command:

```
[domain@localhost:9999 /] undeploy application.ear --all-relevant-server-
groups
Successfully undeployed application.ear
```

You might have noticed that the `undeploy` command uses the `--all-relevant-server-groups` instead of `--all-server-groups`. The reason for this difference is that the deployment may not be enabled on all server groups, so by using this option, you will actually un-deploy it just from all the server groups in which the deployment is enabled.

Deploying an application as `disabled` can be useful if you have some startup beans (which are activated when the application is enabled) and you want to load them, but you don't want to trigger their execution. For example, because the database, or any other Enterprise information system, is temporarily unavailable.

Deploy to a single server group

The other option lets you perform a selective deployment of your application, just on the server groups you have indicated.

```
[domain@localhost:9999 /] deploy application.ear --server-groups=main-
server-group

Successfully deployed application.ear
```

You are not limited to a single server group, but you can separate multiple server groups with a comma; for example:

```
[domain@localhost:9999 /] deploy application.ear --server-groups=main-
server-group,other-server-group

Successfully deployed application.ear
```

 The `tab-completion` will help complete the value for the list of `--server-groups` elected for deployment.

Now, suppose we want to un-deploy the application from just one server group. There can be two possible outcomes. If the application is available just on that server group, you will successfully complete the un-deployment:

```
[domain@localhost:9999 /] undeploy as7project.war --server-groups=main-
server-group

Successfully undeployed as7project.war.
```

On the other hand, if your application is available on other server groups, the following error will be returned by the CLI:

```
C:\WINDOWS\system32\cmd.exe                          _ □ ×
[domain@localhost:9999 /]
[domain@localhost:9999 /] deploy application.ear --all-server-groups
'application.ear' deployed successfully.
[domain@localhost:9999 /] undeploy application.ear --server-groups=main-server-g
roup
Undeploy failed: {"domain-failure-description" => {"Composite operation failed a
nd was rolled back. Steps that failed:" => {"Operation step-3" => "Cannot remove
 deployment application.ear from the domain as it is still used by server groups
 [other-server-group]"}}}
[domain@localhost:9999 /]
```

It seems that something went wrong. As a matter of fact, when you are removing an application from a server group, the domain controller checks that the application is not referenced by any other server group, otherwise the previous command will fail.

You can, however, instruct the domain controller to un-deploy the application, without deleting the content also:

```
[domain@localhost:9999 /] undeploy application.ear --server-groups=main-
server-group --keep-content
```

```
Successfully undeployed application.ear.
```

So, we have learnt quite a lot of available options to deploy applications in a domain. Before moving to the admin console, let's review the CLI deployment options:

Command	Options	Effect
deploy	--all-server-groups	Deploys an application to all server groups
undeploy	--server-groups	Deploys an application to one or more server groups
undeploy	--all-relevant-server-groups	Un-deploys and removes an application from all server groups
undeploy	--server-groups	Un-deploys an application from one server group. Fails if it's referenced in another server group
undeploy	--server-groups –keep-content	Un-deploys an application from one server group, without deleting it

Deploying to an AS domain using the Admin console

Deploying applications using the **Admin** console is pretty intuitive and requires just a few simple steps. Start by logging into the Web application at the default address: `http://localhost:9990/console`.

Then, select the **Runtime** tab (Point **1** in the screenshot). You will see that in the left panel of the screen, there's a **Deployments** menu, which includes the option **Manage Deployments** (Point **2**).

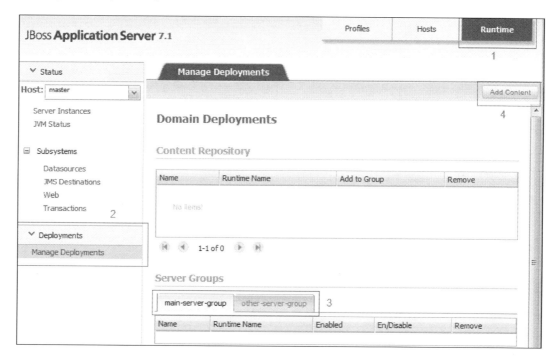

From there, you can use the tabbed menu named **Server Groups** (Point **3**) to check which applications are deployed on the single server groups.

The application can be uploaded using the **Add Content** button (Point **4**), which introduces you to the next dialog:

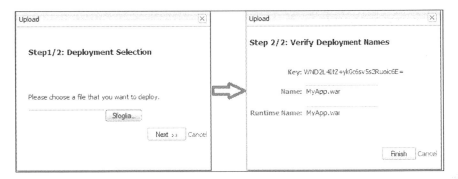

Once you are done with the upload wizard, the application will be uploaded to the domain repository. In order to deploy/un-deploy it to the single server groups, you should select first the server group (Option **1**) on which you want to operate, and then click the **Add to Group** (Option **2**) button.

At this point, the application is deployed but still not enabled. Choose the **Enable** button to complete the deployment of the application.

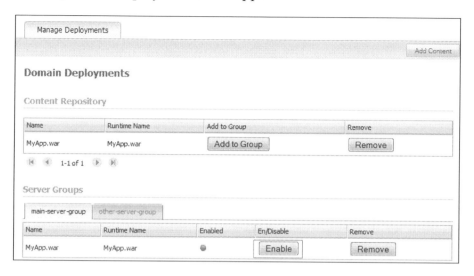

The **Remove** button within the **Server-Groups** area will remove the deployment from the server group selected, while the other **Remove** button within the **Content Repository** will actually delete it from the temporary domain repository where uploaded applications are bundled.

JBoss AS 7 classloading explained

As mandated by Java EE specifications, an application server should ideally give its deployed applications the freedom to use whatever utility library and whatever version of it, regardless of the presence of concurrent applications that want to use the same library.

This is also known as namespace isolation (Java EE 5 specifications, section EE.8.4). However, loading classes from different namespaces can raises some issues, which are not easy to solve, for example, what happens if I pack a newer version of an utility library with my application, while an older version of the same library was loaded by the application server? Or, how can I use two different versions of the same utility library, simultaneously, within the same instance of the application server?

The JBoss AS classloading strategy has changed sensibly through the years: basically, the 4.x releases of the application server used a UnifiedClassLoader, which aimed to reduce communications overhead between running applications, as class data could be shared by reference or simple copies.

One of the major outstanding issues not resolved with the `UnifiedClassLoader` is **classloading dependencies**. The idea being that if one application (A) uses the classes of another application (B), the system should know to re-deploy A when B gets re-deployed, otherwise it will be referencing stale classes. There were actually two different attempts to try to make this work, without the user having to configure anything. Neither attempt really worked and both were dropped.

Since JBoss AS 5.0 was introduced, a new classloader was based on the new **Virtual File System (VFS)**. The VFS was implemented to simplify and unify file handling within the application server. The new classloader, named the VFS classloader, uses VFS to locate JAR and class files. Even though this represented a significant change in how classes are loaded in JBoss AS 5.0, the resulting behavior is much the same as for prior versions of JBoss AS.

A common source of errors is including API classes in a deployment that are also provided by the container. This can result in multiple versions of the class being created and the deployment failing to deploy properly.

Classloading in AS 7 marks a radical departure from previous attempts. Classloading is now based on the JBoss modules project, and any application that is deployed is in effect a **module**. This affirmation raises some questions from a careful reader: which is the module name assigned to a deployed application? And, also, how are dependencies between modules handled by the AS?

Let's answer each question in a separate section.

Getting to know module names

Getting to know the module name is not an academic exercise. As a matter of fact, we can establish dependencies between modules. So, for many cases, it's needed to know which is the module name assigned to an application.

Therefore, applications that are packaged as top-level archives (such as WAR, JAR, and SAR) are assigned the following module name:

```
deployment.[archive name]
```

For example, a web application named `WebExample1.war` will be deployed as the following module name:

```
deployment.WebExample1.war
```

On the other hand, on applications that contain nested modules (such as the EAR archive), every single archive will be assigned a module name using this classification:

```
deployment.[ear archive name].[sub deployment archive name]
```

So, the same web application, if contained in the archive `EnterpriseApp.ear`, will be deployed with the following name:

`deployment.EnterpriseApp.ear.WebExample1.war`

Finding the isolation level

In *Chapter 2, Configuring the Application* Server, we have intentionally deployed an application that used `log4j Api`, adding the `log4j` library into the `WEB-INF/lib folder`. The application was deployed without a hitch, leaving the question: why do we need to add libraries that are already included as a module in the application server (in our case, in the `modules\org\apache\log4j\main` path)?

The general rule is that on JBoss AS 7, every deployed application module is isolated from other modules; this means that, by default, it does not have visibility on the AS modules, nor do the AS modules have visibility on the application.

Using the application server modules is, however, pretty easy and can be summarized in a simple sentence: *add a dependency to the required module and the AS will use it*. The application server automatically adds dependencies, or they need to be signaled by the user:

- The core module libraries (namely the `Enterprise` classes) are qualified as implicit dependencies, so they are automatically added to your application when the deployer detects their usage

- The other module libraries need to be explicitly declared by the user in the application's `MANIFEST` file or in a custom JBoss deployment file named `jboss-deployment-structure.xml` (more about this file in the *Advanced deployment strategies* section).

Implicit dependencies:

Pointing out dependencies for API that are commonly used by the Enterprise application can be tedious. So, as we have anticipated, they are automatically added for you by the application server. Some are added when the application server detects some annotations or configuration files that are typical of that module. For example, adding a `beans.xml` file triggers the automatic **Weld** dependency.

The following mind map shows a synthetic view of the modules that are implicitly added to your application:

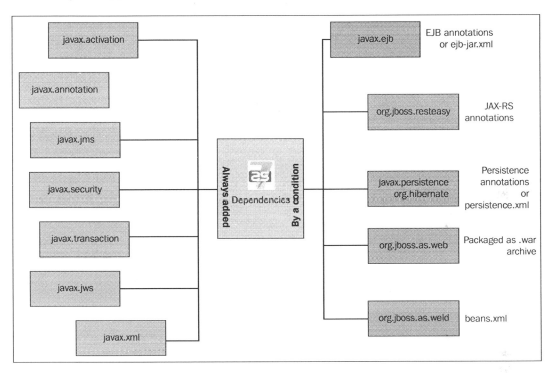

The meaning of this image is simple: if your application uses any of the core modules indicated, then you don't need to specify any dependency, as the application server is able to link the module automatically.

Explicit dependencies

Modules that are not qualified as implicit dependencies need to be declared by the user. In our initial example, the log4j library is not mentioned as an implicit dependency, so we had to package the log4j JAR along with our application. We can, however, instruct the deployer to use the log4j library, which is bundled in the application server distribution. The simplest and recommended approach to achieve it is including in the META-INF/MANIFEST.MF the Dependencies: [module] declaration. In our case, to make your application dependent on log4j, just include in your manifest file the following code:

```
Dependencies: org.apache.log4j
```

Please note that the module name does not always match with the package name of the library. The actual module name is specified in the `module.xml` file by the name attribute of the module element.

Users will typically use the Eclipse (or any other IDE) to update the manifest file, without the need to perform any tedious archive update:

You are not limited to a single dependency, as you can add multiple dependencies separated by a comma. For example, in order to add a dependency on both `log4j` and **Apache Velocity API**, you would use the following:

```
Dependencies: org.apache.log4j,org.apache.velocity
```

You can even export the dependencies used by one application module to other applications, by adding the export keyword. For example, in the earlier application, we're now exporting the dependencies to other modules:

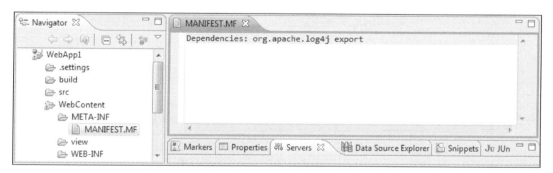

Applications that are marked as dependent to the `deployment.WebApp.war` module will also have access to its dependencies:

> The `export` parameter can also be used to export a dependency to all sub-deployments contained in the ear. Consequently, if you export a dependency from the top-level of the ear (or by a JAR in the `ear/lib` directory), then the dependency will be available to all sub-deployment units as well.

Within the `META-INF/MANIFEST.MF`, you can also specify additional commands that can modify the server deployer's behavior. For example, the optional attribute can be added to specify that the deployment will not fail if the module is not found at deployment time.

Finally, when the `services` keyword is specified, the deployer will try to load services that are placed within the `META-INF/services` of the archive.

> The `service` API has become `public` in Java SE 6. A **service** can be defined as a set of programming interfaces and classes that provide access to some specific application functionality or feature. A **Service Provider Interface (SPI)** is the set of `public` interfaces and `abstract` classes that a service defines.
>
> You can define a service provider by implementing the service provider API. Usually, you will create a JAR file to hold your provider. To register your provider, you must create a provider configuration file in the JAR file's `META-INF/services` directory. When adding the `services` attribute to your `META-INF/MANIFEST.MF`, you will actually be able to load the services contained in the `META-INF/services` directory.
>
> One excellent introduction to the SPI Api is available at: `http://java.sun.com/developer/technicalArticles/javase/extensible`.

Setting up global modules

This option resembles a bit of the old AS approach for loading common libraries, where you used to place them in the folder JBOSS_HOME/common/lib.

If you define a section named global-modules within your standalone.xml/ domain.xml, then you will make the module accessible to other AS modules. For example, instead of declaring a dependency on log4j, you could alternatively use the following section:

```
<subsystem xmlns="urn:jboss:domain:ee:1.0">
  <global-modules>
    <module name="org.apache.log4j" />
  </global-modules>
</subsystem>
```

Although this approach is not generally recommended, as it brings us back to a concept of monolithic application server, it can still yield some benefits. For example, if you are migrating some older applications, and you don't want or simply cannot specify dependencies into the archive.

Advanced deployment strategies

What we have learnt so far can be enough for configuring many kinds of applications. If you are using a complex archive configuration, such as an EAR archive with several modules and dependencies, it would prove useful to define your classloading strategy in a single file.

The configuration file jboss-deployment-structure.xml can do exactly this. The advantages of using this file are many:

- You can define the dependencies of all application modules in a single file
- You can load the modules classes using a finer grained manner by including/ excluding all or part of modules
- You can define classloading isolation policy for your applications packaged in an Enterprise archive

Let's see with some practical examples what jboss-deployment-structure.xml can do for you.

Setting up a single module dependency

We have already learnt how to activate a `log4j` dependency, using the `Dependencies` attribute in the archive's `MANIFEST` file. The same effect can be achieved by using the `jboss-deployment-structure.xml` file. Let's recap the archive structure, which is basically made up of a web application named `WebApp.war`.

As you can see, the file `jboss-deployment-structure.xml` needs to be placed within the `META-INF` folder of the EAR.

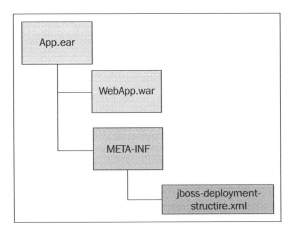

Here's its content:

```
<jboss-deployment-structure>
  <sub-deployment name="WebApp.war">
    <dependencies>
      <module name="org.apache.log4j" />
    </dependencies>
  </sub-deployment>
</jboss-deployment-structure>
```

The file `jboss-deployment-structure` is not for exclusive use of EARs; as a matter of fact, you could also deploy it ithin the `WebApp` application by placing it within the `WEB-INF` folder of the archive. It is, however, applicable only as top-level archive. Thus, if a `jboss-deployment-structure.xml` is placed in the WAR's `WEB-INF` folder and the WAR is packaged in a EAR archive, then the `jboss-deployment-structure.xml` is ignored.

The relevant part of this file is the sub-deployment element, which references the web application, including within it the dependencies element. The expected outcome is that the application server will trigger the dependency to `log4j` API, which will therefore be visible by our web application.

Excluding the server automatic dependencies

Earlier in this chapter, we have shown how the application server is able to trigger some dependencies, automatically, when some conditions are met. For example, if you deploy a JSF application (containing the `faces-config.xml` file), then the JSF 2.1 API implementation is automatically added.

This might not always be the desired option, for example, because you want to provide another release implementation for that module. You can easily achieve this using the exclusion section in the `jboss-deployment-structure.xml`, as shown here:

```
<jboss-deployment-structure>
  <deployment>
    <exclusions>
      <module name="javax.faces.api" />
      <module name="com.sun.jsf-impl" />
    </exclusions>
    <dependencies>
      <module name="javax.faces.api" slot="1.2"/>
      <module name="com.sun.jsf-impl" slot="1.2"/>
    </dependencies>
  </deployment>
</jboss-deployment-structure>
```

Notice in the `dependencies` section we have added our alternate JSF `1.2` implementation, which will be used by your application. Actually, this JSF implementation ships with the application server distribution along with the `javax.faces.api` module path, under the folder specified by the `slot` attribute. In our case, this corresponds to the `JBOSS_HOME/modules/javax/faces/api/1.2` folder.

Isolating sub-deployments

Supposing you have an application that is made up of a web application, an EJB module, and a JAR file containing utility classes. All sub-deployments are placed at the root of the archive, so that they will be able to see each other. This can be convenient, however, supposing that your web application itself contains some implementations of the same EJB. That's absolutely possible since Java EE 6 specification allows your web application to include EJB classes within the `WEB-INF/classes` or `WEB-INF/lib` folder.

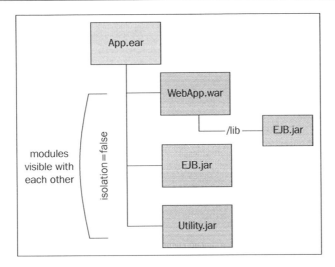

How does the classloader solves this conflict? The application server classloader has a priority list when loading classes that are used to avoid any conflict between loaded classes.

- The maximum priority is given to modules, automatically, by the container, including the Java EE APIs. Libraries that are contained in the modules folder are included in this category.

- Then, libraries that are indicated by the user within the MANIFEST.MF of the packaged archive as **Dependencies** (or in the jboss-deployment-structure.xml file).

- Next, libraries that are packed within the application itself, such as classes contained in WEB-INF/lib or WEB-INF/classes.

- Finally, libraries that are packed within the same EAR archive (in the EAR's lib folder).

So, in this example, the EJB libraries located in the WEB-INF folder will "hide" the implementations of EJB.jar top-level deployment. Whether or not this is the desired action from the container, you can still override it:

```
<jboss-deployment-structure>
  <ear-subdeployments-isolated>false</ear-subdeployments-isolated>
  <sub-deployment name="WebApp.war">
    <dependencies>
      <module name="deployment.App.ear.EJB.jar" />
    </dependencies>
  </sub-deployment>
</jboss-deployment-structure>
```

In this example, we have added a dependency to the `EJB.jar`, which is placed at the root of the archive and which will override the implementation packed within the web application.

Notice the `ear-subdeployments-isolated` element placed at the top of the file. By setting the EAR isolation level, you will be able to indicate if the sub-deployments modules are visible to each other.

The default value for this attribute is `false`, meaning that the sub-deployment modules will be able to see each other. If you are setting isolation to `true`, each module will then be picked up by a different classloader, so, in our example, the web application will not be able to find the classes contained in the `EJB.jar` and `Utility.jar` library.

If you want to keep deployment isolated, but allow visibility for some of them, then you have two choices available:

- Move the library to the `EAR/lib` folder, so that it will be picked up as a separate module
- Specify a dependency using Dependencies or using Class-Path in the `MANIFEST.MF` file of the calling application

From the following image, you can see how you could correctly set up your EAR, by placing common libraries in the `lib` folder, and adding a dependency to the EJB classes:

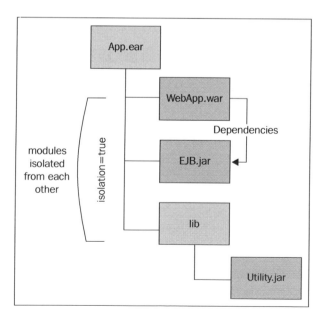

And this is the corresponding configuration required in `jboss-deployment-structure.xml`:

```
<jboss-deployment-structure>

<ear-subdeployments-isolated>true</ear-subdeployments-isolated>
    <sub-deployment name="WebApp.war">
      <dependencies>
        <module name="deployment.App.ear.EJB.jar" />
      </dependencies>
    </sub-deployment>
  </jboss-deployment-structure>
```

> Packaging libraries in a shared library is available, since Java EE 5 is commonly used for holding the JAR files that are used by all modules of the EAR.
>
> The default name for the shared library is `lib`; however, you can override it at any time using the `library-directory` element in the `META INF/application.xml` file. For example, supposing you wanted to use the folder `common` for holding your shared library, then you could add the following to your `application.xml`:
>
> `<library-directory>common</library-directory>`
>
> As a side note, we suggest you avoid placing component-declaring annotations (such as EJB3) in the shared folder, as it can have unintended and undesirable consequences on the deployment process. For this reason, we strongly recommend placing just utility classes in the shared library folder.

Using Class-Path declaration to solve dependencies

Until now, we have solved dependencies between modules using JBoss' way, which we obviously suggest as first choice. Nevertheless, we should also account for Java's portable way to reference one or more library included in the EAR file.

This can be done using the `Class-Path` attribute in the `MANIFEST.MF` file of a module, which needs to reference another library that could not be otherwise visible to the application (think back to the earlier example of a deployment unit with isolation set to `true`).

For example, supposing you needed to reference the Utility.jar application from within your web application, then simply add to your META-INF/MANIFEST.MF the following:

```
Manifest-Version: 1.0
Class-Path: Utility.jar
```

You can actually include more than one library to the Class-Path, keeping them separated by a comma, much the same way you did with the JBoss' Dependencies attribute.

 Unlike the Dependencies attribute, the Class-Path attribute points to the actual JAR filename (and not the module name) to reference dependant libraries.

Choosing between Class-Path approach and JBoss' Dependencies approach is a matter of how your application is structured: using JBoss' Dependencies buys you a richer set of options, in particular the ability to export the Dependencies to other deployments, as we have shown earlier. One more point in favor of the JBoss' Dependencies approach is the ability to reference modules that are not actually packaged within the application; for example, we have seen how to add a dependency to log4j API that are part of the server distribution.

On the other hand, the main advantage of the Class-Path approach relies on application portability. Thus, if a full-portable solution is a priority for you, you could consider switching to the Class-Path manifest attribute.

Summary

In this chapter, we have covered a wide list of concerns related to the deployment of applications. Applications deploy differently, depending if they are targeted on a standalone server or on a domain of servers.

As far as standalone servers are concerned:

- Application can be either deployed automatically or manually. By default, packaged archives are deployed automatically. This means that it's enough to place the archive within the standalone/deployments folder of the application server. Applications that are deployed manually (by default, exploded archives) need some marker files to activate the deployment.

As far as domain servers are concerned:

- Since the application server cannot determine by itself on which server group you want to target the deployment, you need to specify this information when using either the Command Line Interface or the Web Admin interface for deployments.

One of the great advantages of using a domain of servers is the ability to deploy applications on single or multiple server groups, which can even be created and equipped at runtime.

In the other part of this chapter, we have covered the **classloading** mechanism that is used by the application server. Basically, on AS 7, every application is itself a module that is isolated by other modules that are contained in the application server distribution. Modules representing Java EE API classes are implicitly added to your application's classpath as a dependency, so that you don't need any special configuration for deploying a basic Java EE application.

If you want to reference any other module that is contained in the application server, you simply need to specify a `Dependencies` or a within the `META-INF/MANIFEST.MF` file of the application. Enterprise archives can also specify dependencies on other modules by setting the `Class-Path` attribute within the `META-INF/MANIFEST.MF` file.

Should you need to maintain all your dependencies in a single file, you can use the `jboss-deployment-structure.xml`, which is able to define all dependencies within an archive, including the ability to override the default EAR isolation level and filter in/out classes, which are part of the application server deployment.

In the next chapter, we will cover the management of the application server with a close look at the new Command Line Interface and the Web Admin console.

7
Managing the Application Server

In this chapter, we will describe the management tools that can be used to control your application server instances. Obviously, being a complete application server means that JBoss AS implements 100 percent of the Java EE 6 specifications, but it also has additional features that make it a polished product, such as administrative capabilities.

JBoss AS 7 provides several administration channels: one of them is the new CLI, which contains many unique features that make it convenient for daily system administration and for monitoring application server resources.

The management tools also include a Web admin console, which offers an elegant view of the application server subsystems, allowing you to perform administrative tasks in a very simple way.

Within this chapter, we will thus describe the following instruments:

- The **Command Line Interface (CLI)**
- The **Web admin console**

Let's start with the CLI that promises to be your next administrator's Swiss army knife tool.

The Command Line Interface (CLI)

Terminals and consoles were one of the earliest types of communication interfaces between a system administrator and the machine. Due to this long time presence, most system administrators prefer to use the raw power of the command line for performing management tasks. One of the most evident advantages of using a low-level interface, such as a shell, is that tasks can often be executed as a part of batch processing or macros, for repetitive actions.

As we have introduced at the beginning of this book, the CLI is located in the JBOSS_HOME/bin folder and wrapped by `jboss-admin.bat` (Linux users, as well, will use the `jboss-admin.sh` equivalent).

By launching the shell script, you will start with a disconnected session. You can connect at any time with the `connect` [standalone/domain controller] command, which by default, connects to a server controller located at localhost on port 9999.

```
You are disconnected at the moment. Type 'connect' to connect to the
  server or 'help' for the list of supported commands.
[disconnected /] connect
Connected to standalone controller at localhost:9999
```

You can, at any time, adjust the default port where the native interface is running by finding this line into the `standalone.xml/domain.xml` configuration file:

```xml
<management-interfaces>
    <native-interface security-realm="ManagementRealm">
        <socket-binding native="management-native"/>
    </native-interface>
    <http-interface security-realm="ManagementRealm">
        <socket-binding http="management-http"/>
    </http-interface>
</management-interfaces>

<socket-binding-group name="standard-sockets"
default-interface="public">
. . . . . .
<socket-binding name="management-native" interface=
"management" port="9999"/>
<socket-binding name="management-http" interface=
"management" port="9990"/>
. . . . . .
</socket-binding-group>
```

As you can see from the above code snippet, the socket management alias are defined within the management-interfaces section, while the corresponding port is contained in the socket-binding section. A handy switch is `--connect`, which can be used to automatically hook up to your standalone/domain controller:

```
jboss-7.x.x.x/bin/jboss-admin.bat --connect
```

or on a Linux machine:

```
jboss-7.x.x.x/bin/jboss-admin.sh --connect
```

The corresponding command for exiting the CLI is `quit`, which closes the connection to the main controller:

```
[standalone@localhost:9999 /] quit
Closed connection to localhost:9999
```

How to use the CLI

One of the most interesting features of the CLI is its embedded intelligence, which helps us to find the correct spelling of resources and commands, by simply pressing the *Tab* key. You can even use it to find out the parameters needed for a particular command, without the need to go through the reference manual.

This will guide us into the first part of our journey, where we will learn the available commands. So, once you have successfully connected, press the *Tab* key, and it will expand to show the list of available commands and resources. Here's the output of it:

As you can see, there are about 25 commands available. We can, however, distinguish all the interactions that happen with the CLI into two broad categories:

1. **Operations**: These include the resource path (address) on which they are executed.

2. **Commands**: These don't include the resource path and they can, thus, execute an action independently from the path of the current resource.

Navigating through the resources and executing operations

As we said, operations are strictly bound to an application server resource path. The path along the tree of resources is represented by the "/" character, which, as it is, represents the root of the tree, just like for an Unix-Linux file system.

When you are executing operations on the AS resources, you have to use a well-defined syntax:

```
[node-type=node-name (,node-type=node-name)*] : operation-name [(
   [parameter-name=parameter-value (,parameter-name=parameter-value)*] )]
```

It looks a bit awkward at first glance, however, we will try to de-mystify it with the following example:

```
[standalone@localhost:9999 /] /subsystem=deployment-
   scanner/scanner=default:write-attribute(name=scan-interval,value=2500)
{"outcome" => "success"}
```

Here, we are telling the CLI to navigate into the `deployment-scanner` sub-system, under the default scanner resource, and set the scan-interval attribute to `2500` ms, using the `write-attribute` operation.

This example also shows the distinction between resources, attributes, and operations.

A resource is an element of the configuration that is located under a path. All elements, which are classified as resources, can be managed through the AS 7 interfaces. For example, the `deployment-scanner` is a resource located under the `subsystem` path. It has a children elements named `default` scanner. On the single resource, or on the child resources, you can invoke some operations, such as reading or writing the value of an attribute (the `scan-interval`).

Finally, notice that operations are introduced by the `:` prefix, while resources are introduced by the /character. Here's a screenshot that helps to fix the basic terminology concepts:

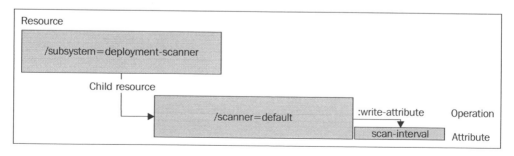

In order to move through the resources path, you can either state the full tree path (as in the earlier example) or use the cd command or also the equivalent cn (change node) to navigate to the path and then issue the desired command. For example, the earlier attribute can also be rewritten as:

```
[standalone@localhost:9999 /] cd /subsystem=deployment-scanner/
scanner=default
```

```
[standalone@localhost:9999 scanner=default] :write-attribute(name=scan-
interval,value=2500)
{"outcome" => "success"}
```

Does modified attributes survive server restart?

If you have been using the earlier JBoss' jmx-console, that's a question we would expect from you. As a matter of fact, most MBeans contacted by the jmx-console didn't alter the server state permanently. When using CLI, every change is persisted into the server configuration file, thus, you must be responsible when you are using this instrument. More power asks more responsibility indeed! Nevertheless, you can, at any time, take a snapshot of your server configuration. See the section *Taking snapshots of the configuration*.

Just like for the operating system shell, by issuing cd . . you move the resource pointer to the parent resource:

```
[standalone@localhost:9999 scanner=default] cd ..
```

```
[standalone@localhost:9999 subsystem=deployment-scanner]
```

You can, at any time, check the resource path where you are located, by issuing either an empty cd command or just pwd, as you do for an Unix shell:

```
[standalone@localhost:9999 scanner=default] pwd
```

```
/subsystem=deployment-scanner/scanner=default
```

Finally, in order to simplify your navigation, we'll close this section, by giving a bird's eye view of the AS tree or resources:

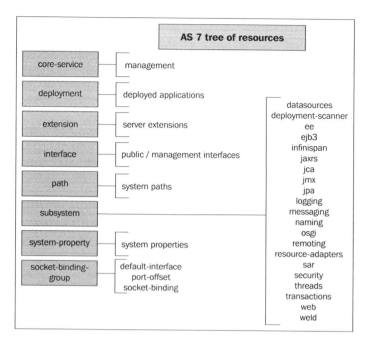

As you can see, the tree of resources includes eight child resources, each one handling one core aspect of the application server. In the *Appendix* of this book, you will find a handy list of useful commands that can be used for your daily system administration. Most of the time, you will explore the sub-system resources, which contain all the application server core modules; other resources that you'll want to learn more about are core-service, which handles management interfaces (such as the CLI itself), or the deployment resource, which can be used to manipulate deployed artifacts, or the `socket-binding-group`, which is the resource you will need to change the ports used by the application server.

Operations which you can issue on a resource

Having learnt the basics of navigation through the resources, let's see the commands that can be issued on a resource. Operations are triggered by the : character — you can get a list of them by using the `tab-completion` feature (*Tab* key). Here's a list of them:

Command	Meaning
read-resource	Reads a model resource's attribute values along with either basic or complete information about any child resources.
read-resource-description	Outputs a description for the selected resource.
read-operation-names	Read the available operation names on the node.
read-operation-description	Outputs a description for the available operations.
read-children-names	Gets the name of all children under the selected resource.
read-children-resources	Reads information about all of a resource's children that are of a given type.
read-children-types	Provides the list of the children located under the selected resource.
read-attribute	Gets the value of an attribute for the selected resource.
write-attribute	Writes an attribute for the selected resource.

The `read-resource` deserves some more explanation. As a matter of fact, without any extra arguments, it provides information about the resource's attribute and the direct child nodes.

For example, here's the resource scanning of the datasource sub-system, which includes the default datasource named ExampleDS.

```
[standalone@localhost:9999 /] /subsystem=datasources:read-resource()
{
  "outcome" => "success",
  "result" => {
    "xa-data-source" => undefined,
    "data-source" => {"java:jboss/datasources/ExampleDS" => undefined},
    "jdbc-driver" => {"h2" => undefined}
  }
}
```

You might have noticed the `undefined` attribute for some elements. As a matter of fact, the information provided by the `read-resource` command is limited to listing the name of child resources. If you want to read information about all child resources, including their corresponding attributes, you have to issue the command with the additional (`recursive=true`) parameter:

```
[standalone@localhost:9999 /] /subsystem=datasources:read-
resource(recursive=true)
{
  "outcome" => "success",
  "result" => {
    "xa-data-source" => undefined,
    "data-source" => {"java:jboss/datasources/ExampleDS" => {
        "background-validation" => undefined,
        "background-validation-millis" => undefined,
        "blocking-timeout-wait-millis" => undefined,
        "connection-properties" => undefined,
        "connection-url" => "jdbc:h2:mem:test;DB_CLOSE_DELAY=-1",
        "driver-name" => "h2",
        "enabled" => true,
      }
    },
    "jdbc-driver" => {"h2" => {
      "driver-module-name" => "com.h2database.h2",
      "driver-name" => "h2",
      "driver-xa-datasource-class-name" => "org.h2.jdbcx.JdbcDataSource"
    }
  }
}
```

As you can see, by adding the `recursive=true` parameter, the CLI has also included the list of configuration parameters, which are stored as children of the datasource element. For the sake of brevity, we have intentionally included just the first few datasource parameters.

Additionally, some resources can produce metrics, which are collected as runtime attributes. These attributes are not showed by default, unless you provide the `include-runtime=true` parameter. For example, the web sub-system typically collects some runtime attributes relative to the `http` connector metrics:

```
[standalone@localhost:9999 connector=http] :read-resource
(include-runtime=true)
{
  "outcome" => "success",
  "result" => {
    "bytesReceived" => "0",
```

```
    "bytesSent" => "0",
    "enable-lookups" => false,
    "enabled" => true,
    "errorCount" => "0",
    "max-post-size" => 2097152,
    "max-save-post-size" => 4096,
    "maxTime" => "0",
    "processingTime" => "0",
    "protocol" => "HTTP/1.1",
    "redirect-port" => 8443,
    "requestCount" => "0",
    "scheme" => "http",
    "secure" => false,
    "socket-binding" => "http",
    "ssl" => undefined,
    "virtual-server" => undefined
  }
}
```

If you want to learn more about a resource, including a short description about itself and its attributes, you can use the read-resource-description, which also includes the resource's runtime attributes. The output can be quite verbose, so here we will just include the head section of it:

```
[standalone@localhost:9999 connector=http] :read-resource-description
{
  "outcome" => "success",
  "result" => {
    "head-comment-allowed" => true,
    "tail-comment-allowed" => true,
    "type" => OBJECT,
    "description" => "A web connector.",
    "attributes" => {
      "name" => {
        "type" => STRING,
        "description" => "A unique name for the connector.",
        "required" => true,
        "nillable" => false,
        "access-type" => "read-only",
        "storage" => "configuration"
      }
    }
  }
}
```

The `read-operation-names` and `read-operation-description` provide the list of available operations on a certain resource and their description. That would produce a synthetic information, just as we have added in the earlier table, so we will not rehash the description.

Next, the `read-children` operations can be used to collect information about child nodes. The `read-children-types` provides information about the child resources and it's pretty similar to a simple `ls` command. For example, on the `root` resource it would produce the following:

```
[standalone@localhost:9999 /] :read-children-types()
{
  "outcome" => "success",
  "result" => [
    "extension",
    "core-service",
    "path",
    "subsystem",
    "system-property",
    "deployment",
    "interface",
    "socket-binding-group"
  ]
}
```

The `read-children-names` delivers information about a single children resource and it's pretty much the same as issuing a `cd "resource"` followed by an `ls` command. For example, supposing we want to know the list of deployed resources on the AS:

```
[standalone@localhost:9999 /] :read-children-names(child-type=deployment)
{
  "outcome" => "success",
  "result" => [
    "Enterprise.ear",
    "EJB.jar",
    "Utility.jar"
  ]
}
```

Finally, the `read-children-resources` command returns information about a child node of a certain type, which needs to be provided as argument. This command is equivalent to executing a `read-resource` operation on each child resource. In the previous example, when issued on an hypothetic `Enterprise.ear` deployment resource, it will provide the sub-deployment information:

```
[standalone@localhost:9999 deployment=Enterprise.ear] :read-children-
  resources(child-type=subdeployment)
{
  "outcome" => "success",
  "result" => {
    "WebApp.war" => {
      "subdeployment" => undefined,
      "subsystem" => {"web" => undefined}
    },
    "Utility.jar" => {
      "subdeployment" => undefined,
      "subsystem" => undefined
    }
  }
}
```

Optionally, you can also include as an argument `include-runtime=true`, to include runtime attributes, and `recursive=true` that provides information about all child resources recursively.

Executing commands with the CLI

As we said, the CLI includes a set of actions as well, which are not bound to your navigation path across the AS tree, but can be issued anywhere to create and modify resources.

For example, the `version` command can be issued to retrieve some basic information about the application server and the environment where JBoss AS is running:

```
[standalone@localhost:9999 /] version
JBoss Admin Command-line Interface
JBOSS_HOME: C:\jboss-as-7.1.0.Alpha1
JAVA_HOME: C:\Program Files\Java\jdk1.6.0_24
java.version: 1.6.0_24
java.vm.vendor: Sun Microsystems Inc.
java.vm.version: 19.1-b02
os.name: Windows 7
os.version: 6.1
```

In most cases, commands are used as an alias for quickly creating some resources, such as JMS destinations and datasources.

Let's see in the following sections how this can be achieved.

Adding a JMS destination

You can add a JMS queue with the `add-jms-queue` command, which requires as mandatory parameter, just the name of the queue (`--name parameter`).

 As you can see, one important difference between operations and command is also the style used to pass parameters. Operations use brackets to pass parameters (for example, `recursive=true`). Commands pass parameters using the format (`--parameter`) borrowed from Unix's operating system shell.

Here's the synopsis of the command:

```
add-jms-queue [--profile=profile_name] --name=queue_name [--
  entries=entry(,entry)*] [--selector=selector_name] [--
  durable=(true|false)]
```

The only mandatory element is `name`, which specifies the `queue` name. The optional `entries` element includes a comma-separated list of JNDI names the queue should be bound under. If not present, the name will be used as the JNDI name. Next, the `selector` parameter can be added to specify a selector on the queue to filter messages. Then, the `durable` parameter specifies whether the queue should be durable or not (the default is `true`). Finally, notice the optional `profile` element, which can be used on domain configurations to specify the `profile` where the `queue` will be created.

The following command creates a new JMS queue named `queue1` and bound under the JNDI `queues/queue1` namespace:

```
add-jms-queue --name=queue1 --entries=queues/queue1
```

The equivalent command for adding a JMS topic is `add-jms-topic`, has the following syntax:

```
add-jms-topic [--profile=profile_name] --name=topic_name [--
  entries=entry(,entry)*]
```

We will not rehash the same description again for topics that are identical, except that has a smaller number of parameters; as a matter of fact the `selector` and `durable` parameters are not included here.

```
add-jms-topic --name=topic1 --entries=topics/topic1
```

Creating and modifying datasources

The CLI provides an useful `data-source` command to create a datasources. As the syntax of this command is a bit more wordy, you might find pretty useful to save it as a CLI script and adapt it to your needs.

Here's the synopsis of the command:

```
data-source [--profile=<profile_name>] add/remove --jndi-name=
<jndi_name> --driver-name=<driver_name> --pool-name=<pool_name>
--connection-url=<connection_url>
```

Except for the `profile_name`, all the other parameters indicated are mandatory. That is, you need to specify if you want to add or remove a datasource. As far as it concerns parameters you need to state, at least, the JNDI name for the datasource (`jndi namc`) , the driver name (`driver-name`), the name of the connection pool (`pool-name`), and the connection URL (`connection-url`).

You can further customize the datasource, just as you would do in your `standalone.xml` file, by adding optional parameters; Let's see a concrete example where we are creating a MySQL datasource.

The first thing we need is providing the JDBC-compliant driver, by deploying the JAR archive. Supposing you are using standalone mode, just copy the JDBC JAR file into the `deployments` folder:

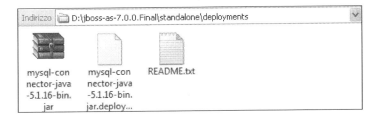

You can alternatively choose to install the JDBC driver as a module, as suggested by the JBoss' JCA team. This procedure is shown in the *Chapter 3, Configuring Enterprise Services*, of this book. For the purposes of this example we are simply deploying the driver as this expedites the installation procedure.

Now, let's verify that the driver has been correctly installed on the datasource subsystem. We can do this by means of the `installed-drivers-list` command on the datasources subsystem:

```
[standalone@localhost:9999 /] /subsystem=datasources:installed-drivers-
list
{
  "outcome" => "success",
  "result" => [
    {
      "driver-name" => "h2",
      "deployment-name" => undefined,
      "driver-module-name" => "com.h2database.h2",
      "module-slot" => "main",
      "driver-datasource-class-name" => "",
      "driver-xa-datasource-class-name" =>
        "org.h2.jdbcx.JdbcDataSource",
      "driver-class-name" => "org.h2.Driver",
      "driver-major-version" => 1,
      "driver-minor-version" => 2,
      "jdbc-compliant" => true
    },
    {
      "driver-name" => "mysql-connector-java-5.1.16-bin.jar",
      "deployment-name" => "mysql-connector-java-5.1.16-bin.jar",
      "driver-module-name" => undefined,
      "module-slot" => undefined,
      "driver-datasource-class-name" => undefined,
      "driver-xa-datasource-class-name" => undefined,
      "driver-class-name" => "com.mysql.jdbc.Driver",
      "driver-major-version" => 5,
      "driver-minor-version" => 1,
      "jdbc-compliant" => false
    }
  ]
}
```

As you can see, there are two drivers installed: the default H2 driver and the MySQL driver that we have just installed.

Ok. Now we are ready to create a new datasource using the MySQL JDBC driver:

```
[standalone@localhost:9999 /] data-source add --jndi-name=java:/MySqlDS -
-pool-name=MySQLPool --connection-url=jdbc:mysql://localhost:3306/MyDB
--driver-name=mysql-connector-java-5.1.16-bin.jar --user-name=myuser -
-password=password --max-pool-size=30
```

In this example, we have just created a MySQL-bound datasource, using a custom pool size of max 30 connections.

 You don't have to remember all datasource parameter names. Just use the *Tab* key to auto-complete the parameter name.

The `data-source` command can be used as well to remove a datasource from the configuration. This can be done by passing the `remove` parameter and the `jndi name` of the `datasource`:

```
[standalone@localhost:9999 /] data-source remove --jndi-
  name=java:/MySqlDS
```

 You can add or remove datasources as well, using operations, which are executed on the datasource system resource. See the *Appendix* of this book, which contains a compendium of most useful CLI commands.

Creating and modifying XA datasources

If you are going to use an XA datasource class for your connections, then since the release 7.1.0 Beta, you need to operate on the resource path of the datasource.

This requires at first creating the datasource with the minimal set of information:

```
/subsystem=datasources/xa-data-source="MySqlDSXA":add(jndi-name="java:/
MySqlDSXA", driver-name="com.mysql", pool-name="mysqlPool")
```

Then, you will add the datasource information as single properties:

```
/subsystem=datasources/xa-data-source=MySqlDSXA/xa-datasource-properties=
ServerName:add(value=localhost)
```

```
/subsystem=datasources/xa-data-source=MySqlDSXA/xa-datasource-properties=
PortNumber:add(value=3306)
```

Now you can finally enable your datasource with:

```
/subsystem=datasources/xa-data-source=MySqlDSXA:enable
```

This was a bit more lenghty procedure however remember that you can use the *<tab>* key when you are creating the datasource to discover the initial properties and as well to add each single property.

When executed with the −1 parameter, the `batch` command provides the list of batch files that are held:

```
[standalone@localhost:9999 /] batch -l
step1
```

In the following table, we include the list of all available commands when you are running in `batch` mode:

Command	Description
batch	Starts a batch of commands. When the batch is paused, reactivates the batch.
list-batch	Lists the commands that have been added to the batch.
run-batch	Executes the currently active batch of commands and exits `batch` mode.
holdback-batch	Saves the currently active batch and exits the `batch` mode, without executing the batch. The held back batch can later be re-activated, by invoking batch commands.
clear-batch	Removes all the existing command lines from the currently active batch. The CLI stays in the `batch` mode after the command is executed.
discard-batch	Discards the currently active batch. All the commands added to the batch will be removed, the batch will be discarded and the CLI will exit the batch mode
edit-batch-line	Replaces existing command line from the currently active batch, with the specified line number with the new one.
remove-batch-line	Removes an existing command line specified with line number argument from the currently active batch.
move-batch-line	Moves existing line from the specified position to the new position, shifting the lines between the specified positions.

Executing scripts in a file

Until now, we have seen CLI commands as part of an interactive session. You can, however, execute commands in no-interactive fashion, adding them in a file, just as a shell script. Suppose you have created a sample `test.cli` file used to issue a `re-deploy` command:

```
connect
deploy Utility.jar --force
```

Then, as Windows user, launch the CLI with the `--file` parameter:

```
jboss-admin.bat --file=test.cli
```

The equivalent command for Unix users will be:

```
./jboss-admin.sh --file=test.cli
```

 Please notice that you can pass the --user and --password arguments to the `jboss-admin.bat`/`jboss-admin.sh` call if you need to authenticate on the management interface.

Another way to execute commands in a non-interactive way, is passing the `--commands` parameter to the CLI, containing the list of commands lines separated by a comma. For example, the previous script can be also executed this way: (Windows users):

```
jboss-admin.bat --commands="connect,deploy Utility.jar --force"
Connected to standalone controller at localhost:9999
'Utility.jar' re-deployed successfully.
Closed connection to localhost:9999
```

The equivalent script for Unix users will be:

```
./jboss-admin.sh --commands="connect,deploy Utility.jar --force"
```

Redirecting non-interactive output

When you are executing the CLI in a non-interactive way, you can redirect the output to a file, which would be otherwise be printed on the screen. Just as for a shell command, use the > operator to redirect the output:

```
jboss-admin.bat --file=test.cli > out.log     # Windows
./jboss-admin.sh --file=test.cli > out.log     # Linux
```

Taking snapshots of the configuration

Well, everyone makes mistakes, but many of them are preventable. Whenever you are performing massive changes to your configuration, it's always a good idea to save copies of your work. That's where snapshots come in; one of the advantages of using the CLI, is the ability to create snapshots of the configuration, which are stored in its `history` folder.

The `history` folder is located just one step under the configuration of the AS. Standalone servers have a `history` folder named `standalone_xml_history` that, at start up, contains the following files:

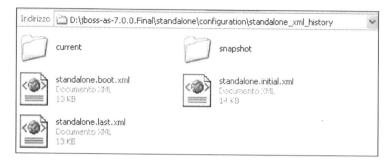

The domain configuration, on the other hand, provides two backup directories both for the domain configuration file and the host configuration file. These folders are named `domain_xml_history` and `host_xml_history`, respectively.

To make the reading not too verbose, we will describe the snapshot mechanisms using a standalone server. The same rules de facto also applies also for domain servers, bearing in mind that the AS takes snapshots of both the `domain.xml` and `host.xml` file.

Let's see now what the history files are about. The `standalone.initial.xml` contains the original AS configuration file. This file is never overwritten by the AS.

 If you need to restore the initial configuration, do not throw away your application server installation! Just replace the `standalone.xml` file with `standalone_xml_history/standalone.initial.xml`.

The `standalone.boot.xml` file contains the AS configuration that was used for the last successful boot of the server. This gets overwritten every time we boot the server successfully.

 If you want to undo all changes in the current session, just replace the `standalone.xml` file with `standalone_xml_history/standalone.boot.xml`.

Finally, the file `standalone.last.xml` contains the last successful configuration, committed by the application server.

What the application server saves for you

Each time you reboot the application server, a copy of your successful boot configuration is stored into the `snapshot` folder using the timestamp naming format `YYYYMMDD-HHMMSSstandalone.xml`. The following is a snapshot taken by the application server on a hot day of August (8th) 2011 at 12:11.

The current folder, on the other hand, is used as temporary folder for storing changes in the configuration that happened in the current session. Each change in the application server configuration model will result in a file named `standalone.v[n].xml` will be created. Here n is the change number applied (`standalone.v1.xml` for the initial configuration, `standalone.v2.xml` for the first change, and so on).

When the application server is restarted, these files are moved into a `timestamped` folder into the `standalone_xml_history` top folder. As you can see from the next screenshot, changes during the last session are moved at reboot into the folder 20110808-122628937:

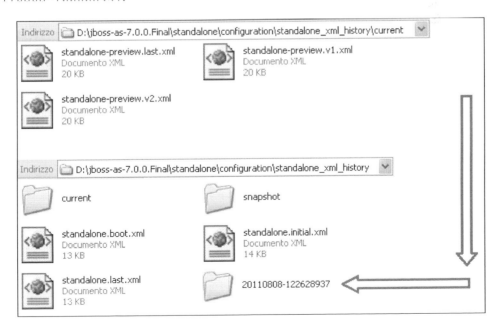

Note: `timestamped` folders are rotated by the application server every 30 days. If you need to store a core view of the application server configuration, you should take snapshots of the AS model. The next section shows how.

Taking your own snapshots

As suggested by the earlier warning, you can also take snapshots on demand whenever you need it. Snapshots created by the user are stored directly in the `snapshot` folder (along with successful server boot's snapshots). In order to take a snapshot of the configuration, just issue the `take-snapshot` command and the CLI will back up your configuration:

```
[standalone@localhost:9999 /] :take-snapshot
{
  "outcome" => "success",
  "result" => {"name" => "C:\\jboss-as-
    7.0.0.Final\\standalone\\configuration\\standalone_xml_history\\
    snapshot\\20110726-223444446standalone.xml"
  }
}
```

You can check the list of available snapshots by using the `list-snapshots` command:

```
[standalone@localhost:9999 /] :list-snapshots
{
  "outcome" => "success",
  "result" => {
    "directory" => "C:\\jboss-as-
      7.0.0.Final\\standalone\\configuration\\standalone_xml_history\\
      snapshot",
    "names" => [
      "20110725-064943007standalone.xml",
      "20110725-222015995standalone.xml",
      "20110726-212857046standalone.xml",
      "20110726-223444446standalone.xml"
    ]
  }
}
```

You can, at any time, delete a particular snapshot using the `delete-snapshot` command, which requires the snapshot name as parameter. Suppose we would need to delete the snapshot we've just created:

```
[standalone@localhost:9999 /] :delete-snapshot(name="20110726-
    223444446standalone.xml")
{"outcome" => "success"}
```

History of CLI

All commands which are executed within a CLI session are stored in an history, much like shell commands for Unix systems. CLI commands are kept in memory and also persisted on the file system in a file named `.jboss-cli-history` placed in the user's home directory. You will notice that the commands entered in previous sessions are part of the history, up to the latest 500 commands (default history size).

If you want to have a look at the CLI history, just issue the `history` command:

```
[standalone@localhost:9999 /] history
```

You can also use the arrow keys to go navigate back and forth in the history of commands and operations, much like you would do with a Linux bash shell.

The history command supports three optional arguments, which can be used to temporarily disable/enable or clear the history. In the following table, we just mention their outcome:

Argument	Effect
disable	Disables history expansion (but will not clear the previously recorded history).
enable	Re-enables history expansion (starting from the last recorded command before the history expansion was disabled).
clear	Clears the in-memory history (but not the file one).

The new Web admin console

Historically, the JBoss AS has always provided a Web-based application to perform some administration and management tasks. Releases 4.x and earlier used the `jmx-console` to read/write and display the value of MBeans, which where the backbone of the application server. The `jmx-console` was indeed a useful tool, however, it also required some degree of experience in order to get started with it. Besides this, the information contained in this application was fragmented across many MBeans. For example, the datasource information was contained into four Mbeans, thus making it cumbersome to manage this resource.

The 5.x and 6.x release proposed a simpler to use approach made up of the Admin console, which was built as a Seam-Based Web application. Although the new Admin console was a neat and simple application, some criticism of it was due to the fact that it consumed a pretty good amount of memory and start up time, as pointed out in my *JBoss AS 5 Performance Tuning* book.

The new AS 7 Web console, which you had already a glimpse in the earlier chapter, is a completely new Web application, powered by the **Google Web Toolkit (GWT)** that uses the HTTP management API to configure a management domain or standalone server.

As many GWT applications, it uses a JSON-encoded protocol and a de-typed, RPC style API to describe and execute management operations against a managed domain or standalone server. For more information about GWT check: `http://code.google.com/intl/it-IT/webtoolkit/`.

Accessing the admin console

It's time to update your bookmarks. JBoss AS 7, by default, does not use anymore port `8080` to serve the admin console. You can access it at the `http://localhost:9990/console` as configured in your `standalone.xml /domain.xml`.

```
<socket-binding name="management-http" interface="management"
port="9990"/>
```

Once logged in with your account you will land on the main application window which, in the standalone mode contains two main tabs: The first one, **Profile**, can be used to model the application server configuration as illustrated by the following screenshot:

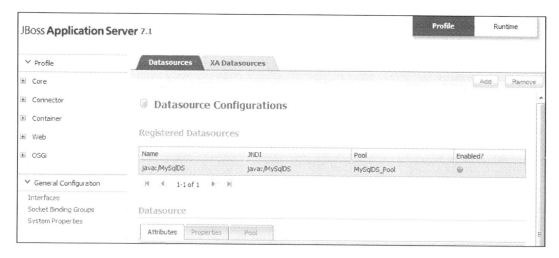

On the other hand, the **Runtime** tab, can be used to manage deployments, as we have learnt in *Chapter 6*. In the next section we will show how easy can be configuring server profiles using the Web admin console:

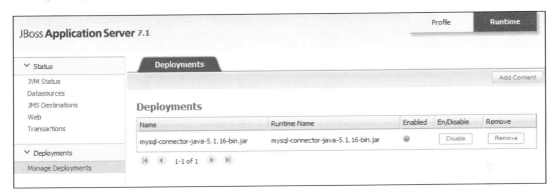

Configuring server profiles

The server profile configuration is located in the left area of the Web application. When running in standalone mode, it can be located under the "Profile" label. When running domain mode, you will need to navigate through the "Profiles" tab and choose one through the "Profile" combo box.

Expanding the Profile label, you can see a set of subsystems which can be configured through the Web interface.

In *Chapter 2*, *Configuring the Application Server*, and *Chapter 3*, *Configuring the Enterprise Server*, of this book, we showed how to configure these resources using the main configuration file. If you are the kind of system administrator who prefers **windows**, **icons**, **menus**, and **pointers** (WIMP) interfaces, then the next sections are for you. The configuration of resources, when using the Web console, is pretty intuitive, so we will just cover the following handy topics:

- Configuring datasources
- Configuring JMS resources
- Configuring Socket Binding groups

Configuring datasources

Clicking on the **Datasources** link, you will switch the main panel to the **Datasource Configurations** panel. This panel contains two upper tabs for configuring **Datasources** and **XADatasources**. Let's see what the first tab contains:

In the middle of the panel, you can find out the list of configured datasources. The actions that can be started, are located in the upper right area of the screen, where you can create a new one by clicking on the **Add button**. In the same part of the screen you can delete a Datasource definition. On the other hand, in the lower part of the GUI you can choose to Edit / Disable / Test a Datasource).

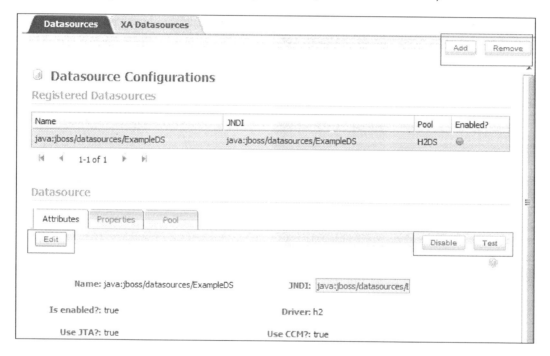

Editing or deleting an existing datasource is a straightforward task, which can be executed with as little as a button click. The same can be said about enabling and disabling the selected datasource. Here, we will rather show how to add a new datasource to your `Profile` configuration, which requires a few simple steps to be completed.

Once you have clicked on the **New Datasource** button, a three-steps wizard will guide you through the creation of the datasource. Let's configure a sample MySQL datasource for this purpose. The first information required will be the datasource name and its JNDI binding. Leaving the **Enabled** check-box on, will make the datasource enabled (default).

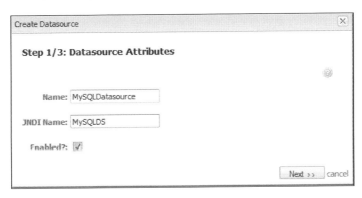

The next step will be selecting the proper JDBC driver for your datasource. Provided that you have successfully installed a JDBC driver on your AS, you will should have it listed as an available driver:

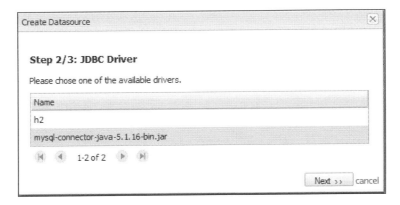

Choose the MySQL JDBC driver and in the next (last) step you will be required to enter the JDBC URL of the datasource along with the **Username** and **Password** credentials.

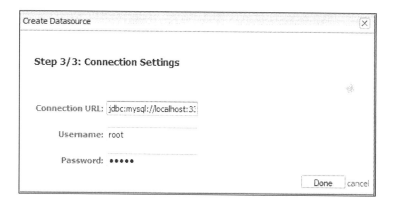

Clicking **Done** completes the wizard and you will be redirected to the main panel, where the new datasource is now enlisted and enabled for use by your applications.

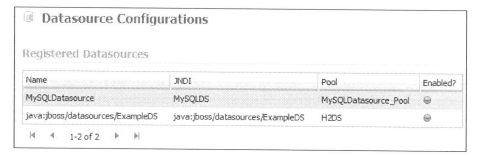

Creating a new XA datasource

As we have shown in the *Command Line Interface* section, an XA datasource requires your JDBC URL to be entered as XA property, in just the same way.

Thus, the datasource JNDI naming and driver selection stays the same as for non-XA datasources. In the next screenshot, we illustrate the last two steps needed to complete the XA datasource creation:

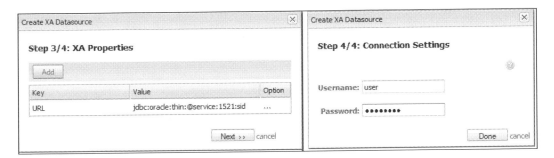

Configuring JMS destinations

Creating new **Queues** and **Topics** using the Web console is even more simple. From the **Profile** menu, select the **Messaging provider** option (**1**). The main panel will switch to the **Messaging canvas**. From there, select the **JMS Destinations** tab (**2**), and the resource you want to create (**Queue** or **Topic**) (**3**). Then, hit the **Add** button (**4**) to create a new one:

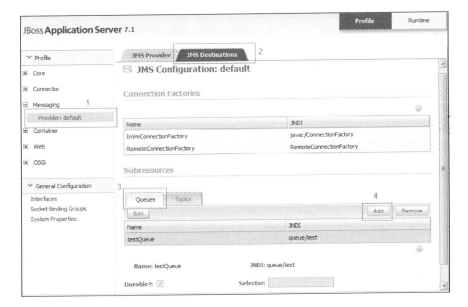

For example, if you need to create a new **Queue**, all you have to do is complete the next simple dialog box, which is shown below:

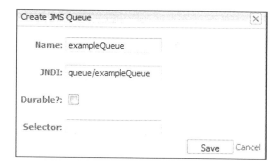

When you hit **Save**, the new JMS resource will be enlisted in the JMS sub-system panel (and as well persisted in the main configuration file).

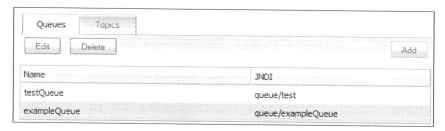

Configuring Socket Binding groups

Changing the Socket Bindings of the application server can be used to solve port conflicts with other applications or even other instances of JBoss AS. If you are running in **domain** mode, the best thing you can do is specify a port offset for your servers, as pointed out in the *Chapter 4, JBoss Web Server Configuration*, which was all about domain servers.

If, however, you are running in standalone mode and you have just to change one or more port address, than you might easily change it from the Web console.

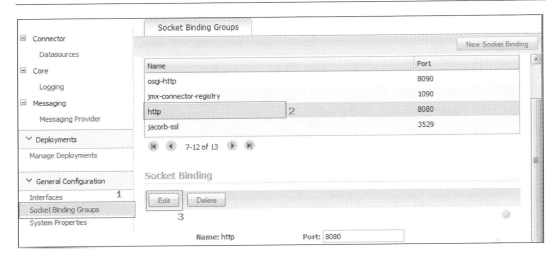

Reach the **Socket Binding groups** (**1**) option, and select the Socket Binding you want to change, for example, the **http** server port (**2**). Then, click on the **Edit** button (**3**) and enter the new port value.

When you are done, click on the **Save** button, which will be added in place of the **Edit** button.

> **Server restart needed?**
>
> Changing the Socket Binding groups does not produce the immediate effect of changing the server port. As a matter of fact the updated configuration must be reloaded by the AS; you could simply restart the application server or, even better, issue the :reload command from your friendly neighbourhood, the Command Line Interface.

CLI or Web console ?

Apparently, this is a pointless question. It's a bit like asking which operating system is better; Linux or Windows. Both management interfaces are powerful instruments, and in some circumstances, one might be a better choice than another.

For example, the CLI provides a huge addition to the application server and with a relatively short amount of time, it will let you put your hands into every resource of the application server, including runtime metrics. Even more add-ons are planned to come in the very next releases of the application server.

On the other hand, the Web console provides a simple and elegant way to manage your AS resources with little or none learning curve. In particular, we have shown in *Chapter 3, Managing the Enterprise Server*, how it can be precious to manage the basic domain functionalities, such as configuring, starting, and stopping server groups and hosts.

Let's examine the excellence of each instrument in a table:

Tool	Best for
Command Line Interface (CLI)	Invaluable instrument for the expert system administrator.
	Reaching in-depth server attributes, such as metrics.
	Perform operations as macros or batches.
Web console	Performing most basic administration tasks, as a handy tool.
	Management of top-level domain resources.

Summary

In this chapter you learned how to manage the application server, using the tools and instruments that are part of the AS distribution.

You became acquainted with the new **Command Line Interface (CLI)**, which is likely to become the favorite interface for many system administrators. The CLI allows to traverse the tree of AS resources and issue commands that can read/ modify or display attributes.

One of the advantages of the CLI is that you can easily build complex management operations, thanks to its tab expansion facility. The CLI also allows to enlist commands in a batch, so that you can execute them in an **all-or-nothing** fashion, which is typical of transactional systems.

The other management tool is the Web interface, which allows us to operate on the server configuration using an intuitive and simple interface. For system administrators that need to perform basic administration tasks, that's the ideal tool, as it does not require much expertise to use it.

At this point, you should have enough expertise to handle complex topics, so in the next chapter we will discuss application server clustering, which is an essential component to provide scalability and high availability to your applications.

8
Clustering

This chapter will cover AS 7 clustering capabilities that serve as an essential component to providing **scalability** and **high availability** to your applications. Actually, there is one more asset that can be achieved using clustering—you can spread the traffic load across several AS instances. **Load balancing**, however, is an orthogonal aspect of any Enterprise application that is generally achieved using a properly configured web server in front of the application server. So, we decided to move this information to the next chapter, while in this chapter we will discuss the following topics:

- We will describe all the available options to set up a cluster either using a standalone configuration or a domain of servers.
- We will show how to effectively configure the cluster-building blocks:
  - The **JGroups** subsystem which is used for the underlying communication between nodes
  - The **Infinispan** subsystem which handles the cluster consistency using its advanced data grid platform
  - The **Messaging** subsystem which uses the HornetQ clusterable implementation

Setting up JBoss clustering

For the benefit of impatient readers, we will show straightaway how to get a cluster of AS 7 nodes up and running.

Earlier JBoss releases had their clustering libraries packed into the `all` server configuration which was *de facto* separated from the common `default` configuration.

We will repeat it once more: in AS 7 you don't have any more server configurations bundled with libraries and configuration files. All you have to do to shape a new server profile is create a new XML configuration file.

Because the standalone server can just hold a single profile, AS 7 ships with a separated configuration file named `standalone-ha.xml`, which contains all the clustering subsystems.

On the other hand, a domain server is able to store multiple profiles into the core `domain.xml` configuration file, hence you can use this file both for clustered domains and for non-clustered domain servers.

 Clustering and domains are, however, two separate concepts which don't interfere with one another. While the aim of clustering is to provide the scalability, load-balancing, high-availability features, a domain is a logical grouping of servers that share a centralized domain configuration and can be managed as a single unit.

That being said, we will now describe the different ways to assemble and start a cluster of standalone servers and domain servers.

Setting up a cluster of standalone servers

A cluster of standalone servers is a common option for a development/test environment. Nothing prevents you from using it also on your production system; however, you would need to arrange some tools for managing your cluster nodes, which are built-in domain of servers.

The possible cluster configurations for standalone servers can be broken in two main scenarios:

- Cluster of AS nodes running on different machines
- Cluster of AS nodes running on the same machine

Let's see each cluster scenario:

Cluster of nodes running on different machines

If each server application is installed on a dedicated machine you are planning a **horizontal-scaled** cluster. In terms of configuration, this one requires the least effort—all you have to do is binding the server to its IP address in the single standalone servers and start the server using a clustered-compliant configuration. Let's build an example with a simple two-node cluster as illustrated in the picture:

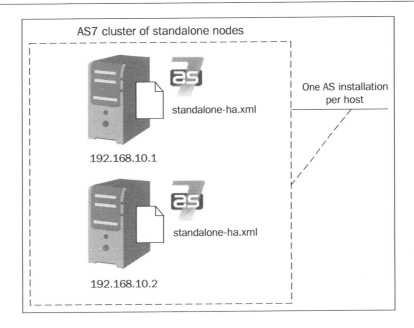

Open the `standalone-ha.xml` file on each AS 7 distribution and reach to the `interfaces` section. Within the nested interface element insert the IP address of the standalone server. For the first machine (`192.168.10.1`), we will define:

```
<interfaces>
        <interface name="management">
            <inet-address value="192.168.10.1"/>
        </interface>
        <interface name="public">
            <inet-address value="192.168.10.1"/>
        </interface>
</interfaces>
```

On the second machine (`192.168.10.2`), we will bind to the other IP address:

```
<interfaces>
        <interface name="management">
            <inet-address value="192.168.10.2"/>
        </interface>
        <interface name="public">
            <inet-address value="192.168.10.2"/>
        </interface>
</interfaces>
```

That's the only thing you needed to change in your configuration. To start the cluster, you have to indicate that your standalone servers will be using the `standalone-ha.xml` configuration file.

```
standalone.bat --server-config=standalone-ha.xml
```

> Starting from Release 7.0.2, the –b option has been resurrected to provide the server binding address. In addition, you can use the –bmanagement flag to specify the management-interface address. The previous configuration can, therefore, be rewritten for the first server as:
>
> ```
> standalone.bat --server-config=standalone-ha.xml –b
> 192.168.10.1 -bmanagement 192.168.10.1
> ```
>
> And for the second server as:
>
> ```
> standalone.bat --server-config=standalone-ha.xml –b
> 192.168.10.2 -bmanagement 192.168.10.2
> ```

In a matter of seconds, your servers will be running, however we didn't find any details about clustering nodes in the console, why? One of the most evident differences between JBoss AS 7 and earlier releases is that the clustering services are started on demand and stop once you don't need them anymore. Hence, simply starting the clustering, without any clustered-enabled application, will not initiate any service or channel.

So, in order to verify our installation, we will deploy a bare bones, cluster-enabled, web application named `Example.war`. To enable clustering of your web applications, you must mark them as **distributable** in the `web.xml` descriptor:

```
<web-app>
   <distributable/>
</web-app>
```

When deploying the application on both machines, you will find out that clustering services are now started and that each machine is able to find out the cluster members.

```
C:\windows\system32\cmd.exe

anisms provided in properties (channelLookup=org.jboss.as.clustering.infinispan.
ChannelProvider, channel-factory=org.jboss.as.clustering.jgroups.JChannelFactory
06fd46259, id=cp11-010-web). Using default JGroups configuration!
19:31:53.361 INFO  [org.jgroups.JChannel] (MSC service thread 1-1) JGroups versi
on: 2.12.1.Final
19:31:56.725 INFO  [org.infinispan.remoting.transport.jgroups.JGroupsTransport]
(MSC service thread 1-1) ISPN00094: Received new cluster view: [cp11-010-36415{0
] [cp11-010-36415]
19:31:56.791 INFO  [org.infinispan.remoting.transport.jgroups.JGroupsTransport]
(MSC service thread 1-1) ISPN00079: Cache local address is cp11-010-36415, physi
cal addresses are [fe80:0:0:0:6df9:69b9:1f11:3c46:64877]
19:31:56.792 INFO  [org.infinispan.factories.GlobalComponentRegistry] (MSC servi
ce thread 1-1) ISPN00128: Infinispan version: Infinispan 'Pagoa' 5.0.0.CR7
19:31:56.852 INFO  [org.infinispan.factories.ComponentRegistry] (MSC service thr
ead 1-1) ISPN00128: Infinispan version: Infinispan 'Pagoa' 5.0.0.CR7
19:31:56.855 INFO  [org.jboss.as.clustering.infinispan.subsystem] (MSC service t
hread 1-1) Started repl cache from web container
19:31:56.962 INFO  [org.jboss.as.clustering.CoreGroupCommunicationService.web] (
MSC service thread 1-1) Number of cluster members: 1
19:31:57.153 INFO  [org.jboss.web] (MSC service thread 1-1) registering web cont
ext: /Example
19:31:57.181 INFO  [org.jboss.as.server.controller] (DeploymentScanner-threads -
2) Deployed "Example.war"
```

Farm deployment

JBoss AS 7 does not use any more the concept of farm deployment. By farm deployment we mean a central repository where you can load (or unload) your applications across the cluster. If you are deploying an application to a domain of servers you can choose on which server groups the application is going to be deployed, hence a farm deployment folder is not needed at all.

If you are going to distribute your application to a set of standalone nodes, your best strategy is creating a CLI script that deploys your application to all your server nodes. For example, create a file named deploy.cli:

```
connect 192.168.10.1
deploy Example.war
connect 192.168.10.2
deploy Example.war
```

Now you can execute this script using the jboss-admin.bat shell (Notice the flags — username and — password for connecting to a remote management interface):

```
jboss-admin.bat --user=username --password=password
--file=deploy.cli
```

Clustering with server nodes on the same machine

The second variant of the standalone configuration comes into picture when your server nodes are located (all or some of them) on the same machine. This scenario applies generally when you are **scaling up** your architecture by adding more hardware resources to your system.

Configuring server nodes on the same machine obviously requires duplicating your AS7 distribution on your filesystem. Then, in order to avoid a port conflict between server distributions, you have to choose between two options:

1. Defining multiple IP address on the same machine.
2. Defining a port offset for each server distribution.

Setting up a cluster on the same machine using multiple IP address

This is also known as **multihoming** and requires some O/S tweaks to get working. Obviously, each operating system uses different approaches to achieve it, which may also vary depending on its version. Being out of the scope of this book to illustrate all possible ways to configure multihoming, we will just show two common scenarios.

When using a Linux box, just issue an `ifconfig` command to activate each IP address:

```
# ifconfig eth0 192.168.10.1 up
# ifconfig eth1 192.168.10.2 up
```

When using a Windows machine, you have to reach, from the network configuration panel, to your Ethernet card's TCP-IP properties. Once there, click on the **Advanced** button and add all addresses that will be part of the cluster:

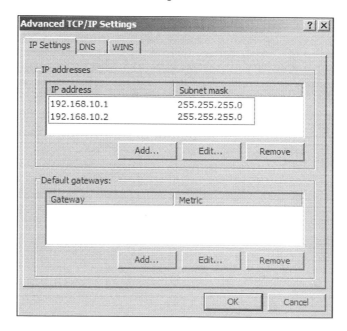

Once you have set up your network interface correctly, it's time to update your `standalone-ha.xml` file. Follow the same steps exposed for multiple host cluster (for each server distribution, reach to the `interfaces` section, and within the nested `interface` element insert the IP address of the standalone server).

In the end, the first server distribution will be bound to the IP Address `192.168.10.1` and the second one to `192.168.10.2`. (as an alternative, use the `-b` and `-bmanagement` switches exposed in the earlier section). The following diagram depicts this scenario:

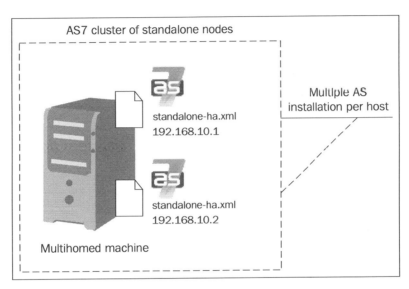

Setting up a cluster on the same machine using port offset

Configuring multihoming is not always a viable choice because it requires some degree of administration experience or maybe because you are lacking in permissions on your machine, in which case, you could still set up a clustering configuration by defining a port offset for your each cluster member.

By defining a port offset for each server, the entire default server binding interfaces will shift to a fixed amount, and hence you will not have two servers engaging the same IP address and the same port.

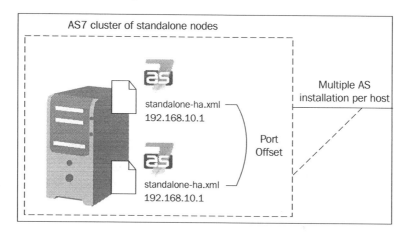

When using this configuration, you can bind each server network address to the same IP address. So, for all your server distributions, we will configure the `standalone-ha.xml` as follows:

```
<interfaces>
        <interface name="management">
            <inet-address value="192.168.10.1"/>
        </interface>
        <interface name="public">
            <inet-address value="192.168.10.1"/>
        </interface>
</interfaces>
```

Then, the first server will use the default socket binding ports:

```
<!--server 1 UNCHANGED -->

<socket-binding-group name="standard-sockets" default-
interface="public">
. . . . . .
</socket-binding-group>
```

While the second one will specify a port-offset element of 150:

```
<!--server 2 -->

<socket-binding-group name="standard-sockets" default-
interface="public" port-offset="150">
. . . . . .
</socket-binding-group>
```

Also, in order to avoid port conflicts, you have to choose a different port for the management interfaces. Again, we will leave the default values for the first server:

```
<!--server 1 UNCHANGED -->

<socket-binding-group name="standard-sockets" default-
interface="public" >
. . . . . . .
        <socket-binding name="management-native"
        interface="management" port="9999"/>
        <socket-binding name="management-http"
        interface="management" port="9990"/>
. . . . . . .
</socket-binding-group>
```

On the second server distribution, we will engage a different port:

```
<!--server 2 -->

<socket-binding-group name="standard-sockets" default-
interface="public" port-offset="150">
. . . . . . .
        <socket-binding name="management-native"
        interface="management" port="19999"/>
        <socket-binding name="management-http"
        interface="management" port="19990"/>
. . . . . . .
</socket-binding-group>
```

Your cluster configuration is complete. Verify it by starting each server distribution by passing it as an argument to the configuration file.

```
standalone.bat --server-config=standalone-ha.xml
```

Setting up a cluster of domain servers

When you are configuring a domain server, you will find that the clustering subsystem is already part of the main configuration file, domain.xml.

As a matter of fact, the AS7 domain deals with clustering just as a different profile used by the application server. Opening the domain.xml file, you will see that the application server ships with two profiles:

- The default profile, which can be used for non-clustered environments
- The ha profile for clustered environments

So, in order to use clustering on a domain, you have at first to configure your server groups to point to the ha profile.

Let's build an example configuration which uses two server groups:

```
<server-groups>
    <server-group name="main-server-group" profile="ha">
            <jvm name="default">
                <heap size="64m" max-size="512m"/>
            </jvm>
            <socket-binding-group ref="ha-sockets"/>
    </server-group>

    <server-group name="other-server-group" profile="ha">
            <jvm name="default">
                <heap size="64m" max-size="512m"/>
            </jvm>
        <socket-binding-group ref="ha-sockets"/>
    </server-group>

</server-groups>
```

As highlighted, in the socket-binding-group element, we are referencing the ha-sockets group, which contains all socket bindings used for a cluster:

```
<socket-binding-group name="ha-sockets" default-interface="public">
    <socket-binding name="http" port="8080"/>
    <socket-binding name="https" port="8443"/>
    <socket-binding name="jgroups-diagnostics" port="0" multicast-
address="224.0.75.75" multicast-port="7500"/>
    <socket-binding name="jgroups-mping" port="0" multicast-
address="230.0.0.4" multicast-port="45700"/>
    <socket-binding name="jgroups-tcp" port="7600"/>
    <socket-binding name="jgroups-tcp-fd" port="57600"/>
    <socket-binding name="jgroups-udp" port="55200" multicast-
address="230.0.0.4" multicast-port="45688"/>
    <socket-binding name="jgroups-udp-fd" port="54200"/>
    <socket-binding name="jmx-connector-registry" port="1090"/>
    <socket-binding name="jmx-connector-server" port="1091"/>
    <socket-binding name="jndi" port="1099"/>
    <socket-binding name="modcluster" port="0"  multicast-
address="224.0.1.105" multicast-port="23364"/>
    <socket-binding name="osgi-http" port="8090"/>
    <socket-binding name="remoting" port="4447"/>
    <socket-binding name="txn-recovery-environment" port="4712"/>
    <socket-binding name="txn-status-manager" port="4713"/>
</socket-binding-group>
```

Your last effort will be defining the servers that are part of the domain (and of the cluster). To ease our work, we will reuse the same domain server list that is contained in the distribution.

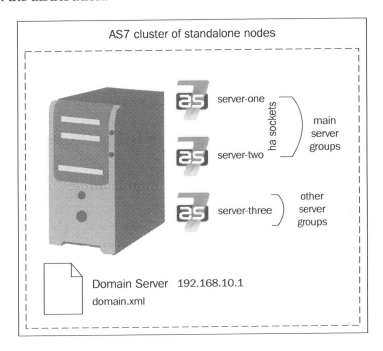

For each server, you have to refer, within your host.xml, to the socket binding group named ha-sockets, which we have just shown:

```
<servers>
  <server name="server-one" group="main-server-group" >
   <socket-binding-group ref="ha-sockets" port-offset="150"/>
    <jvm name="default"/>
  </server>

  <server name="server-two" group="main-server-group"
  auto-start="true" >
    <socket-binding-group ref="ha-sockets" port-offset="250"/>
            <jvm name="default"/>
       </server>

      <server name="server-three" group="other-server-group"
      auto-start="false">
          <socket-binding-group ref="standard-sockets"
          port-offset="350"/>
      <jvm name="default"/>
      </server>
</servers>
```

Your clustered domain is ready for running. Launch your domain of servers using the standard batch script (domain.bat/domain.sh) and the server groups will now point to the ha profile and form a cluster of two nodes.

Troubleshooting clustering

The clustering communication is carried out, by default, using UDP and multicasts information around the cluster. If there are problems, typically it is because of one of the following reasons:

- The nodes are behind a firewall. If your nodes are on different machines then it is possible that the firewall is blocking the multicasts. you can test this by disabling the firewall for each node or adding the appropriate rules.

- You are using a home network or are behind a gateway. Typically home networks will redirect any UDP traffic to the Internet Service Provider, which is then either dropped by the ISP or just lost. To fix this, you will need to add a route to the firewall/gateway that will redirect any multicast traffic back on to the local network instead.

Actually JGroups ships with two test programs that can be used to test multicast communication: McastReceiverTest and McastSenderTest. Start McastReceiverTest, for example:

```
java –classpath jgroups-3.0.0.Final.jar org.jgroups.tests.
McastReceiverTest -mcast_addr 224.10.10.10 -port 5555
```

Then, start McastSenderTest:

```
java –classpath jgroups-3.0.0.Final.jar org.jgroups.tests.McastSenderTest
-mcast_addr 224.10.10.10 -port 5555
```

 The jgroups-3.0.0.Final.jar can be located in the JBOSS_HOME/modules/org/jgroups/main path of your server distribution.

If multicast works correctly, you should be able to type in the McastSenderTest window and see the output in the McastReceiverTest as shown in the following screenshot:

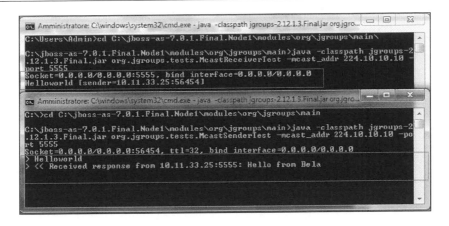

Finally, if you are experiencing troubles with the default multicast address or port, you can change it at any time digging into the `jgroups-udp` socket binding:

```
<socket-binding name="jgroups-udp" port="55200" multicast-
address="${jboss.default.multicast.address:230.0.0.4}" multicast-
port="45688"/>
```

 If you are upgrading from an earlier server release, this command is the equivalent of the AS 5/6 option: `run.sh -c all -u 225.11.11.11 -m 45688`

Configuring JBoss clustering

JBoss AS comes out of the box with clustering support. There is no all-in-one library that deals with clustering, but rather a set of libraries, which cover different kind of aspects.

The following diagram shows the basic clustering architecture adopted by JBoss AS 7:

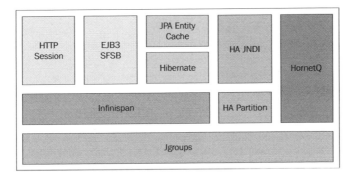

The backbone of JBoss clustering is the **JGroups** library, which provides the communication between members of the cluster using a multicast transmission.

 Multicast is a protocol where data is transmitted simultaneously to a group of hosts that have joined the appropriate multicast group. You can think about multicast as a radio or television streaming where only those tuned to a particular frequency receive the streaming.

The next building block is **Infinispan**, which handles the consistency of your application across the cluster by means of a replicated and transactional JSR-107 compatible cache.

Configuring the JGroups subsystem

The JGroups API handles the communication between nodes in the cluster using a set of reliable communication protocols. Processes can join a group, send messages to all members or single members, and receive messages from members in the group. The system keeps track of the members in every group, and notifies group members when a new member joins, or an existing member leaves or crashes.

Member processes of a group can be located on the same host, within the same Local **Area Network (LAN)**, or across a **Wide Area Network (WAN)**. A member can be in turn part of multiple groups.

The following diagram illustrates a detailed view of JGroups architecture:

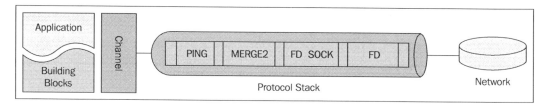

A JGroups process consists basically of three parts, namely the **Channel**, **Building Blocks**, and the **Protocol Stack**.

The **Channel** is a simple socket-like interface used by application programmers to build reliable group communication applications.

Building Blocks are an abstraction interface layered on top of Channels, which can be used instead of Channels whenever a higher-level interface is required.

The **Protocol Stack** contains a list of layers protocols, which need to be crossed by the message. A layer does not *necessarily* correspond to a transport protocol. For example, a layer might take care to fragment the message or to assemble it. What's important is to understand that when a message is sent, it travels down in the stack, while when it's received it traces the way back.

For example, in the previous diagram PING protocol would be executed first, then the MERGE2, followed by FD_SOCK, and finally, the FD protocol. Vice versa, when the message is received, it would meet the FD protocol first, then FD_SOCK, up to PING.

As we said, the JGroups API was already used in earlier JBoss AS releases where developers used to define the JGroups channels in a set of specific configuration files. In JBoss AS 7, the JGroups configuration is embedded into the main standalone. xml/domain.xml configuration file, to be precise into the jgroups subsystem.

There you can find the list of available transport stacks; we'll include here the default UDP stack that is used for communication between nodes.

```xml
<subsystem xmlns="urn:jboss:domain:jgroups:1.0" default-stack="udp">
  <stack name="udp">
    <transport type="UDP" socket-binding="jgroups-udp"
      diagnostics-socket-binding="jgroups-diagnostics"/>
    <protocol type="PING"/>
    <protocol type="MERGE2"/>
    <protocol type="FD_SOCK" socket-binding="jgroups-udp-fd"/>
    <protocol type="FD"/>
    <protocol type="VERIFY_SUSPECT"/>
    <protocol type="BARRIER"/>
    <protocol type="pbcast.NAKACK"/>
    <protocol type="UNICAST"/>
    <protocol type="pbcast.STABLE"/>
    <protocol type="VIEW_SYNC"/>
    <protocol type="pbcast.GMS"/>
    <protocol type="UFC"/>
    <protocol type="MFC"/>
    <protocol type="FRAG2"/>
    <protocol type="pbcast.STREAMING_STATE_TRANSFER"/>
    <protocol type="pbcast.FLUSH"/>
  </stack>
  <stack name="tcp">
    . . . . .
  </stack>
</subsystem>
```

UDP is the default protocol for JGroups and uses multicast (or, if not available, multiple unicast messages) to send and receive messages.

A multicast UDP socket can send and receive datagrams from multiple clients. The interesting and useful feature of multicast is that a client can contact multiple servers with a single packet, without knowing the specific IP address of any of the hosts.

AS 7 migration note

In the AS 5/6 releases, you used to switch between protocol stacks adding to your command line, the property: `-Djboss.default.jgroups.stack=tcp`

One reason why we love AS 7 is that things are much simpler to do. All you have to do is changing the `default-stack` attribute. For example, you could switch to the TCP protocol with as little change as:

```
<subsystem xmlns="urn:jboss:domain:jgroups:1.0"
default-stack="tcp">
```

TCP stacks are typically used when IP multicasting cannot be used in a network (for example, when it is disabled) or when you want to create a network over a WAN (that's conceivably possible, but sharing data across remote geographical sites is a scary option from the performance point of view).

As far as it concerns, the JGroups protocols—a detailed description of all single protocols—would take us far from the scope of this chapter. We will include a short description in the following table, you can find more details on the JGroups home site (`http://jgroups.org/manual/html/index.html`).

Category	Usage	Protocols
Transport	This is responsible for sending and receiving messages across the network.	IDP, TCP, TUNNEL
Discovery	This is used to discover active nodes in the cluster and determine which is the coordinator.	PING, MPING, TCPPING, TCPGOSSIP
Failure Detection	This one is used to poll cluster nodes to detect node failures	FD, FD_SIMPLE, FD_PING, FD_ICMP, FD_SOCK, VERIFY_SUSPECT
Reliable Delivery	This ensures that messages are actually delivered and delivered in the right order (FIFO) to the destination node	CAUSAL, NAKACK,pbcast. NAKACK, SMACK,UNICAST, PBCAST

Category	Usage	Protocols
Group Membership	This is used to notify the cluster when a node joins, leaves or crashes	pbcast.GMS, MERGE,MERGE2, VIEW_SYNC
Flow Control	This is used to adapt the data-sending rate to the data-receipt rate among the nodes	FC
Fragmentation	This fragments messages larger than a certain size.and un-fragments at the receiver's side	FRAG2
State transfer	This one synchronizes the application state (serialized as a byte array) from an existing node with a new-joining node.	pbcast.STATE_TRANSFER, pbcast.STREAMING_STATE_ TRANSFER
Distributed garbage collection	This protocol periodically deletes that have been seen by all nodes from the memory in each node.	pbcast.STABLE

Customizing the protocol stack

If you want to customize your transport configuration at the lowest level, then you could override the default properties used by JGroups or even the single protocol properties. For example, the following configuration snippet can be used to change the default send or receive buffer used by the JGroups UDP stack:

```
<subsystem xmlns="urn:jboss:domain:jgroups:1.0" default-stack="udp">
 <stack name="udp">
   <transport type="UDP" socket-binding="jgroups-udp"
   diagnostics-socket-binding="jgroups-diagnostics">
   <property name="ucast_recv_buf_size">50000000</property>
   <property name="ucast_send_buf_size">1280000</property>
   <property name="mcast_recv_buf_size">50000000</property>
   <property name="mcast_send_buf_size">1280000</property>
 </transport>
    . . . . . . . .
 </stack>
</subsystem>
```

To change the send or receive buffer of the UDP-based JGroups channel, it is important to limit the need for JGroups to retransmit messages by limiting UDP datagram loss.

However, the actual size of the buffer the OS will provide is limited by OS-level maximums. So, as a rule of thumb, you should always configure your OS to take advantage of the JGroups' transport configuration.

If you want to have a look at all the available properties which can be used either at transport level or at the protocol level, consult the JGroups XSD file which is available in the JBOSS_HOME/docs/schema folder of your server distribution.

Configuring the Infinispan subsystem

One of the requisites of a cluster is that data is synchronized across its members so that, in case of failure of a node, the application and its session can continue on other members of the cluster, also known as **High Availability**. Like JBoss AS 6, the new AS 7 uses Infinispan as the distributed caching solution behind its clustering functionality. The Infinispan API replaces the earlier JBoss Cache library and can be either used as standalone data-grid platform (using its native implementation), or it can be embedded into the application server.

As we are interested in the latter option, we will quickly have a look at its configuration, which is contained within the main standalone-ha.xml/domain.xml configuration file.

The following is the backbone of the Infinispan configuration:

```
<subsystem xmlns="urn:jboss:domain:infinispan:1.1"
  default-cache-container="cluster">
  <cache-container name="cluster" default-cache="default">
    <alias>ha-partition</alias>
    <replicated-cache mode="SYNC" name="default" batching="true">
      <locking isolation="REPEATABLE_READ"/>
    </replicated-cache>
  </cache-container>

  <cache-container name="web" default-cache="repl">
    . . . . .
  </cache-container>

  <cache-container name="sfsb" default-cache="repl">
```

```
      .   .   .   .   .
   </cache-container>

   <cache-container name="hibernate" default-cache="local-query">
      .   .   .   .   .
   </cache-container>
</subsystem>
```

One of the key differences with the standalone Infinispan configuration is that the AS 7 Infinispan subsystem exposes multiple `cache-container` elements, while a native Infinispan configuration file contains cache configurations for a single cache container.

Each `cache-container` element, in turn, contains one or more caching policies, which ultimately define how data is synchronized for that specific cache container. The following caching strategies can be used by cache containers:

- **Local**: The entries are stored on the local node only, regardless of whether a cluster has formed. In this mode, Infinispan is typically operating as a local cache.

- **Replication**: Using this, all entries are replicated to all nodes. In this mode, Infinispan is typically operating as a temporary data store and doesn't offer an increased heap space.

- **Distribution**: The entries are distributed to a subset of the nodes only. In this mode, Infinispan is typically operating as a data grid providing an increased heap space.

- **Invalidation**: The entries are stored into a cache store (such as a database) only, and invalidated from all nodes. When a node needs the entry, it will load it from a cache store. In this mode, Infinispan is operating as a distributed cache, backed by a canonical data store such as a database.

In the following sections, we will have a look at some cache configurations which are essential to configure your clustered applications properly, such as `session` caches (the `web` cache and the `sfsb` cache) and the `hibernate` cache.

Configuring session cache containers

The Java Enterprise platform has historically had two competing solutions for storing session data: HTTP Session and Stateful session beans. While the two mechanisms are conceptually different, the way they are implemented, they are quite similar as far as it concerns session synchronization across the cluster. For this reason, we will discuss them in a single section, showing the similarities between them.

So, here's the `cache-container` configuration for the `web` cache and the `sfsb` cache:

```
<cache-container name="web" default-cache="repl">
    <alias>standard-session-cache</alias>

    <replicated-cache mode="ASYNC" name="repl" batching="true">
        <locking isolation="REPEATABLE_READ"/>
        <file-store/>
    </replicated-cache>

    <distributed-cache mode="ASYNC" name="dist" batching="true">
        <locking isolation="REPEATABLE_READ"/>
        <file-store/>
    </distributed-cache>
</cache-container>

<cache-container name="sfsb" default-cache="repl">
    <alias>sfsb-cache</alias>
    <alias>jboss.cache:service=EJB3SFSBClusteredCache
    </alias>

    <replicated-cache mode="ASYNC" name="repl" batching="true">
        <locking isolation="REPEATABLE_READ"/>
        <eviction strategy="LRU" max-entries="10000"/>
        <file-store/>
    </replicated-cache>

</cache-container>
```

As you can see, the `web` cache container configuration can contain one or more caching strategies: the `replicated-cache` and the `distributed-cache`, the former being the default one. In the next section, we will explore in detail the differences and the gotchas between these two cache modes. At the moment, bear in mind that if you want to change the clustering mode, all you have to do is adapting the `default-cache` attribute to your cache mode.

As far as it is concerned the data synchronization across members can be carried out using either synchronous messages (`SYNC`) or asynchronous messages (`ASYNC`).

Synchronous messaging is the least efficient mode as each node will wait for message acknowledgement from all cluster members. However, synchronous mode is needed when all the nodes in the cluster may access the cached data, resulting in a high need for consistency.

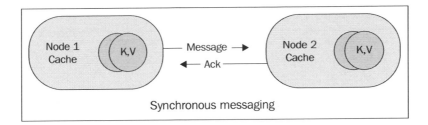

Synchronous messaging

Asynchronous messaging enhances speed rather than consistency and this is particularly advantageous in use cases such as HTTP session replication with sticky sessions enabled. In these scenarios, a session is always accessed on the same cluster node, and only in case of failure is data accessed in a different node.

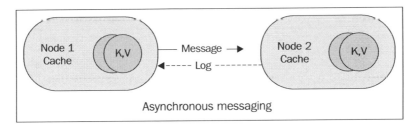

Asynchronous messaging

Inside each cache definition, you should have noticed the `locking-isolation` element that corresponds in semantic to the equivalent database isolation levels. Infinispan only supports `READ_COMMITTED` or `REPEATABLE_READ` isolation levels.

> `REPEATABLE_READ` is the default isolation level used by Infinispan. Using this isolation lock, the transaction acquires read locks on all retrieved data, though phantom reads can potentially occur.
>
> `READ_COMMITTED` provides a significant performance gain over `REPEATABLE_READ`, but data records retrieved by a query are not prevented from modification by some other transaction.

Another element that is included in both caches is `file-store`, which configures the path in which to store the cached data. The default data is written into the `jboss.server.data.dir` directory under a directory named as the cache container name. For example, here's the default `file-store` path for the standalone `web` cache container:

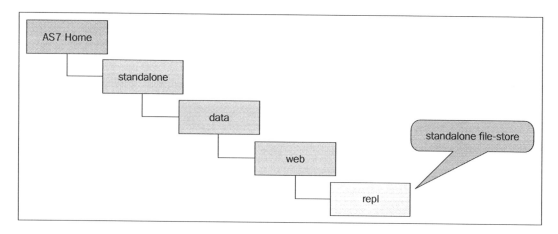

You can, however, customize the `file-store` path using the `relative-to` and `path` element, just as we showed in *Chapter 2* for the path element:

```
<file-store relative-to="..." path="..."/>
```

By having a clear idea of the elements, which include a part of the configuration, we want to hammer on the differences between replicated and distributed caches, without which, you will miss the whole picture.

Choosing between replication and distribution

When using a **replication**, cache Infinispan will store every entry on every node in the cluster grid. This means that entries added to any of these cache instances will be replicated to all other cache instances in the cluster, and can be retrieved from any instance locally.

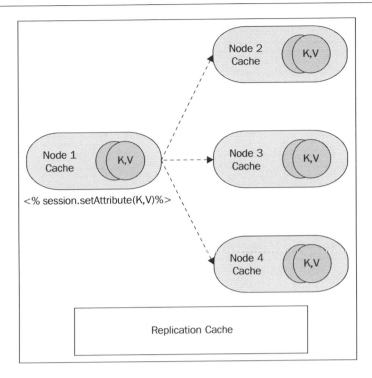

The scalability of replication is a function of cluster size and average data size, so if we have many nodes and/or large data sets, then we hit a scalability ceiling.

If DATA_SIZE * NUMBER_OF_HOSTS is smaller than the memory available to each host, then replication is a viable choice.

On the other hand, when using **distributed** caching, Infinispan will store every cluster entry on a subset of the nodes in the grid thereby allowing to scale linearly as more servers are added to the cluster.

Distribution makes use of a consistent hash algorithm to determine where in a cluster entries should be stored. Hashing algorithm is configured with the number of copies each cache entry should be maintained cluster-wide. The number of copies represents the trade-off between performance and durability of data. The more copies you maintain, the lower performance will be, but also the lower the risk of losing data due to server outages.

You can use the `owners` parameter (default 2) to define the number of cluster-wide replicas for each cache entry.

```
<distributed-cache owners="3" mode="ASYNC" name="dist"
batching="true">

        . . . . .

</distributed-cache>
```

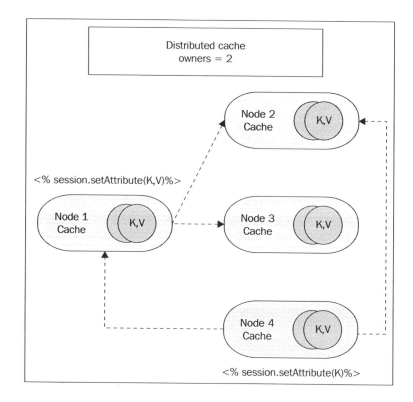

By definition, the choice between replication and distribution depends largely on the cluster size. For example, replication provides a quick and easy way to share state across a cluster; however, it only performs well in small clusters (fewer than ten servers), due to the number of replication messages that need to happen—as the cluster size increases.

In a distributed cache, a number of copies are maintained to provide redundancy and fault tolerance; however, this is typically far fewer than the number of nodes in the cluster. Hence, a distributed cache provides a far greater degree of scalability than a replicated cache.

Does Infinispan use buddy replication?

Buddy replication was the most effective solution for scaling web applications in earlier releases of JBoss AS. The major advantage of buddy replication was that, instead of replicating data across every node of the cluster, it chose a fixed number of backup nodes and only replicated data to these backups.

A quite helpful thing but with one caveat: buddy replication was specifically designed for HTTP-session replication. This in turn requires, for achieving a real performance benefit, the use of session affinity, also known as sticky sessions in HTTP session replication speak.

As we have been using the past tense, you might guess that a buddy replication has been abandoned in JBoss AS 7. The Infinispan's distribution mode is the functional replacement of buddy replication.

While providing a near-linear scalable solution, by using a fixed number of owners to hold the cache data, it does not need session affinity. Hence, it is applicable to a wider set of use cases than HTTP session.

Configuring hibernate cache

The hibernate cache container is a key element of your configuration because it handles the data tier which is the backend of every application. As you probably know, JBoss uses hibernate as default JPA provider, so the concepts described in this chapter apply both for hibernate applications (configured to run on JBoss AS) and for JPA-based applications.

Hibernate caches are conceptually different from the session-based caches because they are based on a different assumption, that is you have a permanent storage for your data (the database files), so it's not necessary to replicate or distribute copies of the Entities across the cluster in order to achieve high availability. You just need to inform your nodes when data has been modified, so it needs to be invalidated.

If a cache is configured for **invalidation** rather than replication, every time data is changed in a cache, other caches in the cluster receive a message informing them that their data is now stale and should be evicted from memory.

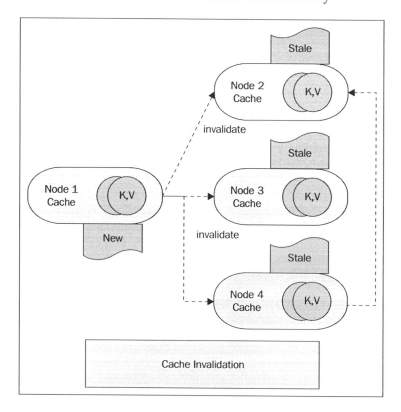

The benefit of this is twofold: network traffic is minimized as invalidation messages are very small compared to replicating updated data, and also that other caches in the cluster look up modified data in a lazy manner, only when needed.

Now let's see in practice how the mechanism works: whenever an new entity or collection is read from database, it's only cached **locally** in order to reduce intra-cluster traffic:

```
<cache-container name="hibernate" default-cache="local-query">
     <local-cache name="local-query">
        <eviction strategy="LRU" max-entries="10000"/>
        <expiration max-idle="100000"/>
     </local-cache>
</cache-container>
```

The `local-query` cache is configured by default to store up to 10000 entries in a LRU vector. Each entry will be evicted from the cache automatically if it has been idle for 100 seconds.

Once that a cache entity is updated, your cache will send a message to other members of the cluster telling them that the entity has been modified. Here, the `invalidation-cache` comes into play:

```
<invalidation-cache mode="SYNC" name="entity">
    <eviction strategy="LRU" max-entries="10000"/>
    <expiration max-idle="100000"/>
</invalidation-cache>
```

By default invalidation uses the same eviction and expiration settings as for local query caching, that is, the maximum number of entries are 10,000 and the idle time before expiration is 100 seconds.

The invalidation too can be synchronous (`SYNC`) or asynchronous (`ASYNC`), and just as in the case of replication, synchronous invalidation blocks until all caches in the cluster receive invalidation messages and have evicted stale data while asynchronous invalidation works in a `fire-and-forget` mode, where invalidation messages are broadcast but doesn't block and wait for responses.

By default, entities and collections are configured to use READ_COMMITTED as cache isolation level. It would, however, make sense to configure REPEATABLE_READ if the application evicts/clears entities from the hibernate session and then expects to repeatedly re-read them in the same transaction. If you really need to use REPEATABLE_READ, you can simply configure entities or collections to use "entity-repeatable" cache.

```
<invalidation-cache mode="SYNC" name="entity">
    . . . . . . .
    <locking isolation="REPEATABLE_READ"/>
</invalidation-cache>
```

The last piece of code contained in the Infinispan subsystems concerns with the `timestamp` cache. The `timestamp` cache keeps track of the last update timestamp for each table (this timestamp is updated for any table modification).

This cache is strictly connected with the query cache, which is used to store the result set of a query made against the database. We will discuss more about query cache in the section named "Entity clustering"; however in short, if the query cache is enabled, any time a query is issued, the query cache is checked before issuing for a query. If the timestamp of the last update on a table is greater than the time the query results were cached, then the entry is removed and the lookup is a miss.

```
<replicated-cache mode="ASYNC" name="timestamps">
        <eviction strategy="NONE"/>
</replicated-cache>
```

By default, timestamps cache is configured with asynchronous replication as clustering mode. Local or invalidated cluster modes are not allowed, since all cluster nodes must store all timestamps. As a result, no eviction/expiration is allowed for timestamp caches either.

Using replication for hibernate cache

There are situations when you could desire to replicate your entity cache across other cluster nodes, instead of using local caches and invalidation. This can be true when the following conditions are met:

- Queries executed are quite expensive.
- Queries are likely to be repeated in different cluster nodes.
- Queries are unlikely to be invalidated out of the cache (Hibernate must invalidate query results from the cache any time any instance of one of the entity classes involved in the query's WHERE clause changes.)

In order to switch to a replicated cache, you have to configure your `default-cache` attribute as follows:

```
<cache-container name="hibernate" default-cache="replicated-cache">
. . . . .
</cache-container>
```

Advanced Infinispan configuration

The caching configuration is essential to get working with a clustered application; Infinispan has, however, wealth of options available to further customize your cache. In this section, we will discuss customizing the thread configuration and the default transport configuration.

Configuring Infinispan threads

Just as for the JGroups transport, you can externalize your Infinispan thread configuration, moving it into the thread pool subsystem. The following thread pools can be configured on a cache-container basis:

Thread pool	Description
transport	This gives the size of the bounded thread pool whose threads are responsible for transporting data across the network.
listener-executor	This gives the size of the thread pool used for registering and getting notified when some cache events take place.
replication-queue-executor	The gives the size of the scheduled replication executor used for replicating cache data.
eviction-executor	This gives the size of the scheduled executor service used to periodically run eviction clean up tasks.

Customizing the thread pool can be advantageous in some cases, for example, if you plan to apply a cache replication algorithm, then it could be worthy to choose the number of threads used for replicating data. In the following example, we are externalizing the thread pools of the web's `cache-container` by defining up to twenty-five threads for transporting data across other nodes and five threads for replicating data.

```
<subsystem xmlns="urn:jboss:domain:infinispan:1.0" default-cache-
container="cluster">

<cache-container name="web" default-cache="repl" listener-
executor="infinispan-listener" eviction-executor="infinispan-eviction"
replication-queue-executor="infinispan-repl-queue">
  <transport executor="infinispan-transport"/>
</cache-container>
</subsystem>
. . . . . . .
<subsystem xmlns="urn:jboss:domain:threads:1.0">
  <thread-factory name="infinispan-factory" priority="1"/>
  <bounded-queue-thread-pool name="infinispan-transport"/>
    <core-threads count="1"/>
    <queue-length count="100000"/>
    <max-threads count="25"/>
    <thread-factory name="infinispan-factory"/>
  </bounded-queue-thread-pool>
  <bounded-queue-thread-pool name="infinispan-listener"/>
    <core-threads count="1"/>
    <queue-length count="100000"/>
    <max-threads count="1"/>
```

```
      <thread-factory name="infinispan-factory"/>
    </bounded-queue-thread-pool>
    <scheduled-thread-pool name="infinispan-eviction"/>
      <max-threads count="1"/>
      <thread-factory name="infinispan-factory"/>
    </scheduled-thread-pool>
    <scheduled-thread-pool name="infinispan-repl-queue"/>
      <max-threads count="5"/>
      <thread-factory name="infinispan-factory"/>
    </scheduled-thread-pool>
  </subsystem>
```

Configuring Infinispan transport

The Infinispan subsystem uses the JGroups subsystem to provide the foundation for the network transport of cache data. By default, cache containers use the `default-stack`, which is defined into the JGroups subsystem.

```
<subsystem xmlns="urn:jboss:domain:jgroups:1.0" default-stack="udp">
</subsystem>
```

You can, however, choose a different transport for each cache container, for example, if you wanted to use TCP as transport for the web cache container:

```
<cache-container name="web" default-cache="repl">
  <transport stack="tcp"/>
</cache-container>
```

The default UDP transport is usually suitable for large clusters or if you are using replication or invalidation as it minimizes opening too many sockets.

The TCP stack performs better for smaller clusters, in particular, if you are using a distribution, as TCP is more efficient as a point-to-point protocol.

Clustering the messaging subsystem

We will conclude the clustering chapter discussing about the messaging subsystem which uses **HornetQ** as JMS provider.

HornetQ clusters allow groups of HornetQ servers to be grouped together in order to share the message processing load. Each active node in the cluster is an active HornetQ server that manages its own messages and handles its own connections.

In order to enable clustering, you need a few simple enhancements to your server configuration file. At first, the JMS server must be configured to be clustered, so you will need to set the `clustered` element at the top of the messaging domain setting it to `true` (this element defaults to `false`).

```
<subsystem xmlns="urn:jboss:domain:messaging:1.1">
  <hornetq-server>
    <clustered>true</clustered>
    . . . . . .
  </hornetq-server>
</subsystem>
```

Next, you need to configure the cluster connections. As a matter of fact, the cluster is formed by each node declaring cluster connections to other server nodes. Behind the scenes, when a node forms a cluster connection to another node, it creates a core bridge connection between it and the other node internally. Once the connection has been established, it can be used to allow messages to flow between the nodes of the cluster and to balance the load.

Let's see a typical cluster connection configuration which can be added to your messaging configuration within your `<hornetq-server>` definition:

```
<cluster-connections>
  <cluster-connection name="mycluster">
    <address>jms</address>
    <connector-ref>netty</connector-ref>
    <retry-interval>500</retry-interval>
    <use-duplicate-detection>true</use-duplicate-detection>
    <forward-when-no-consumers>false</forward-when-no-consumers>
    <max-hops>1</max-hops>
  </cluster-connection>
</cluster-connections>
```

In the previous configuration, we have explicitly specified several parameters, although you might use the defaults for some. You can also reference the `jboss-as-messaging_1_1.xsd` for the full list of available parameters (available in the JBOSS_HOME/docs/schema folder of your server distribution).

The `cluster-connection` instance's `name` attribute obviously defines the cluster connection name which we are going to configure (there can be zero or more cluster connections configured in your messaging subsystem).

The `address` element is a mandatory parameters and determines how messages are distributed across the cluster. In this example, the cluster connection will load balance messages sent to an address that start with `jms`. This cluster connection, will, in effect apply to all JMS queue and topic subscriptions because they map to core queues that start with the substring `jms`.

The `connector-ref` element references the connector which has been defined in the `connectors` section of the messaging subsystem. In this case, we are using the netty connector (See *Chapter 3, Configuring Enterprise Services*, for more information about the available connectors).

The `retry-interval` determines the interval in milliseconds between the message retry attempts. As a matter of fact, if a cluster connection is created and the target node has not been started, or say, it is being rebooted, then the cluster connections from other nodes will retry connecting using the `retry-interval` time.

Next, the `use-duplicate-detection` when enabled will detect any duplicate messages which will be filtered out and ignored on receipt at the target node.

The `forward-when-no-consumers` element, when set to true, will ensure that each incoming message will be distributed round robin even though there are not consumers on some nodes of the cluster.

You can actually specify the connection load balancing policy within the `connection-factory` element. The out-of-the-box policies are **Round-Robin** (`org.hornetq.api.core.client.loadbalance.RoundRobinConnectionLoadBalancingPolicy`) and **Random** (`org.hornetq.api.core.client.loadbalance.RandomConnectionLoadBalancingPolicy`). You can also add your own policy by implementing the interface `org.hornetq.api.core.client.loadbalance.ConnectionLoadBalancingPolicy`.

Here's for example how to use the random policy for a connection factory:

```
<connection-factory name="InVmConnectionFactory">

    . . . .

        <connection-load-balancing-policy-class-
name>    org.hornetq.api.core.client.loadbalance.
RandomConnectionLoadBalancingPolicy
        </connection-load-balancing-policy-class-name>
</connection-factory>
```

Finally, the optional `max-hops` is set to 1 (default), which means messages are only load balanced to other HornetQ serves which are directly connected to this server. (As a matter of fact HornetQ can be configured to also load balance messages to nodes which might be connected to it only indirectly with other HornetQ servers as intermediates in a chain).

Configuring messaging credentials

When starting the cluster, you might have noticed the following warning in the server's console (or log message):

09:29:07,573 WARNING [org.hornetq.core.server.impl.HornetQServerImpl]

(MSC service thread 1-1) Security risk! It has been detected that the cluster admin

user and password have not been changed from the installation default. Please see

the HornetQ user guide, cluster chapter, for instructions on how to do this.

Actually, when creating connections between nodes of a cluster to form a cluster connection, HornetQ uses a cluster user and cluster password. It is imperative that these values are changed from their default values, or remote clients will be able to make connections to the server using the default values. If they are not changed from the default, HornetQ will detect this and pester you with a warning on every start-up.

```
<cluster-user>user</cluster-user>
<cluster-password>password</cluster-password>
```

Summary

In this chapter, we have tested your stamina by discussing lots of topics surrounding clustering. Although the amount of information contained in it was quite abundant, we can resume it in the following key points.

A JBoss AS 7 cluster can be either composed of standalone nodes and as part of a domain of servers.

- Standalone clusters have to define the clustering subsystems in a separate configuration file named `standalone-ha.xml`. So, in order to start a cluster of standalone nodes you have to switch to the `standalone-ha.xml` file.

- Domain server can have multiple profiles associated with it; hence, clustering is contained in one profile named `ha`. In order to start a cluster of domain servers, you have to switch to the `ha` profile.

The communication between cluster nodes is achieved through the **JGroups** API that, by default, uses UDP multicast messages to handle the cluster lifecycle events.

The other building block of a clustered application is demanded to **Infinispan** advanced grid and caching platform.

Every key element of Enterprise applications that need to preserve the consistency of data in the cluster can configure the single cache containers, which are part of the Infinispan subsystems.

- The SFSB's `cache-container` is configured to replicate stateful session bean data across the cluster nodes.

- The web's `cache-container` is configured as well to replicate HTTP Session data across the cluster nodes.

- The **hibernate's** `cache-container` uses a more complex approach by defining a `local-query` strategy for handling local entities, then an `invalidation-cache` mechanism when data is updated and other cluster nodes need to be informed. Finally, a `replicated-cache` is used to replicate the query timestamps.

Finally, we have covered the messaging subsystem which can be easily clusterable by setting the `clustered` element to true. This way, messages will be transparently load-balanced across your JMS servers. You can fine-tune your cluster connections by defining a `cluster-connection` section which will determine how messages are distributed across the cluster.

9
Load-balancing Web Applications

In the previous chapter, we illustrated the first important advantage of clustered applications, which is the ability to maintain unaffected services for any predefined number of clients. It is also known as high availability.

In this chapter, we will cover the second main concern of clustering, which is the ability to make several servers participate in the same service and do the same work. In other words, how to load-balance the number of requests across the available servers.

Historically, the JBoss AS has inherited the load-balancing libraries from his "cousin" Tomcat, which is itself a part of the application server modules. This module, mod_jk, is still available for use in the new application server era; however, new specific instruments are available for the AS 7. In particular, mod_cluster project, which is a part of the AS 7 modules, provides a level of intelligence and granularity unmatched in other load-balancing solutions.

Having made this a short premise, we will, at first, introduce the advantages of using a web server in front of your web applications, and then we will cover the following topics:

- Connecting JBoss AS 7 using mod_jk and mod_proxy
- Connecting JBoss AS 7 using mod_cluster API

Using Apache web server with JBoss AS 7

In real-world projects, it's common to find Apache web server as a front door to your application server. The advantages of such an architecture are as follows:

- **Speed**: Apache is generally faster at serving static content than JBoss Web server.

- **Security**: The application server, which contains sensitive data, can then be placed in a protected area and, from a security point of view, you only need to worry about the Apache server. Essentially, Apache becomes a smart proxy server.

- **Load balancing and clustering**. By using Apache as a frontend you can handle traffic to multiple JBoss Web server instances. If one of your JBoss AS fails, the communication transparently continues to another node in the cluster.

Connecting Apache and JBoss AS can be done by means of several libraries: in the past, most projects have adopted either Tomcat's mod_jk library or Apache's mod_proxy libraries. Because the installation of either mod_jk or mod_proxy does not differ from earlier AS releases, we will just include a quick setup guide for your reference.

If, however, you are planning to set up a high-performance, dynamic cluster of web servers, we suggest you migrate to the newer mod_cluster API, which is discussed in the second part of this chapter.

Configuring mod_jk

mod_jk is the most-used solution for fronting JBoss AS with Apache web server. All requests first come to the Apache web server. The Apache web server accepts and processes any static resource requests, such as requests for HTML pages or graphical images. Then, with the help of mod_jk, the Apache web server redirects requests for any JSP or Servlet component to a JBoss Web server instance(s). Sending the request over the network using the AJP protocol performs this redirection.

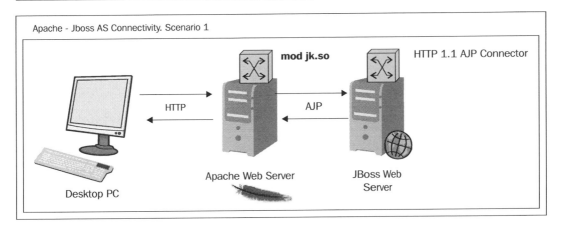

Apache - Jboss AS Connectivity. Scenario 1

In order to install mod_jk, at first, download the appropriate Tomcat Connector for your Apache web server installation from `http://tomcat.apache.org/download-connectors.cgi`.

Then, modify the Apache configuration file (`APACHE_HOME/conf/httpd.conf`) and add a single line at the end of the file:

```
Include conf/mod-jk.conf
```

Next, create a new file named `APACHE_HOME/conf/mod-jk.conf`, which will contain the mod_jk configuration:

```
# Load mod_jk module
# Specify the filename of the mod_jk lib
LoadModule jk_module modules/mod_jk.so

# Where to find workers.properties
JkWorkersFile conf/workers.properties

# Where to put jk logs
JkLogFile logs/mod_jk.log

# Set the jk log level [debug/error/info]
JkLogLevel info

# Mount your applications
# Send everything for context /myapp to worker1 (ajp13)
JkMount   /myapp/* loadbalancer
JkShmFile logs/jk.shm
```

Please note that the following two settings are most important:

- The `LoadModule` directive must reference the `mod_jk` library you have just downloaded. Change the `modules` path to any other path you are using to store libraries.

- The `JkMount` directive tells Apache which URLs it should forward to the `mod_jk` module (and, in turn, to the web container). In the previous file, all the requests with the URL path `/myapp/*` are sent to the `mod_jk` connector. This way, you can configure Apache to server-static contents directly and only use `mod_jk` for Java applications. If you plan to use `mod_jk` for every web application, you can also forward all URLs using "/*".

Next, you need to configure the `mod_jk` workers file `conf/workers.properties`. This file specifies where the different web servers are located and, possibly, how calls should be load-balanced across them. For a one-node setup, the file could look like this:

```
# Define worker list using ajp13
worker.list=loadbalancer,status
# Set properties for worker1 (ajp13)
worker.worker1.type=ajp13
worker.worker1.host=192.168.0.1
worker.worker1.port=8009

# Set properties for worker2 (ajp13)
worker.worker1.type=ajp13
worker.worker1.host=192.168.0.2
worker.worker1.port=8009

worker.loadbalancer.balance_workers=worker1,worker2
worker.loadbalancer.sticky_session=1
```

In the `workers.properties` file, each node is defined using the `worker.XXX` naming convention, where XXX represents an arbitrary name you choose for each web server containers. For each worker, you must specify the hostname (or IP address) and the port number of the AJP13 connector running in the web server.

On the JBoss side, you have to add the AJP connector, which is not inserted by default:

```
<subsystem xmlns="urn:jboss:domain:web:1.1">
            <connector name="http" protocol="HTTP/1.1" socket-
binding="http" scheme="http"/>
```

```
          <connector name="AJP" protocol="AJP/1.3"
          socket-binding="ajp" />

          <virtual-server name="localhost">
              <alias name="example.com"/>
          </virtual-server>
  </subsystem>
```

Then, in the `socket-binding-group`, you have to choose a port for the AJP connector. In our example, it will be listening on port 8009:

```
<socket-binding-group name="standard-sockets"
  default-interface="default">
  <socket-binding name="http" port="8080"/>

  <socket-binding name="ajp" port="8009"/>

  . . . .
</socket-binding-group>
```

Configuring mod proxy

Since **Apache 1.3**, there's support for an optional module, named `mod_proxy`, that configures Apache to act as a proxy server. This can be used to forward requests for particular web applications such as Tomcat or JBoss, without having to configure a web connector such as `mod_jk`.

So, `mod_proxy` just requires including the following directives in your Apache's `httpd.conf` file:

```
LoadModule proxy_module modules/mod_proxy.so
```

Then, include two directives in your `httpd.conf` file for each web application that you wish to forward to JBoss AS. For example, to forward an application at context path `/myapp`:

```
ProxyPass        /myapp  http://localhost:8080/myapp
ProxyPassReverse /myapp  http://localhost:8080/myapp
```

This tells Apache to forward URLs of the form `http://localhost/myapp/*` to the JBoss HTTP connector listening on port 8080.

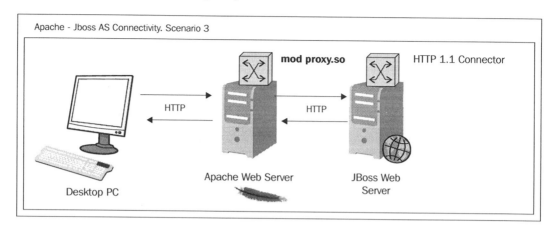

As shown in the previous diagram, Apache's `mod_proxy` is TCP-based and uses the HTTP, so you don't need to add anything else in your JBoss configuration. By definition, this is the simplest way to put Apache in front of JBoss, but also the slowest way to do it

In **Apache 2.2**, there's support for another module, named `mod_proxy ajp`, which can be used in much the same way as `mod_proxy`. However, it uses AJP protocol to proxy Apache requests to JBoss AS. In order to use it, add the following directive to your Apache configuration:

```
LoadModule proxy_ajp_module modules/mod_proxy_ajp.so
```

Then, enable proxy pass to JBoss AS with this directive:

```
ProxyPass / ajp://localhost:8009/
```

```
ProxyPassReverse / ajp://localhost:8009/
```

Here, we are simply redirecting all traffic ("/") to the web server listening on localhost at port 8009.

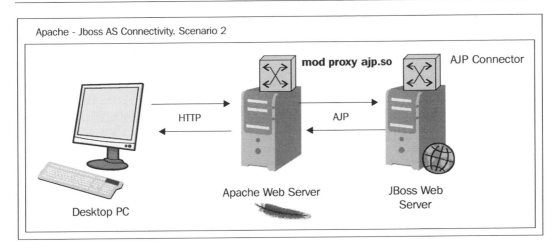

Apache - Jboss AS Connectivity. Scenario 2

Since `mod_proxy_ajp` runs on a dedicated port, you have to activate it on your JBoss side:

```
<subsystem xmlns="urn:jboss:domain:web:1.1">
        <connector name="http" protocol="HTTP/1.1"
        socket-binding="http" scheme="http"/>

        <connector name="AJP" protocol="AJP/1.3" socket-
binding="ajp" />

        <virtual-server name="localhost">
            <alias name="example.com"/>
        </virtual-server>
    </subsystem>
. . . . . .
<socket-binding-group name="standard-sockets" default-
interface="default">
        <socket-binding name="http" port="8080"/>

        <socket-binding name="ajp" port="8009"/>
. . . .
</socket-binding-group>
```

Load-balancing with mod_cluster

Mod_cluster is an HTTP-based load balancer, which, like `mod_jk`, can be used to forward a request to a set of application server instances. The advantage of using `mod_cluster` against `mod_jk` and `mod_proxy` can be summarized in these key points:

1. Dynamic clustering configuration.
2. Server-side pluggable load metrics.
3. Lifecycle notifications of application status.

Let's see each point in more detail. As we have just learnt, when using a standard load balancer like `mod_jk`, you have to provide a static list of nodes that are used to spread load. This is a very limiting factor, especially if you have to deliver upgrades to your configuration by adding or removing nodes or you simply need to upgrade releases used by single nodes. Besides this, using a flat cluster configuration can be tedious and prone to errors, especially if the number of cluster nodes is high.

When using `mod_cluster`, you are able to dynamically add or remove nodes to your cluster because cluster nodes are discovered through an advertising mechanism. In practice, the `mod_cluster` libraries on the **httpd** side send UDP messages on a multicast group, which is subscribed by AS7 nodes. This allows AS7 nodes the automatic discovery of **httpd** proxies where application lifecycle notifications are sent.

The next diagram illustrates the concept better:

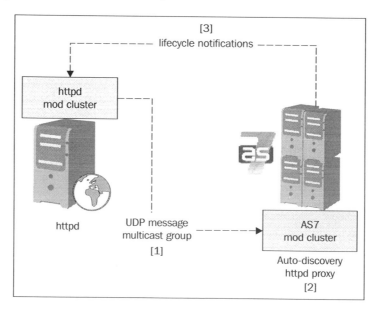

This is exceptionally useful in **cloud environments** where hosts can be added or removed at any time and simply cannot be managed by traditional instruments such as mod_jk.

Another key feature of mod_cluster resides in the load metrics, which are determined on the server side using pluggable policies with appropriate load factors. Load metrics are then sent to the **httpd** side as circumstances change. As a consequence, mod_cluster provides a far more robust architecture then traditional **httpd**-based load balancers where metrics are statically held on the proxy.

Finally, one more advantage provided by mod_cluster over mod_jk is the ability to intercept lifecycle events such as un-deployment or redeployment, which, as we have just seen, are synchronized between the **httpd** side and the application server-side.

Installing mod_cluster

mod_cluster is implemented as a core AS 7 module, which is a part of the distribution and, on the **httpd** side, as a set of libraries installed on the Apache web server.

On the JBoss AS 7 side, you can find already bundled the mod cluster's 1.1.3 module as part of the clustered configuration file. You can find it either in the standalone-ha.xml file or in the domain.xml configuration file:

```
<subsystem xmlns="urn:jboss:domain:modcluster:1.0">
        <mod-cluster-config advertise-socket="modcluster"/>
</subsystem>
```

This is just a bare-bones declaration that references its socket-binding through the advertise-socket element:

```
<socket-binding name="modcluster" port="0" multicast-
address="224.0.1.105" multicast-port="23364"/>
```

In the next section of this chapter, we will show how to customize the module configuration; for the time being, the great news is that you don't have to install anything on the application server to get started.

On the Apache web server side, we have to install the core libraries, which are used to interact with **mod_cluster**. This is a very simple procedure: point the browser to the appropriate download page for your **mod_cluster** release. For mod cluster 1.1.3, the correct download page is located at http://www.jboss.org/mod_cluster/downloads/1-1-3.

From there, download the binaries for your platform, which contains a built-in **httpd** server and its modules. For example, if you are planning to run Apache web server on a Windows 32-bit machine, download the following binaries:

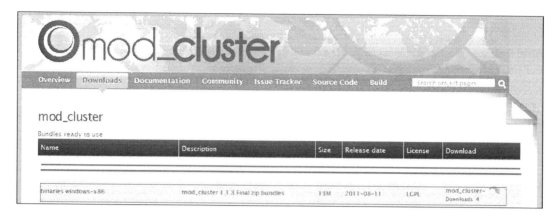

Once the binaries are downloaded extract the archive to a folder, for example, `C:\modcluster`. Then, navigate into the extracted folder. As you can see, mod cluster binaries consist essentially of a bundled Apache web server with all required libraries installed.

> The bundled Apache web server configuration, however, requires defining from scratch all the web server key elements, such as server root, binding ports, loaded modules, and directories configuration. I personally find it much more immediate to use my own Apache web server 2.2 installation; just pick up the modules from the **mod_cluster** bundle.

So, whether you choose to use your own Apache web server or the bundled one, you have to load the following libraries into your `httpd.conf` file.

This is the list of modules that are needed for `mod_cluster` to get working:

```
LoadModule proxy_module modules/mod_proxy.so
LoadModule proxy_ajp_module modules/mod_proxy_ajp.so
LoadModule slotmem_module modules/mod_slotmem.so
LoadModule manager_module modules/mod_manager.so
LoadModule proxy_cluster_module modules/mod_proxy_cluster.so
LoadModule advertise_module modules/mod_advertise.so
```

These libraries are located in the bundled Apache distribution (in our example, `C:\mod_cluster\httpd-2.2\modules`). You have to copy all the previous modules into your Apache distribution, as shown by the following screenshot:

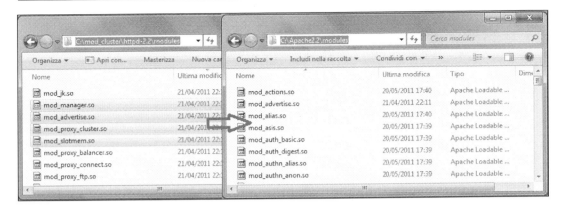

Each of these modules covers an important aspect of the load balancing: mod_proxy and mod_proxy_ajp are the core modules, which forward requests to cluster nodes using either the HTTP/HTTPS protocol or the AJP protocol.

Next, mod_manager is a module that reads information from AS 7 and updates the shared memory information in conjunction with mod_slotmem. The mod_proxy_cluster is the module that contains the balancer for mod_proxy. Finally, the mod_advertise is an additional module that allows **httpd** to advertise via multicast packets—the IP and port—where the mod_cluster is listening.

The next part of the configuration that we need to add is the core load-balancing configuration:

```
Listen 192.168.10.1:8888
<VirtualHost 192.168.10.1:8888>

    <Location />
        Order deny,allow
        Deny from all
        Allow from 192.168.10.
    </Location>

  KeepAliveTimeout 60
  MaxKeepAliveRequests 0

  ManagerBalancerName mycluster
  ServerAdvertise On

</VirtualHost>
```

Basically, you have to replace the `192.168.10.1` IP address with the one where your Apache web server listens for requests, and the port value of 8888 with the one you want to use for communicating with JBoss AS.

As it is, the Apache Virtual Host allows incoming requests from the sub-network `192.168.10`.

The `KeepAliveTimeout` directive allows reusing the same connection within 60 seconds. The number of requests per connection is unlimited, since we are setting `MaxKeepAliveRequests` to 0. The `ManagerBalancerName` provides the balancer name for your cluster (defaults to `mycluster`).

Most important for us is the `ServerAdvertise` directive, which sets to **On** and uses the advertise mechanism to tell the JBoss AS to whom it should send the cluster information.

In-depth on the advertising mechanism

The default multicast IP address and port used for advertising are `224.0.1.105:23364`. These values match the AS 7 bindings defined in the `socket-binding name`:

```
<socket-binding name="modcluster" port="0" multicast-
address="224.0.1.105" multicast-port="23364"/>
```

Bear in mind that if you change these values, you have to match it on the httpd side with the `AdvertiseGroup` directive:

```
AdvertiseGroup 224.0.1.105:23364
```

You can also refine the time elapsed between multicasting advertising messages with the `AdvertiseFrequency` directive, which defaults to 10 seconds:

```
AdvertiseFrequency 5
```

Now, restart Apache web server and the single application server nodes.

If you have correctly configured the mode cluster on the **httpd** side, you will see that each JBoss AS node will start receiving UDP multicast messages from `mod_cluster`:

Managing mod_cluster with the CLI

There are a couple of options that can be used to manage and retrieve runtime information from your cluster. Your first option is the command-line management interface, which can be used to trigger a set of commands available in the mod_cluster subsystem.

The first command you need to learn is list-proxies, which returns merely the hostnames (and port) of the connected proxies:

```
[standalone@localhost:9999 subsystem=modcluster] :list-proxies
{
    "outcome" => "success",
    "result" => [
        "CP11-010:8888",
        "CP12-010:8888"
    ]
}
```

While this can be useful for a quick inspection of your cluster members, you can get detailed info with the read-proxies-info command that actually sends an INFO message to the **httpd** server:

```
[standalone@localhost:9999 subsystem=modcluster] :read-proxies-info
{
    "outcome" => "success",
    "result" => [
```

```
        "CP11-010:8888",

        "Node: [1],Name: de6973fe-b63d-31dc-a806-04ec16870cfa,Balancer:
mycluster,LBGroup: ,Host: 192.168.10.1,Port: 8080,Type:
http,Flushpackets: Off,Flushwait:

 10,Ping: 10,Smax: 65,Ttl: 60,Elected: 0,Read: 0,Transfered: 0,Connected:
0,Load

 : 1

Vhost: [1:1:1], Alias: default-host

Vhost: [1:1:2], Alias: localhost

Vhost: [1:1:3], Alias: example.com

Context: [1:1:1], Context: /, Status: ENABLED
 ",

        "CP12-010:8888",

        "Node: [1],Name: re5673ge-c83d-25dv-y104-02rt16456cfa,Balancer:
mycluster,LBGroup: ,Host: 192.168.10.2,Port: 8080,Type:
http,Flushpackets: Off,Flushwait:

 10,Ping: 10,Smax: 65,Ttl: 60,Elected: 0,Read: 0,Transfered: 0,Connected:
0,Load

 : 1

Vhost: [1:1:1], Alias: default-host

Vhost: [1:1:2], Alias: localhost

Vhost: [1:1:3], Alias: example.com

Context: [1:1:1], Context: /, Status: ENABLED
 "


    ]
}
```

 The `mod_cluster` subsystem also provides the `read-proxies-configuration` command, which can provide slightly more verbose information about your cluster. For the sake of brevity, we will omit printing its output.

The list of proxies that are part of your cluster can also be modified with the CLI. For example, you can use the `add-proxy` command to add a proxy that has not been "captured" by the mod cluster's `httpd` configuration.

```
[standalone@localhost:9999 subsystem=modcluster] :add-proxy(host= CP15-
022, port=9999)

{"outcome" => "success"}
```

At the same time, you can remove proxies from the list using the corresponding `remove-proxy` command:

```
[standalone@localhost:9999 subsystem=modcluster] :remove-
proxy(host=CP15-022, port=9999)
{"outcome" => "success"}
```

Managing your web contexts with CLI

You can use the CLI to manage your web contexts. For example, the `enable-context` command can be used to tell Apache that a particular web context is able to receive requests:

```
[standalone@localhost:9999 subsystem=modcluster] :enable-
context(context=/myapp, virtualhost=default host)
{"outcome" => "success"}
```

The corresponding `disable-context` command can be used to prevent Apache from sending *new* requests:

```
[standalone@localhost:9999 subsystem=modcluster] :disable-
context(context=/myapp, virtualhost=default-host)
{"outcome" => "success"}
```

Rather, if you want to stop Apache from sending requests from a web context, you can use the `stop-context` command:

```
[standalone@localhost:9999 subsystem=modcluster] :stop-context(context=/
myapp, virtualhost=default-host, waittime=50)
{"outcome" => "success"}
```

Adding native management capabilities

If you are not able (or simply don't want) to use the CLI, then you can alternatively configure Apache web server to provide some native management capabilities through the browser.

In order to do that, all you need to add is the `mod_cluster_manager` application context:

```
<Location /mod_cluster_manager>
      SetHandler mod_cluster-manager
      Order deny,allow
      Deny from all
      Allow from 192.168.10
</Location>
```

You can test your `mod_cluster` manager application by pointing to the `mod_cluster_manager` web context at:

`http://192.168.10.1:8888/mod_cluster_manager.`

In our example, the `mod_cluster` manager displays information about all the JBoss AS 7 nodes that have been discovered through multicast announcements.

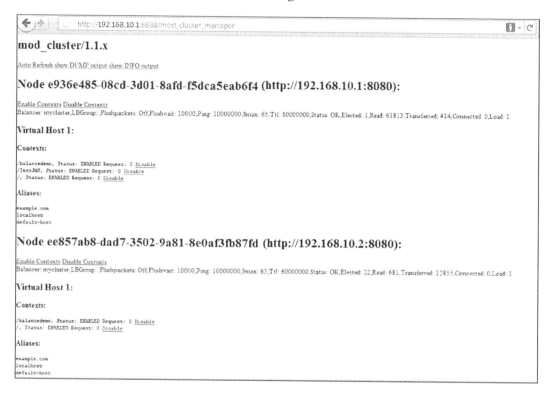

As you can see, in the `mod_cluster` manager page you have plenty of useful information, such as the number of hosts that are currently active (in our example, two nodes) and the web context that are available. By default, all web contexts are mounted automatically (not requiring an explicit mount as for `mod_jk`), but you can, at any time, exclude or include them by clicking on the **Disable/Enable** link, which is placed next to the web context.

Managing web contexts using the configuration file

For the sake of completeness, we will add one more option that can be used to manage your web context, by using your application server configuration file. By default, all web contexts are enabled; however, you can exclude web contexts from the main configuration file using the `excluded-contexts` directive:

```
<subsystem xmlns="urn:jboss:domain:modcluster:1.0">
    <mod-cluster-config excluded-contexts="ROOT, webapp1"/>
</subsystem>
```

Troubleshooting mod_cluster

Installing `mod_cluster` requires just a few steps on the **httpd** side to get working; however, just in case you cannot get ahead with it, you can find some clues by allowing a verbose output on the administration console:

```
AllowDisplay On
```

When setting this directive, you can get some information about the single modules loaded into **httpd**:

mod_cluster/1.1.x

start of "httpd.conf" configuration
mod_proxy_cluster.c: OK
mod_sharedmem.c: OK
Protocol supported: http AJP
mod_advertise.c: OK
Server: CP11-010
Server: CP11-010 VirtualHost: 192.168.0.1:8888 Advertising on Group 224.0.1.105 Port 23364 for (null)://(null):0 every 10 seconds
end of "httpd.conf" configuration

Should you find any module that exhibits an **OK** in the display page, you have at least a clue to investigate.

One more possible cause of errors is advertising messages that could potentially hit a firewall. Remember that advertisement messages use UDP port 23364 and multicast address 224.0.1.105. In order to verify if advertising is an issue, you could try to turn it off by setting the following in the **httpd** side:

```
ServerAdvertise Off
```

This directive should be matched on the application server side by the `proxy-list` element, which defines the list of **httpd** servers with which the AS will initially communicate:

```
<mod-cluster-config proxy-list="192.168.10.1:8888">
 . . . .
 </mod-cluster-config>
```

Finally, don't forget to check the **httpd** logs directory for the `error.log` file and see if it contains any descriptive error. For example, a common source of errors that can be found on a Windows machine is triggered by Apache's **Dynamic Shared Objects (DSO)**:

[Tue Aug 23 10:29:24 2011] [warn] proxy: No protocol handler was valid for the URL /balancedemo. If you are using a DSO version of mod_proxy, make sure the proxy submodules are included in the configuration using LoadModule.

This kind of error can be solved by loading the additional proxy module used for your protocol, in this case, the `proxy_http_module` module:

```
LoadModule proxy_http_module ./modules/mod_proxy_http.so
```

Testing mod_cluster

Having completed and verified the installation of mod cluster, we can now test it with minimal web application. The sample application packaged as `balancer.war` contains simply an `index.jsp` page, which dumps a message on the console.

```
<%
Integer counter = (Integer)session.getAttribute("counter");
if (counter == null) {
   session.setAttribute("counter",new Integer(1));
}
else {
   session.setAttribute("counter",new Integer(counter+1));
}
System.out.println("Counter"+session.getAttribute("counter"));out.
println("Counter "+session.getAttribute("counter"));
%>
```

Now, open your browser and point to the **httpd** proxy address we have configured at:

```
http://192.168.10.1:8888/balancer
```

As you can see, mod cluster follows the **sticky session** policy; that is, once a session is started on one server, subsequent requests are sent to the same node:

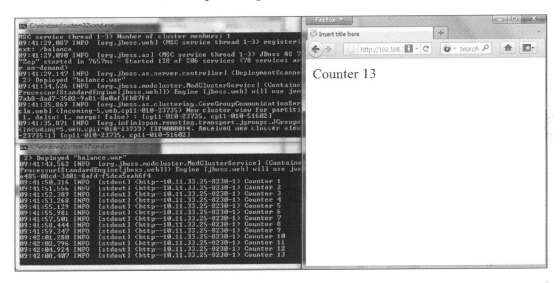

Load-balancing between nodes

We will run one more test in order to verify how mod_cluster distributes the load between several different clients. For the purpose of our test, we will need a software that can launch a minimal amount of requests. We will use JMeter, which is a Java desktop application designed to load and test functional behavior and measure performance. JMeter can be downloaded from: http://jakarta.apache.org/site/downloads/downloads_jmeter.cgi.

In short, a JMeter test plan consists of one or more Thread groups, logic controllers, listeners, timers, assertions, and configuration elements.

For the purpose of our example, we will just create the following elements:

- A **Thread Group**, which is configured to run 100 subsequent requests
- An **HTTP Request** element, which contains the information about the web application end point

Additionally, you should add a **Listener** element, which collects the test plan result in a table/graph in order to analyze it.

Now, from the top menu launch **Run | Start** and the JMeter test will be executed.

Running the test demonstrates that the requests are roughly split between the two servers. As a matter of fact, an HTTP Request element, by default, treats every request as a single session that ends at the request.

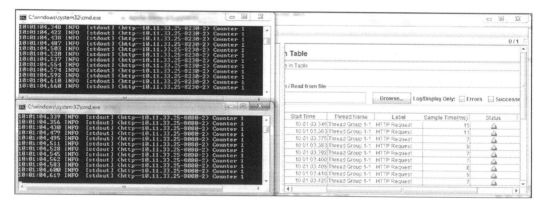

Using load metrics

The built-in configuration of `mod_cluster` distributes requests using a fixed load factor. That is, it corresponds to the default configuration, which is:

```
<subsystem xmlns="urn:jboss:domain:modcluster:1.0">
  <mod-cluster-config>
    <simple-load-provider load="1"/>
  </mod-cluster-config>
</subsystem>
```

You can, however, customize the load-balancing using dynamic attributes, which are a set of metrics that can be included in a `dynamic-load-provider` element. For example:

```
<subsystem xmlns="urn:jboss:domain:modcluster:1.0">
  <mod-cluster-config advertise-socket="mod_cluster">
    <dynamic-load-provider history="10" decay="2">
      <load-metric type="cpu" weight="2" capacity="1"/>
      <load-metric type="sessions" weight="1" capacity="512"/>
    </dynamic-load-provider>
  </mod-cluster-config>
</subsystem>
```

The most important factors when computing load balancing are the `weight` and `capacity` properties. The `weight` (default is 1) indicates the impact of a metric with respect to the other metrics. In the previous example, the CPU metric will have twice the impact on the sessions that have a load factor metric of 1.

The `capacity`, on the other hand, can be used for a fine-grained control on the load metrics. By setting a different capacity to each metric, you can actually favor one node instead of another while preserving the metric weights.

The list of supported load metrics is resumed in the following table:

Metric	Factor used to compute metric
cpu	CPU load
mem	System memory usage
heap	Heap memory usage as a percentage of max heap size
sessions	Number of web sessions
requests	Amount of requests/sec
send-traffic	Amount of outgoing requests traffic
receive-traffic	Amount of incoming requests POST traffic
busyness	The percentage of connector Threads from the Thread Pool that are busy servicing requests
connection-pool	The percentage of connections from a JCA connection pool that are in use

The above metrics can also be set using the CLI. For example, supposing that you want to add a metric that is based on the amount of heap used by the proxy. Here's what you need to issue:

```
[standalone@192.168.10.1:9999 /] /subsystem=modcluster:add-
metric(type=heap)
{"outcome" => "success"}
[standalone@192.168.10.1:9999 /] /subsystem=modcluster:read-
resource(name=mod-clu

ster-config)
{
    "outcome" => "success",
    "result" => {
        "advertise-socket" => "modcluster",
        "dynamic-load-provider" => {
            "history" => 9,
            "decay" => 2,
            "load-metric" => [{
                "address" => "[(\"subsystem\" => \"modcluster\")]",
                "operation" => "add-metric",
                "type" => "heap"
            }]
        }
    }
}
```

At any time, the metric can be removed using the `remove-metric` command:

```
[standalone@192.168.10.1:9999 /] /subsystem=modcluster:remove-
metric(type=heap)
{"outcome" => "success"}
```

Example setting dynamic metrics on a cluster

In the following example, we have a very simple cluster comprising two nodes. Each node has the same JVM operating defaults, and each one is running on two identical machines.

We will, however, simulate some memory-intensive operation on the first node so that the amount of heap memory used differs from one server to another:

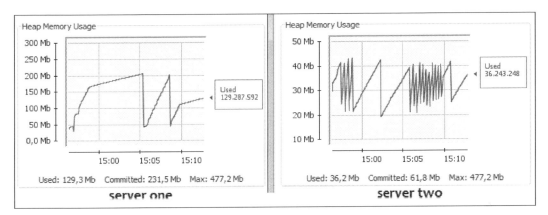

This is a very common scenario in Enterprise applications where each functionality may have a different impact on memory, for example, holding data temporarily in the HTTP session.

In such a case, using a round-robin approach to distribute a request may, in the end, lead to an Out-of-Memory scenario on some nodes of your cluster. You can, however, mitigate this effect largely with a simple configuration of the loading metrics:

```
<subsystem xmlns="urn:jboss:domain:modcluster:1.0">
  <mod-cluster-config advertise-socket="mod_cluster">
    <dynamic-load-provider history="10" decay="2">
      <load-metric type="heap" weight="2" />
      <load-metric type="mem"  weight="1" />
      <load-metric type="cpu"  weight="1" />
    </dynamic-load-provider>
  </mod-cluster-config>
</subsystem>
```

When using this configuration on both nodes, the heap memory usage has twice the impact of other enlisted metrics (operating system memory and CPU speed).

The outcome of this configuration change is that the server two collects 55 percent of the requests over the 45 percent landed on the first server:

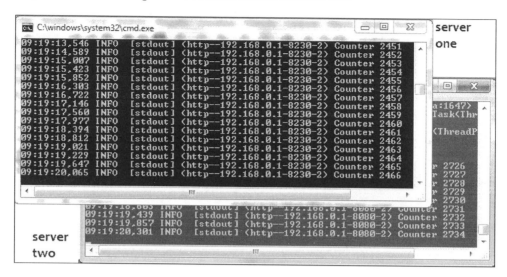

By setting the appropriate capacity, you can further achieve a better level of granularity to node-weighting. For example, setting on the first server a higher capacity:

```
<load-metric type="heap" weight="2" capacity="512"/>
```

And to the second one a low capacity:

```
<load-metric type="heap" weight="2" capacity="1"/>
```

Then, the outcome of the test would be different, as the second server now delivers more response than the first one, counter-balancing the weight metric:

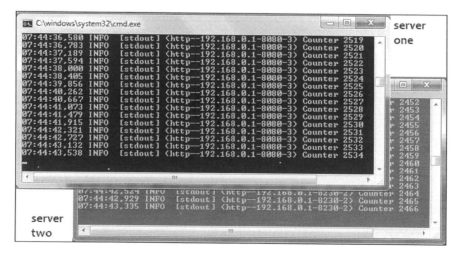

The capacity of each metric defaults to 512 and should be configured such that `0 <= (load / capacity) >= 1`.

Configuring clustering in your applications

At the time of writing this book, the application clustering configuration had not been finalized in all components. Although web applications and the persistence API is ready for clustering, some components (chiefly EJB 3 session beans) are still missing clustering capabilities.

With the help of the JBoss development team, we could, however, produce all the necessary information needed for configuring clustering in your applications. As this information might be subject to change, we suggest you check the AS 7.1 documentation at: `https://docs.jboss.org/author/display/AS71/High+Availability+Guide`.

Now, we will complete our journey through the clustering system, discussing:

- Session bean clustering
- Entity clustering
- Web application clustering

Clustering session beans

In *Chapter 3, Configuring Enterprise Services*, we recapped the difference between **Stateless Session Beans (SLSB)** and **Stateful Session Beans (SFSB)**.

SLSB are not able to retain state between invocations, so the main benefit of clustering an SLSB is to balance the load between an array of servers. Consequently, the clustering policies are pretty simple and requires at most adding a `@org.jboss.ejb3.annotation.Clustered` annotation.

```
@Stateless
@Clustered
public class ClusteredBean {
   public void doSomething() {
   // Do something
   }
}
```

If you want to further specialize your SLSB, then you can choose the load-balancing algorithm used to distribute the load between your EJBs. These are the available load-balancing policies for your SLSB:

Load-balancing policy	Description
Round robin	It is the default load-balance policy. The smart proxy cycles through a list of JBoss Server instances in a fixed order.
RandomRobin	Under this policy, each request is redirected by the smart proxy to a random node in the cluster.
FirstAvailable	It implies a random selection of the node, but subsequent calls will stick to that node until the node fails. The next node will again be selected randomly.
FirstAvailableIdenticalAllProxies	Same as FirstAvailable, except that the random node selection will then be shared by all dynamic proxies.

Then, you can apply the load-balancing policy as in the following example:

```
@Clustered(loadBalancePolicy="FirstAvailable")
```

Clustering SFSB is not too different from the stateless counterpart. At the minimum, all you have to include is a **@Clustered** annotation at class level:

```
@Stateful
@Clustered
public class ClusteredBean {
  public void doSomething() {
  // Do something
  }
}
```

By default, SFSBs use the cache-container named sfsb, which replicates sessions across all nodes. Should your application server node fail while sessions are running, the EJB proxy will detect it and choose another node where session data has been replicated. You can, however, reference a custom cache container used by your SFSB with the org.jboss.ejb3.annotation.CacheConfig annotation:

```
@Stateful
@CacheConfig(name="custom-sfsb")
@Clustered
public class ClusteredBean {
  . . . .
}
```

And, this is the corresponding `cache-container` that uses a distributed cache:

```
<cache-container name="custom-sfsb" default-cache="dist-cache">
   <alias>dist-sfsb-cache</alias>

  <distributed-cache owners="3" mode="ASYNC"
    name="dist" batching="true">
      <locking isolation="REPEATABLE_READ"/>
      <file-store/>
  </distributed-cache>
</cache-container>
```

Clustering entities

Entities do not provide remote services like session beans, so they are not concerned with the load-balancing logic or session replication. You can, however, use a cache for your entities to avoid roundtrips to the database. JBoss AS7EJB 3.0 persistence-layer JPA implementation is based on the Hibernate framework and, as such, this framework has a complex cache mechanism, which is implemented both at **Session** level and at **SessionFactory** level.

The latter mechanism is called **second-level caching**. The purpose of a JPA/ Hibernate second-level cache is to store entities or collections locally retrieved from the database or to maintain results of recent queries.

 The key characteristic of the second-level cache is that it can be used across sessions. This differentiates it from the session cache, which only (as the name says) has session scope.

Enabling the second-level cache for your Enterprise applications needs some properties to be set. If you are using JPA to access the second-level cache, all you have to add in the `persistence.xml` configuration file is:

```
<shared-cache-mode>ENABLE_SELECTIVE</shared-cache-mode>
<properties>

   <property name=
     "hibernate.cache.use_second_level_cache" value="true"/>
   <property name="hibernate.cache.use_minimal_puts" value="true"/>
</properties>
```

The first element, `shared-cache-mode`, is the JPA 2.0 way to specify whether the entities and entity-related state of a persistence unit will be cached. The `shared-cache-mode` element has five possible values, as indicated in the following table:

Shared Cache mode	Description
ALL	Causes all entities and entity-related state and data to be cached.
NONE	Causes caching to be disabled for the persistence unit.
ENABLE_SELECTIVE	Allows caching if the `@Cacheable` annotation is specified on the entity class.
DISABLE_SELECTIVE	Enables the cache and causes all entities to be cached except those for which `@Cacheable(false)` is specified.

The property named `hibernate.cache.use_minimal_puts` performs some optimization on the second-level cache, by reducing the amount of writes in the caches at the cost of some additional reads.

In addition, if you plan to use the Hibernate Query cache in your applications, you need to activate it with a separate property:

```
<property name="hibernate.cache.use_query_cache" value="true"/>
```

For the sake of completeness, we will also include here the configuration needed for using Infinispan as a caching provider for **native** Hibernate applications. This is the list of properties you have to add to your `hibernate.cfg.xml`:

```
<property name="hibernate.cache.region.factory_class"
    value="org.hibernate.cache.infinispan.JndiInfinispanRegionFactory"/>
<property name="hibernate.cache.infinispan.cachemanager"
    value="java:jboss/infinispan/hibernate"/>
<property name="hibernate.transaction.manager_lookup_class"
    value="org.hibernate.transaction.JBossTransactionManagerLookup"/>
<property name="hibernate.cache.use_second_level_cache" value="true"/>
<property name="hibernate.cache.use_minimal_puts" value="true"/>
```

As you can see, the configuration is a bit more verbose because you have to tell Hibernate to use Infinispan as a caching provider. This requires setting the correct Hibernate transaction factory, using the `hibernate.transaction.factory_class` property.

Next, the property `hibernate.cache.infinispan.cachemanager` exposes the CacheManager used by Infinispan. By default, Infinispan binds in the JNDI a shared CacheManager under the key `java:jboss/infinispan/hibernate`. This will be in charge to handle the second-level cache on the cached objects.

Finally, the property `hibernate.cache.region.factory_class` tells Hibernate to use the Infinispan second-level caching integration, using the previous Infinispan CacheManager found in JNDI as the source for Infinispan cache's instances.

Caching entities

Unless you have set `shared-cache-mode` to `ALL`, Hibernate will not cache entity automatically. You have to select which entities or queries need to be cached. This is definitely the safest option since indiscriminate caching can actually hurt performance. The following example shows how to do this for JPA entities using annotations.

```
import javax.persistence.*;
import org.hibernate.annotations.Cache;
import org.hibernate.annotations.CacheConcurrencyStrategy;

@Entity
@Cacheable
@Cache(usage = CacheConcurrencyStrategy.TRANSACTIONAL, region
="properties")

public class Property {

@Id
@Column(name="key")
private String key;

@Column(name="value")
private String value;

// Getter & setters omitted for brevity
}
```

The `@javax.persistence.Cacheable` dictates whether the Hibernate shared cache should be used for instances of the entity class and is applicable only when the `shared-cache-mode` is set to one of the selective modes.

The `@org.hibernate.annotations.Cache` annotation is the older annotation used to achieve the same purpose of `@Cacheable`. You can still use it for defining which strategy for controlling concurrent access to cache contents Hibernate should use.

The `CacheConcurrencyStrategy.TRANSACTIONAL` provides support for an Infinispan fully-transactional JTA environment.

If there are chances that your application data is read but never modified, you can apply the `CacheConcurrencyStrategy.READ_ONLY` that does not evict data from the cache (unless performed programmatically).

```
@Cache(usage=CacheConcurrencyStrategy.READ_ONLY)
```

Finally, the other attribute that can be defined is the caching region where entities are placed. If you do not specify a cache region for an entity class, all instances of this class will be cached in the `_default` region. Defining a caching region can be useful if you want to perform a fine-grained management of caching areas.

Caching queries

The query cache can be used to cache data from a query so that if the same query is issued again, it will not hit the database but return the cached value.

 Note that the query cache does not cache the state of the actual entities in the result set; it caches only the identifier values and results of value type.

In the following example, the query result set named `listUsers` is configured to be cached using the `@QueryHint` annotation inside a `@NamedQuery`:

```
@NamedQueries(
{
@NamedQuery(
name = "listUsers",
query = "FROM User c WHERE c.name = :name",
hints = { @QueryHint(name = "org.hibernate.cacheable", value =
"true") }
)
})
public class User {

@Id
@Column(name="key")
private String key;

@Column(name="name")
private String name;

. . . . .
}
```

Use the query cache with caution because it might have a bad impact on your application if used blindly. First of all, the query cache will increase the memory requirements if your queries (stored as key in the query cache map) are made up of hundreds of characters.

Another important reason is that the result of the query cache is constantly invalidated each time there's a change in the underlying database. This will lead to a very poor hit ratio of the query cache if entities are constantly modified. Therefore, it is advisable to turn on the query cache only when you have a mostly read application.

Clustering web applications

Clustering web applications requires the least effort for the developer. As we have just discussed, all you need to switch on clustering in a web application is adding the following directive in the `web.xml` descriptor:

```
<web-app>
    <distributable/>
</web-app>
```

By default, clustered web applications will use the **web** cache contained in the Infinispan configuration. One thing you can customize is setting up a specific cache per deployment unit. This can be achieved by adding to `jboss-web.xml` the `replication-config` directive containing the cache name to be used:

```
<jboss-web>
   <replication-config>
      <cache-name>web.dist</cache-name>
   </replication-config>
</jboss-web>
```

The previous configuration should obviously reference a cache defined in the main configuration file:

```
<cache-container name="web" default-cache="repl">
   <alias>standard-session-cache</alias>

   <distributed-cache mode="ASYNC" name="web.dist" batching="true">
       <locking isolation="REPEATABLE_READ"/>
       <file-store/>
   </distributed-cache>
</cache-container>
```

Summary

In this chapter, we have shown instruments that can be used to distribute the load of an application across a set of nodes, also known as load balancing.

Load balancing is not an exclusive feature of clustered applications because it can be applied to any kind of applications that are running over multiple AS, although it's commonly used as a front door to your cluster of nodes.

In the first half of this chapter, we have illustrated how to use the mod_jk and mod_proxy libraries in the AS7. Both approaches are still viable in the new application server:

- mod_jk requires some configuration both on the **httpd** side and on the AS side. On the other hand, when using mod_jk you can achieve a better level of granularity.

- mod_proxy is a more immediate solution, as it requires simply configuring the end points in the **httpd** side.

In the second half of the chapter, we have shown the recommended approach to load-balancing calls between applications, which are using mod_cluster.

The main advantage of using mod cluster verses traditional load balancers is that it does not use a static configuration of worker nodes, but it can register application servers and their applications dynamically using a multicast-based advertising mechanism.

This can be especially useful in a cloud environment where you cannot rely on a flat list of nodes, but you should be able to add or remove nodes dynamically. Without mod cluster, you would need to stop or start your set of nodes at each configuration upgrade.

Finally, another major asset of mod cluster is that you can use a dynamic set of metrics, which are calculated on the server side, to define the load between server nodes. In particular, you can give an advantage to servers that, for example, have higher sets of memory, connections, Threads, or any other user-defined metric.

10
Securing JBoss AS 7

Security is a key element of any Enterprise application. You must be able to control and restrict who is permitted to access your applications and what operations users may perform.

The Java Enterprise Edition (Java EE) specification defines a simple role-based security model for Enterprise Java Beans (EJBs) and web components. The implementation of JBoss security is delivered by PicketBox framework (formerly known as JBoss security), which provides the authentication, authorization, auditing, and mapping capabilities to Java applications.

Because the number of topics that are concerned with security could cover a book by themselves, we had to confine our focus on those that are likely to interest the majority of administrators and developers. More in detail, we will cover the following topics:

- A short introduction to Java security API
- The foundation of JBoss AS 7 security subsystem
- Defining login modules and their integration with the Enterprise components (for example, web applications EJB)
- How to secure the AS 7 management interfaces
- How to use the **Secure Sockets Layer** (**SSL**) to encrypt web applications

Approaching Java security API

Java EE security services provide a robust and easily configured security mechanism for authenticating users and authorizing access to application functions and associated data. To better understand the topics related to security, we should, at first, give some basic definitions:

Authentication is the process by which it's verified who is currently executing an application, regardless of whether it's an EJB or a Servlet). Authentication is usually performed by means of a login form contained in a web application or standalone application.

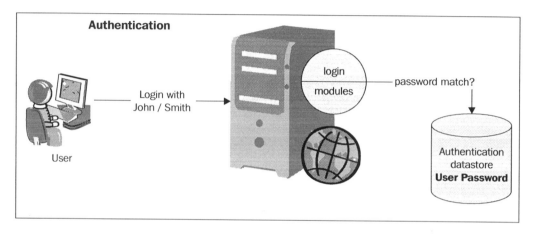

Authorization is the process by which you can verify that users have the rights (permissions) to access system resources. Authorization, therefore, presupposes that authentication has occurred, otherwise it would be impossible to grant any access control if you don't know who the user is.

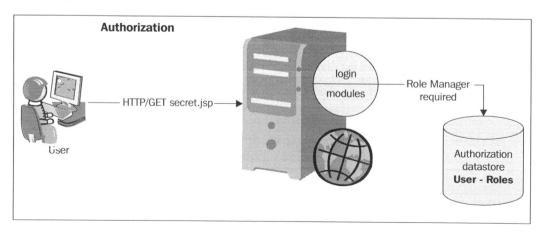

In Java EE, the component containers are responsible for providing application security. A container, basically, provides two types of security: **declarative** and **programmatic**. Let's see them all:

- **Declarative security** expresses an application component's security requirements by means of **deployment descriptors and/or annotations**. Because deployment descriptor information contained in an external file, it can be changed without the need to modify the source code.

  For example, Enterprise JavaBeans components use an EJB deployment descriptor that must be named `ejb-jar.xml` and placed in the META-INF folder of the EJB JAR file.

  Web components use a web application deployment descriptor named `web.xml` located in the WEB-INF directory.

  In Java EE5, you can apply declarative security, also by means of **annotations**. Annotations are specified within a class file and, when the application is deployed, this information is translated by the application internally — the application server translates this information.

  By using annotations, you are exempted from writing boilerplate (or useless) code because this can be generated by external tools from the source external tools from the source code can generate this. This leads to a declarative programming style, where the programmer says what should be done and tools emit the code to do it. It also eliminates the need for maintaining side files that must be kept up to date with changes in source files. Instead, the information is maintained in the source file.

- **Programmatic security** is embedded in an application and is used to make security decisions. It can be used when declarative security alone is not sufficient to express the security model of an application. The Java EE security API allows the developer test whether or not the current user has access to a specific role, using these calls:

  - `isUserInRole()` for Servlets, JSPs (adopted in `javax.servlet.http.HttpServletRequest`)
  - `isCallerInRole()` for EJBs (adopted in `javax.ejb.SessionContext`)

In addition, there are other API calls that provide access to the user's identity, such as:

- ○ `getUserPrincipal()` for Servlets, JSPs (adopted in javax.servlet. http.HttpServletRequest)

- ○ `getCallerPrincipal()` for EJBs (adopted in javax.ejb. SessionContext)

Using these APIs, you can develop a complex authorization model arbitrarily.

 Annotation security encompasses both the **declarative** and **programmatic** security concepts.

Rather than embedding security into your business component, the JEE security model is declarative: this means that you describe the security roles and permissions in a standard XML descriptor. This isolates security from business-level code because security tends to be more a function of where the component is deployed than an inherent aspect of the component's business logic.

The default implementation of the declarative security model is based on **Java Authentication and Authorization Service (JAAS)** login modules and subjects. The security proxy layer allows custom security that cannot be described using the declarative model to add an EJB in a way that is independent of the EJB business object.

JBoss uses the PicketBox framework, which builds on top of the Java Authentication and Authorization Service, and secures all the Java EE technologies running in the application.

JBoss AS 7 security subsystem

JBoss security is qualified as an extension to the application server and it's included by default, both in standalone servers and in domain servers:

```
<extension module="org.jboss.as.security"/>
```

The following is the default security subsystem contained in the server configuration file:

```
<security-domains>
    <security-domain name="other" cache-type="default">
        <authentication>
            <login-module code="UsersRoles" flag="required"/>
        </authentication>
```

```
    </security-domain>
    <security-domain name="jboss-web-policy" cache-type="default">
        <authorization>
            <policy-module code="Delegating" flag="required"/>
        </authorization>
    </security-domain>
    <security-domain name="jboss-ejb-policy" cache-type="default">
        <authorization>
            <policy-module code="Delegating" flag="required"/>
        </authorization>
    </security-domain>
</security-domains>
```

As you can see, the configuration is pretty short as it relies largely on default values, especially for high-level structures such as the security management area.

> A security domain does not explicitly require an authorization policy. If a security domain does not define an authorization module, the default `jboss-web-policy` and `jboss-ejb-policy` authorization are used. In such a case, the **Delegating** authorization policy takes places, which simply delegates the authorization to another module declared as `<module-option>`. See this link for more information about this topic: `http://tinyurl.com/7upybe8`.

By defining your own security management options, you could, for example, override the default Authentication/Authorization managers with your implementations. Because it's likely that you will not require to override these interfaces, we will rather concentrate on the `security-domain` element, which is a core aspect of JBoss security.

A **security domain** can be imagined as a Customs Office for foreigners. Before the request crosses JBoss AS borders, the security domain performs all the required authorization and authentication checks, and eventually notifies the caller if he/she can proceed or not.

Security domains are generally configured at server startup or in a running server and subsequently bound to the JNDI tree under the key `java:/jaas/`. Within the security domain, you can configure login authentication modules so that you can easily change your authentication provider by simply changing its login module.

The following table describes all the available login modules, including a short description of them:

Login module	Description
Client	This login module is designed to establish caller identity and credentials when AS is acting a client. It should never be used as part of a security domain used for actual server authentication.
Database	This login module loads user/role information from a database.
Certificate	This login module is designed to authenticate users based on X509Certificates.
CertificateRoles	This login module extends the Certificate login module to add role-mapping capabilities from a properties file.
DatabaseCertificate	This login module extends the Certificate login to add role mapping capabilities from a database table.
DatabaseUsers	It is a JDBC-based login module that supports authentication and role mapping.
Identity	This login module simply associates the principal specified in the module options with any subject authenticated against the module
Ldap	This login module loads user/role information from an LDAP server.
LdapExtended	This login module is an alternate LDAP login module implementation that uses searches for locating both the user to bind the authentication as well as the associated roles.
RoleMapping	This login module is used to map roles that are the end result of the authentication process to one or more declarative roles.
Simple	This login module is used to quickly set up the security for testing purposes.
Kerberos	This login module is used uses Sun's Kerberos login module as a mechanism for authentication.
SPNEGOUsers	This login module works in conjunction with SPNEGOAuthenticator to handle the authentication.
AdvancedLdap	This login module is a refactoring of the LdapExtLoginModule, which is able to separate the login steps (find or authenticate ormap roles) so that any of the actions can be taken separately.
AdvancedADLdap	This login module is an extension of the AdvancedLdapLoginModule, which is also able to query the primary group of the user being authenticated.
UserRoles	This login module is a simple Properties Map-based login module that consults two Java Properties-formatted text files for username to password("users.properties") and username to roles("roles.properties") mapping.

Activating a login module is a two-step procedure:

1. First you need to define the login module within your `standalone.xml/domain.xml` configuration file.

2. Then you need to tell your applications to use a login module to perform authentication and authorization.

 In earlier releases of the application server, the login module was configured in a separate file named `login-config.xml`. Porting earlier login modules into the new application server is not too complex as the format of the login module is pretty much the same as the new application server.

So, we will now expand these bullet points in separate sections. Let's see first how to define some commonly-used login modules, and then we will apply them to Java EE components, such as servlets, EJB, and web services.

Using the UserRoles login module

The `UserRoles` is one of the simples security domain which can be implemented for testing purposes in your applications. It is based on two files:

- `users.properties`—containing the list of username and passwords
- `roles.properties`—containing the mapping between the users and the roles

Here is a sample `UserRoles` configuration, which stores the security files in the application server's configuration directory:

```
<security-domain name="basic" cache-type="default">
 <authentication>
   <login-module code="UsersRoles" flag="required">
       <module-option name="usersProperties" value="${jboss.server.
config.dir}/users.properties"/>
       <module-option name="rolesProperties" value="${jboss.server.
config.dir}/roles.properties"/>
   </login-module>
 </authentication>
</security-domain>
```

All you need to do to get running with your security domain, is adding the two files into the specified path (for the standalone by default `JBOSS_HOME/standalone/configuration`) with some credentials within it. For example, the `users.properties` could be:

```
admin=admin
```

And the `roles.properties`:

```
admin=Manager
```

This means that authenticating with the admin/admin credentials would assign the role of manager to the user.

Using the database login module

A database security domain follows the same logic exposed in the earlier example; just, it stores the credentials within the database. In order to run this example, we are referring to a `MySqlDS` datasource which we reated earlier in *Chapter 3, Configuring Enterprise Services*:

```
<security-domain name="mysqldomain" cache-type="default">
    <authentication>
        <login-module code="Database" flag="required">
            <module-option name="dsJndiName" value="java:/
MySqlDS"/>
            <module-option name="principalsQuery" value="select
passwd from USERS where login=?"/>
            <module-option name="rolesQuery" value="select role,
'Roles' from USER_ROLES where login=?"/>
        </login-module>
    </authentication>
</security-domain>
```

In order to get working with this configuration, you have first have to create the required tables and insert some sample data in it:

```
CREATE TABLE USERS(login VARCHAR(64) PRIMARY KEY, passwd VARCHAR(64))
CREATE TABLE USER_ROLES(login VARCHAR(64), role VARCHAR(32))

INSERT into USERS values('admin', 'admin')
INSERT into USER_ROLES values('admin', 'Manager')
```

As you can see, the admin user will map again to the Manager role. One caveat of this configuration is that it uses clear-text passwords in the database, so before rolling this module production you should consider adding additional security to your login module. Let's see how to do this in the next section.

Encrypting passwords

Storing passwords in the database as clear-text string is not considered a good practice; as a matter of fact, a database has even more potential security holes then a regular file system. Think about, for example, a DBA which added a public synonym for some tables, forgetting that one of those tables was holding sensitive information such as the application passwords! You need to be sure that no potential attackers will ever be able to deliver the following query:

Fortunately, securing application passwords is relatively easy: you can add a few extra options to your login module, specifying that the stored passwords are encrypted using a **message digest algorithm**. For example, in the `mysqlLogin` module, you should add the following highlighted options at the end:

```
<login-module code="Database" flag="required">
    <module-option name="dsJndiName" value="java:/MySqlDS"/>
    <module-option name="principalsQuery" value="select passwd from
USERS where login=?"/>
    <module-option name="rolesQuery" value="select role, 'Roles' from
USER_ROLES where login=?"/>
  <module-option name="hashAlgorithm" value="MD5"/>
  <module-option name="hashEncoding" value="BASE64"/>
  <module-option name="hashStorePassword" value="true"/>
</login-module>
```

Here, we have specified that the password will be hashed against an **MD5** hash algorithm; you can alternatively use any other algorithm allowed by your JCA Provider, like SHA, for example.

For the sake of completeness, we include here a small application, which uses the `java.security.MessageDigest` and the `org.jboss.security.Base64Util` class to generate the base-64 hashed password to be inserted in the database:

```
public class Hash {

    public static void main(String[] args)
      {
          String password = args[0];
          MessageDigest md = null;
```

```
        try
        {
           md = MessageDigest.getInstance("MD5");
        }
        catch(Exception e)
        {
           e.printStackTrace();
        }
        byte[] passwordBytes = password.getBytes();
        byte[] hash = md.digest(passwordBytes);
    String passwordHash = org.jboss.security.Base64Utils.
tob64(hash);
        System.out.println("password hash: "+passwordHash);
    }


    }
```

Running the main program with **admin** as argument, generates the hash **X8oyfUbUbfqE9IWvAW1/3**. This hash will be your updated password for the admin user into our database:

Using an LDAP login module

The **Lightweight Directory Access Protocol (LDAP)** is the *de facto* standard for providing directory services to applications. An LDAP server can provide a central directory information for:

- User credentials (login and password)
- User directory information (such as names and e-mail addresses)
- Web directories

The action in LDAP takes place around a data structure known as an **entry**. An entry has a set of named component parts called **attributes** that hold the data for that entry. To use database terms, they are like the fields in a database record.

An entry's content and structure are defined by its object. Its object class defines an entry's content and structure. The object class (along with server and user settings) specifies which attributes must and may exist in that particular entry.

All entries stored in an LDAP directory have a unique **Distinguished Name**, or **DN**. The DN for each LDAP entry is composed of two parts: the **Relative Distinguished Name (RDN)** and the **location** within the LDAP directory where the record resides.

In practice, the RDN is the portion of your DN that is not related to the directory tree structure, and is in turn, composed of one or several attribute name/value pairs. Let's see a concrete example in an organization:

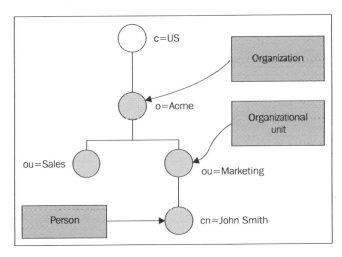

In the previous diagram, "cn=John Smith" (where cn stands for "common name") could be an RDN. The attribute name is cn and the value is John Smith.

On the other hand, the DN for John Smith would be: cn=John Smith, ou=Marketing, o=Acme, c=US (where ou is short for organizational unit, o is short for organization, and c is for country).

Connecting LDAP to JBoss AS

That being said, connecting to JBoss AS and LDAP can be done by means of several LDAP login modules. The first and obvious thing we need is a running instance of an LDAP server available. Today, there is a huge number of LDAP servers (both commercial and open source) available, and maybe, you have already configured one to run in your company. Just in case you don't have one, or simply don't want to add sample data to it, we suggest you having a look at **Apache Directory Service** (http://directory.apache.org/), which is an excellent solution for getting started with LDAP but also for building complex directory infrastructures.

Once installed, we suggest you using the **Apache Directory Studio** (available at the same link) to create a directory infrastructure quickly. The simplest way to create a directory from scratch is by means of an LDAP'S **Data Interchange Format File (LDIF)** file. Within this file, you can mention all entries which will be loaded by the LDAP engine.

 A quick shortcut for importing an LDIF file from Apache studio is in the **File menu**: **File** | **Import** | **LDIF** into **LDAP**.

Here's a basic LDIF file we will use:

```
dn: dc=example,dc=com
objectclass: top
objectclass: dcObject
objectclass: organization
dc: example
o: MCC

dn: ou=People,dc=example,dc=com
objectclass: top
objectclass: organizationalUnit
ou: People

dn: uid=admin,ou=People,dc=example,dc=com
objectclass: top
objectclass: uidObject
objectclass: person
uid: admin
cn: Manager
sn: Manager
userPassword: secret

dn: ou=Roles,dc=example,dc=com
objectclass: top
objectclass: organizationalUnit
ou: Roles

dn: cn=Manager,ou=Roles,dc=example,dc=com
objectClass: top
objectClass: groupOfNames
cn: Manager
description: the JBossAS7 group
member: uid=admin,ou=People,dc=example,dc=com
```

Once you have imported this information into the LDAP server, you will end up with the following small directory:

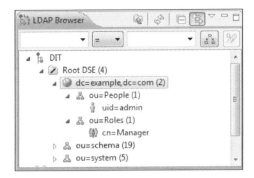

Within this directory, we have just one user registered as **admin**, belonging to the **Manager** role, just like other login modules we have shown in the earlier sections.

Now we will configure the LDAP connection on JBoss AS 7. For our purpose, we will use the `LdapExtended` login module implementation that uses searches for locating both the user to bind for authentication and the associated roles. The roles query will follow distinguished names (DNs) recursively to navigate a hierarchical role structure.

```
<login-module code="LdapExtended" flag="required">

    <module-option name="java.naming.factory.initial"  value-"com.sun.
jndi.ldap.LdapCtxFactory"/>
    <module-option name="java.naming.provider.url" value="ldap://
localhost:10389"/>
    <module-option name="java.naming.security.authentication"
value="simple"/>
    <module-option name="bindDN" value="uid=admin,ou=system"/>
    <module-option name="bindCredential" value="secret"/>
    <module-option name="baseCtxDN" value="ou=People,dc=example,dc=c
om"/>
    <module-option name="baseFilter" value="(uid={0})"/>
    <module-option name="rolesCtxDN" value="ou=Roles,dc=example,dc=c
om"/>
    <module-option name="roleFilter" value="(member={1})"/>
    <module-option name="roleAttributeID" value="cn"/>
    <module-option name="searchScope" value="ONELEVEL_SCOPE"/>
    <module-option name="allowEmptyPasswords" value="true"/>

</login-module>
```

The following is a brief description of the module properties:

- `bindDN`: The DN used to bind against the LDAP server for the user and roles queries, in our case `"uid=admin,ou=system"`.

- `baseCtxDN`: It is the fixed DN of the context to start the user search from. In our example it is `"ou=People,dc=example,dc=com."`

- `baseFilter`: It is a search filter used to locate the context of the user to authenticate. The input `username`/`userDN` as obtained from the login module will be substituted into the filter anywhere a `"{0}"` expression is seen.

- `rolesCtxDN`: It is the fixed DN of the context to search for user roles. Consider that this is not the Distinguished Name of where the actual roles are; rather, this is the DN of where the objects containing the user roles are.

- `roleFilter`: It is a search filter used to locate the roles associated with the authenticated user. An example search filter that matches on the input username is `"(member={0})."` An alternative that matches on the authenticated userDN is `"(member={1})."`

- `roleAttributeID`: It is the name of the role attribute of the context which corresponds to the name of the role.

- `searchScope`: It sets the search scope to one of the strings. `ONELEVEL_SCOPE` searches directly under the named roles context.

- `allowEmptyPasswords`: It is a flag indicating if empty(length==0) passwords should be passed to the LDAP server.

Securing web applications

Okay! Now, we have learnt some commonly used login modules. These login modules can be used by any Java EE application, so it's time to show a concrete example. In this first section, we will show how to apply a login module into a web application in order to provide a basic web authentication.

Basic access authentication is the simplest way to provide a username and password when making a request through a browser.

It works by sending an encoded string containing the user credentials. This Base64-encoded string is transmitted and decoded by the receiver, resulting in the colon-separated username and password string.

Turning on web authentication requires, at first, defining the security-constraints into the web application configuration file (web.xml):

```
<web-app>
. . . . . .
<security-constraint>
    <web-resource-collection>
        <web-resource-name>HtmlAuth</web-resource-name>
        <description>application security constraints
        </description>
    <url-pattern>/*</url-pattern>
        <http-method>GET</http-method>
        <http-method>POST</http-method>
    </web-resource-collection>
  <auth-constraint>
    <role-name>Manager</role-name>
  </auth-constraint>
    </security-constraint>
    <login-config>
        <auth-method>BASIC</auth-method>
        <realm-name>AS 7 sample Realm</realm-name>
    </login-config>

<security-role>
    <role-name>Manager</role-name>
</security-role>
</web-app>
```

The previous configuration will add a security constraint on any JSP/Servlet of the web application that will restrict access to users authenticated with the role **Manager**.

 Supposing we are using the **Database** login module, then the role **Manager** will be granted to user that have authenticated with the admin/admin credentials.

Next configuration tweak needs to be performed on JBoss web deployment's descriptor: WEB-INF/jboss-web.xml. There you need to declare the **security domain**, which will be used to authenticate the users.

```
<jboss-web>
    <security-domain>java:/jaas/mysqldomain</security-domain>
</jboss-web>
```

Pay attention to the `security-domain` element. It is necessary to prefix the domain name with `java:/jaas/` and the name itself must be exactly the same as the one you typed into the security-domain's `name` attribute. The following diagram resumes the whole configuration sequence applied to a Database login module:

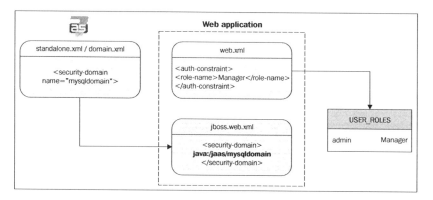

Once you have deployed your application, the outcome of this action should be a blocking popup, requesting user authentication.

Logging in with "*admin/admin*" will grant access to the application with the **Manager** role.

Securing EJBs

Securing applications by means of a web login form is the most frequent option in Enterprise applications. Nevertheless, the HTTP protocol is not the only choice available to access applications. For example, EJBs can be accessed by remote clients using RMI-IIOP protocol. In such a case, you should further refine your security policies by restricting access to the EJB components, which are usually involved in the business layer of your applications.

How does security happen at EJB level?

Authentication must be performed before any EJB method is called. **Authorization**, on the other hand, occurs at the beginning of each EJB method call.

One vast area of improvement introduced in Java EE 5 concerns the use of annotations, which can be also used to perform the basic security checks. The available annotations are five:

- `@org.jboss.ejb3.annotation.SecurityDomain`: It specifies the **Security Domain**, which is associated with a specific class.

- `@javax.annotation.security.RolesAllowed`: It specifies the list of roles permitted to access method(s) in an EJB.

- `@javax.annotation.security.RunAs`: It assigns a role dynamically to the EJB during the invocation of the method. It can be used, for example, if we need to allow a *temporarily* permission to access certain methods.

- `@javax.annotation.security.PermitAll`: When specified, this annotation allows all roles to access a particular bean method. The purpose of this annotation is to widen security access to some methods in situation where you don't exactly know what role will access the EJB. (imagine that some modules have been developed by the third party and they access your EJB with some not well-identified roles).

- `@javax.annotation.security.DenyAll`: When specified, this annotation denies access to all roles. Same considerations as for @PermitAll.

In the following example, we are restricting access to the EJB named `SecureEJB` only to the authorized role, **Manager**:

```
import org.jboss.ejb3.annotation.SecurityDomain;
import javax.annotation.security.RolesAllowed;

@Stateless

@SecurityDomain("mysqlLogin")
@RolesAllowed( { "Manager" })
   public  class SecureEJB {
   . . . . . .
   }
```

Be careful! There is a more than one SecurityDomain annotation available in the server's class path. As shown, you have to include org. jboss.ejb3.annotation.SecurityDomain. The @RolesAllowed annotation, on the other hand, needs importing javax.annotation. security.RolesAllowed.

Annotations can also be applied at method level; for example, if we needed a special role named SuperUser for inserting a new User, then we would tag the method as follows:

```
@RolesAllowed( { "SuperUser" })
    public void createUser(String country,String name) {
        User customer = new User ();
        customer.setCountry(country);
        customer.setName(name);
        em.persist(customer);
    }
```

Securing web services

Web services authorization can be basically carried out in two ways, depending if we are dealing with a POJO-based web Service or EJB-based web services.

Security changes to POJO Web Services are identical to those we have introduced for Servlets or JSP, consisting in defining the security-constraints into web.xml and login modules into jboss-web.xml.

If you are using a web client to access your web service that's all you need to get authenticated. If you are using a standalone client you will need, in turn, to specify the credentials to the JAX-WS Factory as shown in this snippet:

```
JaxWsProxyFactoryBean factory = new JaxWsProxyFactoryBean();

factory.getInInterceptors().add(new LoggingInInterceptor());
factory.getOutInterceptors().add(new LoggingOutInterceptor());

factory.setServiceClass(POJOWebService.class);
factory.setAddress("http://localhost:8080/pojoService");
factory.setUsername("admin");
factory.setPassword("admin");
    POJOWebService client = (POJOWebService) factory.create();

client.doSomething();
```

What about EJB-based Web Services? The configuration is slightly different; because the security domain is not specified into the web descriptors, we have to provide it by means of annotations:

```
@Stateless
@WebService(targetNamespace = "http://www.packtpub.com/",
    serviceName = "SecureEJBService")
@WebContext(authMethod = "BASIC",
        secureWSDLAccess = false)
@SecurityDomain(value = "mysqldomain")
    public  class SecureEJB {

    . . . .
    }
```

As you can see, the @WebContext annotation basically reflects the same configuration options of POJO-based Web Services, with BASIC authentication and unrestricted WSDL access.

The @SecurityDomain annotation should be familiar to you, because we have introduced it to illustrate how to secure an EJB. As you can see, it's a replacement for the information contained in the jboss-web.xml file, except that the security domain is referenced by mysqldomain directly.

> The previous security configuration can be also specified by means of the META-INF/ejb-jar.xml and META-INF/jboss-ejb3.xml files, in case, you prefer using XML deployment descriptors.

Securing the AS 7 management interfaces

One of the most obvious tasks for the system administrator who cares about security is restricting access to the server management interfaces. Without a security policy, every user can gain access to the application server and modify its properties.

> Starting from the release 7.1.0 Beta of the application server, security is enabled by default on the AS management interfaces to prevent unauthorized **remote** access to the application server.
>
> **Local** clients of the application server are, on the other hand, still allowed to access the management interfaces without any authentication.

The attribute which is used to switch on security on the management interface is a `security-realm` which needs to be defined within the `security-realms` section:

```
<management>
    <security-realms>
     <security-realm name="ManagementRealm">
            <authentication>
                <properties path="mgmt-users.properties"
                relative-to="jboss.server.config.dir"/>
            </authentication>
        </security-realm>
    </security-realms>
    <management-interfaces>
        <native-interface security-realm="ManagementRealm">
            <socket-binding native="management-native"/>
        </native-interface>
        <http-interface security-realm="ManagementRealm">
            <socket-binding http="management-http"/>
        </http-interface>
    </management-interfaces>
</management>
```

With the default configuration, the properties are stored in the `mgmt-users.properties` which can be found in the `configuration` directory of your server.

 Users can be added to this property file at any time; even the updates after the server has started are detected automatically.

By default, this management realm expects the entries to be in the following format:

```
username=HEX( MD5( username ':' realm ':' password))
```

This means that each user is associated with an hex-encoded hash that consists of the username, the name of the realm, and the password.

To add new users to the property file, you can use an utility script contained in the `bin` folder of the AS 7.1 installation named `add-user.sh` (Linux) or `add-user.bat` (Windows). As you can see from the following screenshot, the `add-user` shell requires three pieces of information for the new user:

- **Realm**: This is the name of the realm used to secure the management interfaces. If you just press *Enter*, the user will be added in the default realm named `ManagementRealm`.

- **Username:** This is the username we are going to add (it needs to be alpha numeric).

- **Password:** This is the password field which needs to be different from the username.

Here, we have just added the user **francesco** in the default realm, resulting in the following property added to `mgmt-users.properties` of your standalone and domain configuration:

```
francesco=5b9b0917f340b6a9842651867b3deb6f
```

You can now connect to a remote AS 7 management interface using this user:

For the sake of completeness, you can also add users using a non-interactive shell, which could be convenient when you need to add a batch of users on your server distribution. This approach works by passing the username, password, and optionally the realm name to the `add-user` script:

```
add-user.bat myuser mypassword realm1
```

Securing the transport layer

If you were to create a mission critical application with just the bare concepts we have learnt until now, you are not guaranteed to be shielded from all security threats. For example, if you needed to design a payment gateway, where the credit card information is transmitted by means of an EJB or Servlet, using just the authorization and authentication stack is really not enough.

In order to prevent disclosure of critical information to unauthorized individuals or systems, you have to use a protocol that provides **encryption** of the information. Encryption is the conversion of data into a form that cannot be understood by unauthorized people. Conversely, **decryption** is the process of converting encrypted data back into its original form, so it can be understood.

The protocols, which are used to secure the communication, are **SSL** and **TLS**, the latter being considered a replacement for the older SSL.

The differences between the two protocols are minor and very technical; in short, TLS uses *stronger* encryption algorithms and has the ability to work on different ports. For the rest of our chapter, we will refer to SSL for both protocols.

There are two basic techniques for encrypting information: **symmetric encryption** (also called **secret key** encryption) and **asymmetric encryption** (also called public key encryption).

Symmetric encryption is the oldest and best-known technique. It is based on a secret key, which is applied to the text of a message to change the content in a particular way. As long as both the sender and recipient know the secret key, they can encrypt and decrypt all messages that use this key. These encryption algorithms typically work fast and are well suited for encrypting blocks of messages at once.

One significant issue with symmetric algorithms is the requirement of a safe administrative organization to distribute keys to users. This generally results in more overhead from the administrative aspect while the keys remain vulnerable to unauthorized disclosure and potential abuse.

For this reason, a mission-critical enterprise system usually relies on the asymmetric encryption algorithms, which tend to be easier to employ, manage, and make it ultimately more secure.

Asymmetric cryptography, also known as **Public key cryptography**, is based on the concept that the key used to encrypt is not the same used to decrypt the message. In practice, each user holds a couple of keys: the **public key** which is distributed to other parties and the **private key** which is kept in secret. Each message is encrypted with the recipient's public key and can only be decrypted (by the recipient) with his/her private key.

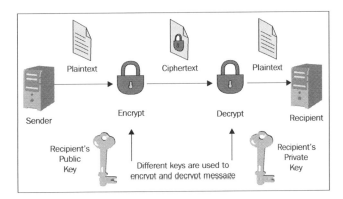

Using asymmetric encryption you can be sure that your message cannot be disclosed by a third-party, however, you *still* have one vulnerability.

Suppose you want to exchange some valuable information with a business partner and so you are requesting his/her public key by telephone or by e-mail. A fraudulent user intercepts your e-mail or simply listens to your conversation and quickly sends you a fake e-mail with his/her public key. Now, even if your data transmission is secured, it will be directed to the wrong person!

In order to solve this issue, we need a document that verifies that the public key belongs to an individual: this document is called **digital certificate** or public key certificate. A digital certificate consists of a formatted block of data that contains the name of the certificate holder (which may be either a user or a system name) and the holder's public key, as well as the digital signature of a **Certification Authority** (CA) for authentication. The certification authority attests that the sender's name is the one associated with the public key in the document.

Public key certificates are commonly used for **secure interaction with websites**. By default, the web browser ships with a set of predefined CA; they are used to verify that the public certificate served to the browser when you enter a secure site, has been actually issued by the owner of the website. In short, if you connect with your browser to `https://www.abc.com` and your browser doesn't give certificate warning; then, you can be sure that you can safely interact with the entity in charge of the site unless that site or your browser has been hacked. But this is another story.

Simple authentication and client authentication

In the previous example, we have depicted a simple authentication (also called server authentication). In this scenario, the only party, which needs to prove its identity, is the server.

SSL, however, is able to perform a **mutual authentication** (also called client or two-way authentication) in case the server requests a client certificate during the SSL handshake over the network.

The client authentication requires a client certificate in **x.509** format from a CA. The x.509 format is an industry-standard format for SSL certificates. In the next section, we will explore the available tools to generate digital certificates and also how to have your certificates signed by a CA.

Enabling the Secure Socket Layer on JBoss AS

JBoss AS uses the **Java Secure Socket Extension (JSSE))**, which is bundled in the J2SE to leverage the SSL/TLS communication.

An Enterprise application can be secured at two different locations: at **HTTP level** and **RMI level**. HTTP communication is handled by the web subsystem within the `standalone.xml/domain.xml` file. Securing the RMI transport is, on the other hand, not always a compelling requirement of your applications. Actually, in most production environments, JBoss AS is placed behind a firewall.

As you can see from the following diagram, this implies that your EJBs are not directly exposed to un-trusted networks, which usually connect through the web server placed into a *demilitarized* zone.

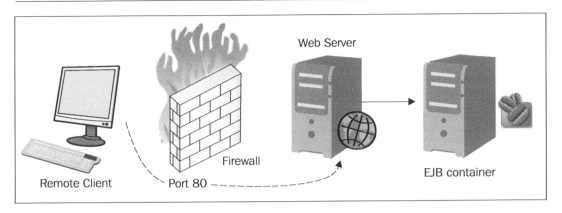

In order to get started with JBoss AS and SSL, we need, first of all, a tool which generates a public key/private key pair in the form of an X509 certificate for use by the SSL server sockets. This is covered in the next section.

Certificate management tools

One tool that can be used to set up a digital certificate is keytool, a key and certificate management utility that ships with the Java SE. It enables users to administer their own public/private key pairs and associated certificates for use in self-authentication (where the user authenticates himself or herself to other users or services) or data integrity and authentication services, using digital signatures. It also allows users to cache the public keys (in the form of certificates) of their communicating peers.

The keytool stores the keys and certificates in a file termed as keystore, a repository of certificates used for identifying a client or a server. Typically, a keystore contains one client or one server's identity, which are protected by using a password. Let's see an example of keystore generation:

```
keytool -genkey -keystore jboss.keystore -storepass mypassword
-keypass mypassword -keyalg RSA -validity 180  -alias as7book  -dname
"cn=Francesco Marchioni,o=PackPub,c=GB"
```

This command creates the keystore named jboss.keystore in the working directory, and assigns it the password mypassword. It generates a public/private key pair for the entity whose "distinguished name" has a common name of Francesco Marchioni, organization of PacktPub and two-letter country code of GB.

The aftermath of this action will be a **self-signed certificate** (using the RSA signature algorithm) that includes the public key and the distinguished-name information. This certificate will be valid for 180 days, and is associated with the private key in a keystore entry referred to by the alias as as7book.

A **self-signed certificate** is a certificate that has not been not verified by a CA and hence leaves you vulnerable to the classic **man-in-the-middle** attack. A self-signed certificate is only suitable for in-house use or for testing while you wait for your real one to arrive.

Securing the HTTP communication with a self-signed certificate

Now let's see how you can use this `keystore` file to secure your JBoss web channel. Open the server configuration file (`standalone.xml/domain.xml`) and reach the web subsystem.

Now, update the connector information by adding the `ssl` element which contains the `keystoreFile` and `keyStorePass` information with data from your certificate:

```
<subsystem xmlns="urn:jboss:domain:web:1.0" default-virtual-
server="default-host">
  <connector name="http" protocol="HTTP/1.1" socket-binding="https"
scheme="https" secure="true">
    <ssl key-alias="as7book" password="mypassword" certificate-key-
file="jboss.keystore" cipher-suite="ALL" protocol="TLS"/>
    . . . .
  </connector>
</subsystem>
```

You have to restart JBoss AS to activate changes. You should see at the bottom of your console the following log which will inform you about the new HTTPS channel running on port 8443.

INFO [org.apache.coyote.http11.Http11Protocol] (MSC service thread 1-4) Starting Coyote HTTP/1.1 on http--127.0.0.1-8443

The following screen is what will be displayed by the Internet Explorer browser if you try to access any web application on the secured channel (for example, if we deployed the `SecuredApp` via `https://localhost:8443/SecuredApp`).

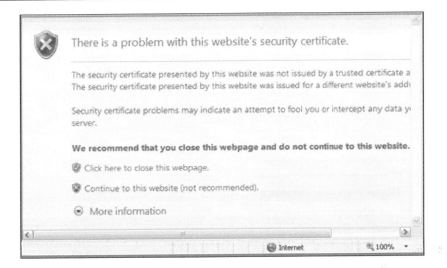

What happened? once you have established a secure connection with the web server, the server certificate has been sent to the browser. Because the certificate **has not been signed** by any recognized CA, the browser security sandbox warns the user about the potential security threat.

This is an in-house test, so we can safely proceed by choosing **Continue to this website**. That's all you need to do in order to activate the Secure Socket Layer with a self-signed certificate.

Securing the HTTP communication with certificate signed by a CA

Having your certificate signed requires issuing a **certificate-signing request (CSR)** to a CA, which returns a signed certificate to be installed on your server. This implies a cost for your organization, which depends on how many certificates you are requesting, the encryption strength and other factors.

So, at the first generate a **CSR** using the newly created `keystore` and `keyentry`:

```
keytool -certreq -keystore jboss.keystore -alias as7book -storepass
mypassword -keypass mypassword  -keyalg RSA  -file certreq.csr
```

This will create a new certificate request named `certreq.csr`, bearing the format:

```
-----BEGIN NEW CERTIFICATE REQUEST-----
. . . . . .
-----END NEW CERTIFICATE REQUEST-----
```

The previous certificate needs to be transmitted to the CA. For example supposing you have chosen **Verisign** (`http://www.verisign.com`) as CA:

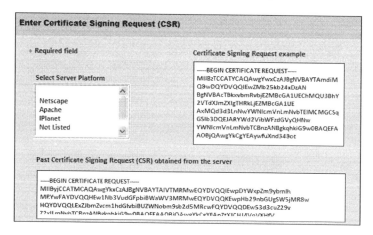

At the end of the enrollment phase, the CA, which will return a signed, certificate that needs to be imported into your keychain. Suppose that you have saved your CA certificate in a file named `signed_ca.txt`:

```
keytool -import -keystore jboss.keystore -alias testkey1 -storepass
mypassword -keypass mypassword -file signed_ca.txt
```

Here, the the `-import` option is used to add a certificate or certificate chain to the list of trusted certificates as specified by the `-keystore` parameter and identified by the `-alias`. The parameter `-storepass` specifies the password which is used to protect the integrity of the `keystore`. If the `-keypass` option is not provided at the command line, and the private key password is different from the `keystore` password, the user is prompted for it.

Now, your web browser will recognize your new certificate as being signed by a CA, so it won't complain that it cannot validate the certificate.

Summary

We started this chapter discussing about the basic concepts of security and the difference between authentication and authorization.

Authentication is used to verify the identity of a user while authorization is used to check if the user has the rights to access a resource.

JBoss uses the PicketBox framework, sitting on top of Java Authentication and Authorization Service (JAAS) which secures all the Java EE technologies running in the application. The core section of the security subsystem is contained in the security-domain element, which performs all the required authorization and authentication checks.

Then, we took a close look at the login modules used to store the user credentials and their associated role. Each login module can be used by Enterprise applications in either programmatic or declarative way. While programmatic security can provide a fine-grained security model, you should consider using declarative security, which allows a clean separation between the business layer and the security policies.

Thereafter, we showed how to secure the management interfaces, namely the new command line interface, by adding a security realm to them.

Finally, we covered in the last section of this chapter about how to encrypt the communication channel using the Secure Socket Layer and the certificates produced by the keytool java utility.

In the next chapter, we will end our journey in the new application server by learning how to configure and distribute our Enterprise applications on a JBoss AS 7 server running on the cloud.

11
Taking JBoss AS 7 in the Cloud

This book has been written during a period of big changes in the application server itself and in the projects related to it. One of the most dazzling changes in this turbulent 2011 is the landing of the OpenShift project which promises to deliver Java EE 6 compliant applications on the cloud with few simple steps. So we couldn't miss this opportunity to show to our readers how you can promote your Enterprise applications worldwide using this new exciting project.

Since the concepts of cloud computing are relatively new we will at first introduce a minimal background to the reader, then we will dive headlong into the OpenShift project which is split into two main areas:

- The OpenShift Express service, which will be your starting objective for leveraging cloud applications
- The OpenShift Flex service which can be used by advanced users for rolling in production your cloud applications

Introduction to cloud computing

What is cloud computing? We're hearing this term everywhere, but what does it really mean? We have all used the cloud knowingly or unknowingly. If you have Gmail, Hotmail, or any other popular mailing service then you have used the Cloud. Simply put, cloud computing is a set of pooled computing resources and services delivered over the Web. When you diagram the relationships between all the elements it resembles a cloud.

Client computing, however, is not a completely new thing in the computer industry. Those of you who have been in the trenches of IT for a decade or two should remember that the first type of client-server application were the mainframe and terminal applications. At that time, storage and CPU was very expensive and the mainframe pooled both types of resources and served them to thin-client terminals.

With the advent of the PC revolution, which brought mass storage and cheap CPUs to the average corporate desktop, the file server gained popularity as a way to enable document sharing and archiving. True to its name, the file server served storage resources to the clients in the enterprise, while the CPU cycles needed to do productive work were all produced and consumed within the confines of the PC client.

In the early 1990s, the budding Internet finally had enough computers attached to it that academics began seriously thinking about how to connect to those machines together to a create massive, shared pools of storage and compute power that would be much larger than what any one institution could afford to build. This is when the idea of "the grid" began to take shape.

Cloud Computing versus Grid Computing

In general, the terms grid and cloud seem to be converging due to some similarities; however there are a list of important differences between them which are often not understood, generating confusion and clutter within the marketplace.

Grid Computing requires the use of software that can divide and farm out pieces of a program as one large system image to several thousand computers. Hence, it may or may not be in the cloud depending on the type of use you make of it. One concern about the grid is that if one piece of the software on a node fails, other pieces of the software on the other nodes may fail too. This is alleviated if that component has a failover component on another node, but problems can still arise if the components rely on other pieces of software to accomplish one or more grid computing tasks.

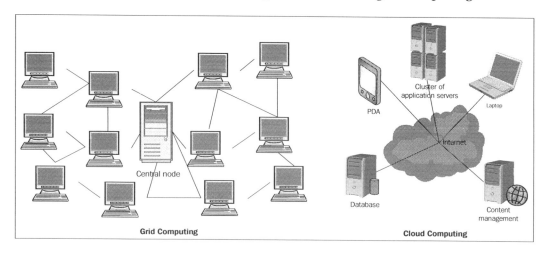

Cloud Computing evolves from grid computing and provides on-demand resource provisioning. With cloud computing, companies can scale up to massive capacities in an instant without having to invest in a new infrastructure, train new personnel, or license new software. If the users are systems administrators and integrators, they care how things are maintained in the cloud. They upgrade, install, and virtualize the servers and applications. If the users are consumers, they do not care how things are run in the system.

Grid and Cloud: similarities and differences

Cloud computing and grid computing, however, do bear some similarities, and as a matter of fact, they are not always mutually exclusive. In fact, they are both used to economize computing by maximizing existing resources.

However, the difference between the two lies in the way the tasks are computed in each respective environment. In a computational grid, one large job is divided into many small portions and executed on multiple machines. This characteristic is fundamental to a grid; not so much to a cloud.

Cloud computing is intended to allow the user to avail various services without investing in the underlying architecture. Cloud services include the delivery of software, infrastructure, and storage over the Internet (either as separate components or a complete platform) based on the effective user demand.

Advantages of cloud computing

Having gone through the basics of cloud computing, we should now account for the benefits which are guaranteed when you transition to a cloud computing approach:

- **On demand service provisioning**: By using self-service provisioning, customers can get cloud services easily, without going through a lengthy process. The customer simply requests a number of computing, storage, software, process, or other resources from the service provider.

- **Elasticity**: This particular characteristic of cloud computing — its elasticity — means that customers no longer need to predict traffic, but can promote their sites aggressively and spontaneously. Engineering for peak traffic becomes a thing of the past.

- **Cost reduction**: As a matter of fact, companies are often challenged to increase the functionality of IT while minimizing capital expenditures. By purchasing just the right amount of IT resources on demand, the organization can avoid purchasing unnecessary equipment.

- **Application programming interfaces** (**APIs**): The accessibility to software that enables machines to interact with cloud software in the same way the user interface facilitates interaction between humans and computers. Cloud computing systems typically use REST-based APIs.

Along with these advantages, cloud computing also bears some disadvantages or potential risks, which you must account for.

The most compelling threat is that sensitive data processed outside the Enterprise brings with it an inherent level of risk, because outsourced services bypass the "physical, logical, and personnel controls" IT shops exert over in-house programs. In addition, when you use the cloud, you probably won't know exactly where your data is hosted. In fact, you might not even know what country it will be stored in, leading to potential issues with local jurisdiction.

As Gartner Group suggests (`http://www.gartner.com`), you should always ask providers to supply-specific information on the hiring and oversight of privileged administrators. Besides this, the cloud provider should provide evidence that encryption schemes were designed and tested by experienced specialists. It is also important to understand if the providers will make a contractual commitment to obey local privacy requirements on behalf of their customers.

Types of cloud computing

Another classification of cloud resources can be made on the basis of the location where the cloud is hosted:

- **Public cloud**: It represents the IT resources offered as a service and shared across multiple organizations, managed by an external service provider
- **Private cloud**: It provides the IT resources dedicated to a single organization and offered on demand
- **Hybrid cloud**: It is a mix of private and public clouds managed as a single entity to extend capacity across clouds as needed

The decision between the different kinds of cloud computing is a matter of discussion between experts and it generally depends on several key factors. For example, as far as security is concerned, although public clouds offer a very secure environment; private clouds offer an inherent level of security that meets even the highest of standards. In addition, you can add security services such as **Intrusion Detection Systems** (IDS) and dedicated firewalls.

A private cloud might be the right choice for large organization carrying a well-run data-center with a lot of spare capacity. It would be more expensive to use a public cloud even if you have to add new software to transform that data center into a cloud.

On the other hand, as far as scalability is concerned, one negative point of private clouds is that their performance is limited to the number of machines in your cloud cluster. Should you max out your computing power, another physical server will need to be added. Besides this, public clouds are typically delivering a *pay-as-you-go* model, where you pay by the hour for the computing resources you use. This kind of utility pricing is an economical way to go if you're spinning up and tearing down development servers on a regular basis.

So, by definition, the majority of public cloud deployments are generally used for web servers or development systems where security and compliance requirements of larger organizations and their customers are not an issue.

As opposed to public clouds, private clouds are generally preferred by mid-size and large enterprises because they meet the security and compliance requirements of those larger organizations that also need dedicated high-performance hardware.

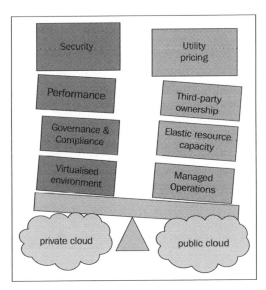

Layers of cloud computing

Cloud computing can be broadly classified into three layers of cloud stack, also known as Cloud Service Models or SPI Service Model:

Infrastructure as a Service (IaaS): This is the base layer of the cloud stack. It serves as a foundation for the other two layers, for their execution. It includes the delivery of computer hardware (servers, networking technology, storage, and data center space) as a service. It may also include the delivery of operating systems and virtualization technology to manage the resources. IaaS makes the acquisition of hardware easier, cheaper, and faster.

Amazon EC2 is a good example of an IaaS. In Amazon EC2 (Elastic Compute Cloud), your application will be executed on a virtual computer (also known as an instance). You have your choice of virtual computer, meaning that you can select a configuration of CPU, memory, and storage that is optimal for your application.

Platform as a Service layer (PaaS) offers a development platform for developers. The end users write their own code and the PaaS provider uploads that code and presents it on the Web.

By using PaaS, you don't need to invest money to get that project environment ready for your developers. The PaaS provider will deliver the platform on the Web, and in most cases, you can consume the platform using your browser. There is no need to download any software. This combination of simplicity and cost efficiency empowers small and mid-size companies, or even individual developers, to launch their own Cloud SaaS.

Facebook is a social application platform where third parties can write new applications that are made available to end users. Another example is provided by OpenShift provider that enables developers to upload their server-side applications on JBoss AS OpenShift provider that enables developers to upload their server-side applications on JBoss AS 7 provides another example.

The final segment in cloud computing is **Software as a Service (SaaS)** which is based on the concept of renting software from a service provider rather than that of buying it yourself. The software is hosted on centralized network servers to make the functionality available over the Web or Intranet. Also known as "software on demand," it is currently the most popular type of cloud computing because of its high flexibility, great services, and enhanced scalability and less maintenance. Yahoo! mail, Google docs, and CRM applications are all instances of SaaS.

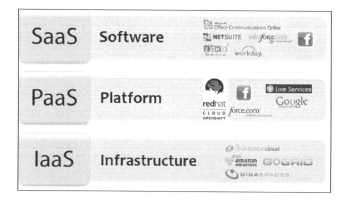

You might wonder if it's possible that some services can be defined both as a *platform* and as a *software*. The answer is, of course, yes! For example, we have mentioned Facebook: we might define Facebook both as a platform where various services can be delivered and also as business applications (Facebook API), which are developed by the end user.

JBoss cloud infrastructure

Up until the last few months, it was common to hear that JBoss AS was still missing a cloud platform while other competitors such as SpringSource already had a solid cloud infrastructure.

Well, although it's true that the application server was missing a consolidated cloud organization, but this does not mean that there was little or no interest on the subject. If you have a look at the JBoss world 2010 labs, there has been a lot of discussing about cloud. One first effort exhibited at JBoss labs was **CirrAS** (`http://www.jboss.org/stormgrind/projects/cirras`), a set of appliances that could automatically deploy a clustered JBoss AS server in the Cloud. Built using the BoxGrinder project (`http://boxgrinder.org/`), CirrAS composed of a set of three appliances: a front-end appliance, a back-end appliance, and management appliance. Unfortunately, the project didn't grow any further and, up to August 2011, the portfolio of JBoss cloud applications was still minute.

At that time, RedHat announced the availability of OpenShift platform for deploying and managing Java EE applications on JBoss AS 7 servers running the cloud. Finally, it's time for the application server to spread its wings over the clouds!

OpenShift is the first PaaS to run CDI applications and plans support for Java EE 6, extending the capabilities of PaaS to even the richest and most demanding applications. OpenShift delivers two kinds of services for rapidly deploying Java applications on the cloud:

- **Express** is a free cloud-based platform for deploying new and existing Java EE, Ruby, PHP, and Python applications in the cloud in a matter of minutes.
- **Flex** is a cloud-based application platform for Java EE and PHP applications which can be deployed on dedicated hosting, running middleware components. Flex is an ideal platform for those who require a great degree of control and choice over their middleware components with valuable features including versioning, monitoring, and auto-scaling.

OpenShift also provides the **Power** platform where you can deploy applications to the cloud that are written to Linux (that is, written in C, or using many binary components) and anything that builds on Linux.

Starting with OpenShift Express

OpenShift Express enables you to create, deploy, and manage applications within the cloud. It provides disk space, CPU resources, memory, network connectivity, and an Apache or JBoss server. Depending on the type of application you are building, you also have access to a template filesystem layout for that type (for example, PHP, WSGI, and Rack/Rails). OpenShift Express also generates a limited DNS for you.

The first thing needed to get started with OpenShift Express is an account, which can be obtained with a very simple registration procedure at: `https://openshift.redhat.com/app/user/new/express`.

Once you've registered and confirmed your e-mail, the next step will be installing on your Linux distribution the client tools needed to deploy and manage your applications in the cloud.

 It is, however, possible to use the **cgywin** tool to emulate the same installation procedure; however, it does require installing a set of tools, such as Openssh, Ruby, and Git, which makes it a bit lengthier, so we don't suggest it as a first choice.

Installing OpenShift client tools

For this purpose, we suggest you use either **Fedora 14** (or higher) or **Red Hat Enterprise 6** (or higher).

Then you need to grab a copy of the `openshift.repo` file, which contains the base URL of rpm files and keys necessary to validate them. This file should be available at: `https://openshift.redhat.com/app/repo/openshift.repo`.

Now, copy this file into the `/etc/yum.repos.d/` filesystem using either `sudo` or root access privileges:

```
$ sudo mv openshift.repo /etc/yum.repos.d/
```

And then install the client tools:

```
$ sudo yum install rhc
```

The `sudo` command is a safe way to execute a command as the super user. In order to use `sudo`, you have to add your user to the list of allowed **sudoers**. From any terminal window type:

```
visudo
```

Then, in the editor, add the following line (replacing with the actual username)

```
user ALL=(ALL) ALL
```

Create an OpenShift Express domain

Before you can create an application, you need to create a **domain**. OpenShift Express uses non-strict domains (that is, there is no preceding period), and the domain name forms part of the application name. The syntax for the application name is `applicationName-domainName.rhcloud.com`.

Each username can only support a single domain, but you can create multiple applications within this domain. If you need multiple domains, you need to create multiple accounts using different usernames.

To create a new domain, run the `rhc-create-domain` command. For example, supposing you were to create the `as7sample` domain for the user `fmarchioni@fmailbox.com`:

```
$ rhc-create-domain -n as7sample -l fmarchioni@fmailbox.com -p password
```

In this command line, the `-n` option specifies the name of the domain that you want to create. The `-l` option is the e-mail address that you used to apply for your OpenShift Express account and `-p` as its password.

Recent enhancements allow domain and application creation via the UI and even from JBoss Tools IDE. Check the Openshift knowledge base at: http://tinyurl.com/6tzx3rd.

When this command is executed for the first time, a SSH handshake happens between your client tool and OpenShift Express. After that, the SSH keys (stored in the user home) will be used for communication with OpenShift Express:

```
[francesco@localhost ~]$ ls -al .ssh
-rw-------.   francesco francesco  222 sep 18.25 config
-rw-------.   francesco francesco 1675 sep 17.29 libra_id_rsa
-rw-r--r--.   francesco francesco  413 sep 17.29 libra_id_rsa.pub
-rw-r--r--.   francesco francesco 3325 sep 10.10 libra_known_hosts
```

 What if I need to develop my application from different hosts?

As explained before, communication between your computer and OpenShift Express happens over SSH using secure keys. So, in order to use your domain from different machines you need to copy SSH keys and the SSH configuration file from one machine to another so that you can use OpenShift Express on multiple computers. You should also copy the express configuration file which is located at $HOME/.openshift/express.conf.

Create your first OpenShift Express application

Having registered a domain, we will now use it to create an application. OpenShift is able to deliver a set of different server applications: you can mix and match Java, PHP, Perl, Python, and Ruby to your heart's content. What really matters is that you deploy applications on a JBoss AS 7.0 platform using the Java EE 6 web profile.

Actually, the configuration of the JBossAS7 server used by the OpenShift Express JBoss cartridge is a simple modification of the JBoss 7.0.2. Final release (upgraded to 7.1.0 Alpha just before this book was going to be printed). The OpenShift Express release does contain some limitations concerning the amount of memory and the number of processes which can be spawned by the application server.

From a conceptual point of view, an application can be seen as a container for one or more server-side components. The command used to create an application is `rhc-create-app`, which accepts multiple options. For a complete list of options run:

```
$ rhc-create-app --help
```

Supposing we want to create an application named `example` using our credentials, we will issue:

```
$ rhc-create-app -a example -l fmarchioni@fmailbox.com -p password -t
jbossas-7.0 -r /home/francesco/example
```

Here, the `-a` option points to the application name, the `-l` flag stands for the user login name, `-p` is the password, `-t` is the application type (which, in our case, will be a JBoss 7.0 application), finally the `-r` option is used to point to a folder on your local filesystem where OpenShift will store all the data-related to your application. Part of that data will be a local copy of the Git-versioning system. In the next section, we will return more in detail on the local repository.

When you issue the `rhc-create-app`, the SSL handshake will take place:

```
Creating remote application space: example

Contacting https://openshift.redhat.com


RESULT:

Successfully created application: example


Adding rhcloud.com to ~/.ssh/config

Warning: Permanently added 'example-as7sample.rhcloud.com,50.17.130.104'
(RSA) to the

list of known hosts.

Receiving objects: 100% (19/19), done.

Confirming application example is available

  Attempt # 1


Success!  Your application is now published here:


  http://example-as7sample.rhcloud.com/
```

Okay. Now, your domain contains an application namespace which can be verified by pointing to the URL where it has been published: `http://example-as7sample.rhcloud.com/`.

In order to deploy artifacts in your application namespace, we need to use the Git local repository which has been created for us.

 Git is a free and open source, distributed version control system designed to handle everything from small to very large projects with high speed and efficiency. It is available at `http://git-scm.com`.

If you look beneath the application's `example` folder, you will notice something familiar in it:

```
example
|
|--- deployments
|
|--- pom.xml
|
|--- src
|
|--- .openshift
```

As you can imagine, the `deployments` folder performs the same task of the equivalent `JBOSS_HOME/standalone/deployments` directory. Applications placed in it will be candidate for uploading in the OpenShift repository.

So, now we need to create an application and deploy it there. As our first example, we will deploy a simple cloud service which renders a text file as a PDF—something that you might have searched for on the Internet at least once in your life!

This application consists just of a Servlet which translated the request into a PDF response, using the **iText** library (available at: `http://itextpdf.com/download.php`)

```java
package sample;

import java.io.IOException;

import javax.servlet.*;
import javax.servlet.annotation.WebServlet;
import javax.servlet.http.*;

import com.itextpdf.text.*;
import com.itextpdf.text.pdf.PdfWriter;
```

```java
@WebServlet("/TexttoPdf")
public class TexttoPdf extends HttpServlet {
  private static final long serialVersionUID = 1L;

  public void init(ServletConfig config) throws ServletException{
    super.init(config);
  }

  public void doGet(HttpServletRequest request,
      HttpServletResponse response)
  throws ServletException, IOException{
    doPost(request, response);
  }

  public void doPost(HttpServletRequest request,
      HttpServletResponse response)
  throws ServletException, IOException{
    String text = request.getParameter("text");
    response.setContentType("application/pdf");
    Document document = new Document();
    try{
      PdfWriter.getInstance(document,
          response.getOutputStream());
      document.open();

      document.add(new Paragraph(text));

      document.close();
    }catch(DocumentException e){
      e.printStackTrace();
    }
  }

}
```

The application obviously needs an HTML/JSP page which carries the text to parse in a text area:

```html
<form action="TexttoPdf" method="post">

    <textarea cols="80" rows="5" name="text">
      This text will be converted in PDF.
    </textarea>

    <input type="submit" value="Convert to PDF">
</form>
```

Next, we will package the application into a file named `createpdf.war` and we will bring it to the cloud. For this purpose, let's copy the `createpdf.war` file into the `deployments` folder using the `cp` command:

```
$ cp createpdf.war /home/francesco/example/deployments
```

 Following the standard AS 7 deployment rules, exploded applications will also need marker files to trigger actual deployment. Marker files are placed in the `deployments` folder of your local repository and will be uploaded to the AS 7 server instance.

We need to add and commit our application to the Git repository using the `git add` and `git commit` command:

```
$ git add deployments/createpdf.war
```

```
$ git commit -m "First application on the cloud" deployments/ createpdf.war
```

```
 [master 1637c21] Deploy createpdf application
 1 files changed, 0 insertions(+), 0 deletions(-)
 create mode 100644 deployments/createpdf.war
```

In practice, with the `git add` command, we tell Git to take a snapshot of the file `createpdf.war`. You can permanently store the contents of the index in the repository with `git commit`.

Your application has now been moved on the remote Git repository. The command `git push` will actual deploy the application on JBoss AS 7:

```
git push
```

Finally, we are able to access our application using the OpenShift application name and domain, in addition to the web context: `http://example-as7sample.rhcloud.com/createpdf`

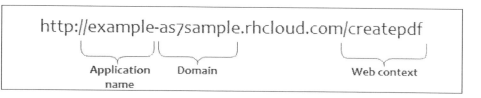

Launching our application generates as result a PDF file: your first cloud application!

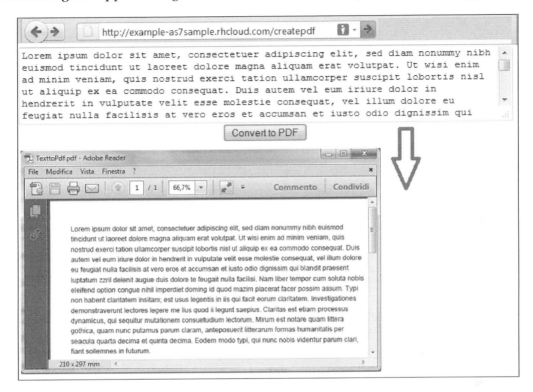

Having completed the first application in the next sections, we will now show you how to manage your Openshift Express applications and introduce some advanced features.

Watching what's happening on the server

When you deploy or run your applications you might be interested to know what is happening on the server side. The most basic form of control on your application server is the console which produces some information, such as when an application is deployed or if it encountered any error.

Tailing for the application server logs is quite simple and you just need to use the `rhc-tail-files` for this. For instance, our example application can be watched using this shell:

```
$ rhc-tail-files -a example -p password


Contacting https://openshift.redhat.com
```

```
Attempting to tail files: example/logs/*

Use ctl + c to stop


==> example/logs/boot.log <==

14:41:17,500 INFO   [org.jboss.modules] JBoss Modules version 1.0.1.GA

14:41:17,785 INFO   [org.jboss.msc] JBoss MSC version 1.0.0.GA

14:41:17,834 INFO   [org.jboss.as] JBoss AS 7.0.0.Final "Lightning"
starting

14:41:17,836 DEBUG [org.jboss.as.config] Configured system properties:


. . . . . . . . . . . .


==> example/logs/server.log <==

14:41:18,706 INFO   [org.jboss.as.connector.subsystems.datasources]
(Controller Boot Thread) Deploying JDBC-compliant driver class org.
h2.Driver (version 1.2)

14:41:18,712 INFO   [org.jboss.as.connector.subsystems.datasources]
(Controller Boot Thread) Deploying non-JDBC-compliant driver class com.
mysql.jdbc.Driver (version 5.1)

14:41:18,732 INFO   [org.jboss.as.clustering.infinispan.subsystem]
(Controller Boot Thread) Activating Infinispan subsystem.

14:41:18,860 INFO   [org.jboss.as.naming] (Controller Boot Thread)
Activating Naming Subsystem

14:41:18,877 INFO   [org.jboss.as.naming] (MSC service thread 1-1)
Starting Naming Service
```

Managing AS 7 applications

Working in the cloud may be perceived a bit difficult, at first, because you don't
have your standard instruments to manage your applications. At the time of writing,
the only available instrument to manage your applications is a command line,
however a new web interface has been announced which will further simplify
your application's administration.

In order to control your applications, you can use the rhc-ctl-app command, which
accepts besides user credentials and info, the -c command, which allows basic
application control.

The following is the list of available commands which can be used to manage your applications (you can get, at any time, the list of available options using the -help flag):

Option	Description
start	It starts an application in the cloud.
stop	It stops an application that is currently running in the cloud.
restart	It restarts an application in the cloud.
reload	It reloads an application in the cloud.
status	It displays the current status of an application in the cloud.
destroy	It removes an application from the cloud.

For example, supposing you want to delete your just created application example, you could use the following shell:

```
$ rhc-ctl-app -l fmarchioni@fmailbox.com -p mypassword -a example -c
destroy
Contacting https://openshift.redhat.com
!!!! WARNING !!!! WARNING !!!! WARNING !!!!
You are about to destroy the example application.

This is NOT reversible, all remote data for this application will be
removed.
Do you want to destroy this application (y/n): y
Contacting https://openshift.redhat.com
API version:    1.1.1
Broker version: 1.1.1

RESULT:
Successfully destroyed application: example
```

Configuring your applications on the cloud

As we have anticipated, when you create an application, you will have a local repository, which can be used for advanced cloud configuration. We have formerly discussed about the deployments folder. Besides this, there are some more interesting things in your Git repository. Looking under the .openshift folder, we see the following files:

```
[francesco@localhost .openshift]$ ls -al
drwxrwxr-x. francesco francesco 4096 10 sep 10.10 action_hooks
drwxrwxr-x. francesco francesco 4096 10 sep 10.42 config
drwxrwxr-x. francesco francesco 4096 10 sep 10.10 markers
```

The `action_hooks` contains a script named `build` which will be executed after `git push` and before the application is started.

 You can use the build script for performing some application initialization, such as creating tables or setting some variables. Check out this: `http://tinyurl.com/3hp6yg7`.

The other folder named `markers` can be used to send some hints to the maven compiler. For example, the `skip_maven_build` marker file will instruct the maven compiler to skip the build process.

Most importantly, the `config` folder contains the following structure under it:

```
[francesco@localhost config]$ ls -al
drwxrwxr-x. francesco francesco 4096 sep 10.57 modules
-rw-rw-r--. francesco francesco 9495 sep 10.10 standalone.xml
```

Here, the `standalone.xml` file will be used as a configuration for your applications. You can actually use it to customize your application environment, though there are some limitations: for example, you cannot exceed the Java max heap at 128MB, and 83MB of PermGen.

Besides this, OpenShift Express users running the application are limited to about 100 processes, which translate to a max of 80 or so Java threads, so excessive thread creation can eat up available processes and begin to cause `java.lang.OutOfMemoryErrors` with a failure to create native thread cause.

In the next section, we will show how to modify the standard configuration by enabling the MySQL datasource contained in it.

Finally, the `modules` folder can be used to inject modules into your JBoss AS 7 environment, emulating the same folder, which we described in the local AS 7 distribution.

OpenShift storage management

Well, every Enterprise application needs a storage for its data and OpenShift makes no exception to it. OpenShift Express provides up to 128MB of storage space for your application. You can also use your allocated storage space to store databases.

At the time of writing, the databases available on the Flex Platform are MySQL and PDOMySql (A PHP Database object). In order to embed the MySql database in your application, you have to pass the `-e` option to the `rhc-ctl-app` command, as shown next:

```
$ rhc-ctl-app -a example -l fmarchioni@fmailbox.com -e add-mysql-5.1

API version:     1.1.1
Broker version: 1.1.1

RESULT:

Mysql 5.1 database added.  Please make note of these credentials:

  Root User: admin

  Root Password: SH-v4VuAZ_Se

  Database Name: example


Connection URL: mysql://127.1.23.129:3306/
```

Now, we will need to configure a datasource on the application server. This will be much easier than you think: as a matter of fact, your standalone.xml already contains a datasource for MySQL database. You just have to enable it and use the credentials that have been displayed on the console:

```
<datasource jndi-name="java:jboss/datasources/MysqlDS"
  enabled="true" use-java-context="true" pool-name="MysqlDS">
  <connection-url>
    jdbc:mysql://127.1.23.129:3306/example
  </connection-url>
  <driver>mysql</driver>
  <security>
    <user-name>admin</user-name>
    <password>SH-v4VuAZ_Se</password>
  </security>
</datasource>
```

Okay, now you have a datasource registered under the java:jboss/datasources/MysqlDS JNDI namespace that is available for use by your applications.

Moving to OpenShift Flex

The Flex framework is not surprisingly a more flexible instrument to deploy your application on the cloud. When using the Flex platform you have direct control over your PaaS environment, made up of a cluster of nodes.

The first difference with the Express platform is that OpenShift Flex provides a graphical user interface (GUI) that you can use to create, deploy, configure, manage, and monitor your cloud environment. Although OpenShift Flex is designed for commercial use, you can start your cloud environment with a free trial period.

At the time of writing, you need to link your OpenShift Flex account with an Amazon EC2 account. Navigate to the AWS home page at: `https://console.aws.amazon.com/ec2/home`.

Enter your e-mail address and password and sign in. Next, you will be taken to the payment gateway, which requires entering credit card information. Don't worry, you will not be billed during your trial period!

Once completed, the website displays a numerical security code; use your phone keypad to enter this code when prompted by the automated call from Amazon.

Now, return to your Flex Console and enter your Amazon account. Click on **Try it** and Flex will link it to your OpenShift Flex account:

As a first step, you will define the name and the shape of your cluster of nodes:

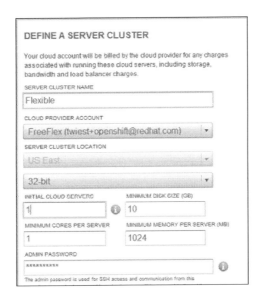

Once you have defined the cluster name and the capabilities of your cloud of servers, you will be interviewed shortly with some basic questions about your plans with cloud and OpenShift. We will not detail this process and move to the application setup.

Creating a sample application

You are now ready to rock with the Flex platform. There are basically two ways to get started: you can either deploy a ready-made application, such as the Seam booking example. See `http://docs.jboss.org/seam/latest/reference/en-US/html/tutorial.html`), or you can deploy your own application.

Adding pre-built application is quite a straightforward task and it's entirely driven by the Flex console. We will rather show how to deploy one of your applications. To make it more interesting, we will add it as a requirement to store some data in a no-SQL database like **MongoDB**.

So, reach the **Applications** tab option in the upper area of the screen. You will see there are at the moment no running applications in your cluster. Click on the **Add application** button.

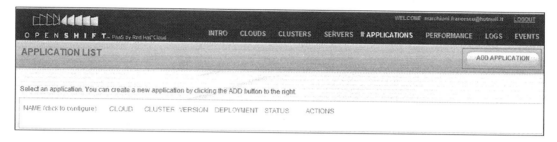

From there, choose an appropriate application name, such as **NoSqlApp**; flag the **Create New** option and select an application version. (this is to enable support for multiple versions in later releases of OpenShift Flex. Choose **1** in our case). Click on **Submit**.

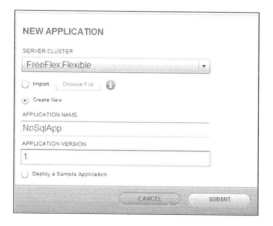

Now, your application should be enlisted in the main application list. By clicking on the application name, you will be linked to the main application menu, which is composed of the following tabs:

- **Overview**: This gathers generic information about the application components and, most important, it informs us the DNS name of the application, which we will use it to reach it from the browser.

- **Components**: This window contains the components, which will be installed along the application, including application server components, JDK and additional frameworks like Infinispan cache or MongoDB database.

- **Files**: These contain information about the application files. The application files can be added from here, or even from an SSH session.

- **Configure**: It can be used to configure the specific components used by your application. For example, if you are using a MySQL database, you will configure in this tab the connection properties.

- **Deploy changes**: This window is used to deploy your application files on the cluster.

Our first step will be selecting the resources used by our application, so move to the **Components** menu. Here, select JBoss AS 7.0.0 (or higher) and a JDK 1.6. In the **Other components** frame, choose to add MongoDB component.

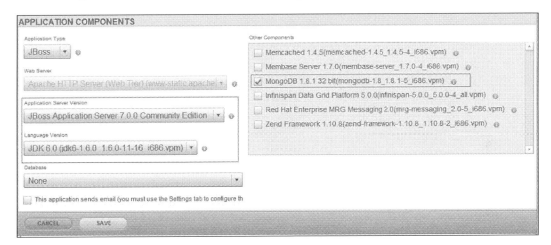

Fine, we will now deploy a simple application, which stores data in the no-SQL MongoDB and performs some basic searches.

Create a new Dynamic Web project, which contains the following Servlet in it:

 In order to compile this project, you will need to download the MongoDB JDBC driver, which is available at: `https://github.com/mongodb/` `mongo-java-driver/downloads`. Package the JAR within the `WEB-INF/lib` folder of your application.

```java
package sample;

import java.io.*;

import javax.servlet.*;
import javax.servlet.annotation.WebServlet;
import javax.servlet.http.*;

import com.mongodb.*;


@WebServlet("/MongoServlet")
public class MongoDBServlet extends HttpServlet {

  Mongo m = null;

  public void init(ServletConfig config)
  {
    try {
      m = new Mongo( "localhost" );
      System.out.println("Connected");
    } catch (Exception e) {

      e.printStackTrace();
    }
  }


  protected void doGet(HttpServletRequest request, HttpServletResponse
response) throws ServletException, IOException {
      PrintWriter out = response.getWriter();
      String name = request.getParameter("name");
      String surname = request.getParameter("surname");
      String department = request.getParameter("department");
      String wage = request.getParameter("wage");

      DB db = m.getDB( "test" );

      BasicDBObject doc = new BasicDBObject();

      doc.put("name",name);
      doc.put("surname",surname);

      DBCollection coll = null;
```

```
    coll = db.getCollection("employee");

    if (coll == null) {
      coll = db.createCollection("employee", doc);
    }
    BasicDBObject info = new BasicDBObject();

    info.put("department", department);
    info.put("wage", new Integer(wage));

    doc.put("info ", info);

    coll.insert(doc);
    coll.insert(info);

    out.println("Inserted DBObject "+coll);
    DBCursor cur = coll.find();
    out.println("Documents contained:" );
    while(cur.hasNext()) {
      out.println(cur.next());
      out.println();
    }
  }


  protected void doPost(HttpServletRequest request,
HttpServletResponse response) throws ServletException, IOException {
    doGet(request,response);
  }

}
```

As you can see, this Servlet basically connects to default **test** DB instance of MongoDB and, if not found, creates a collection of **employee** objects which include information about the employee's name, surname. This information is linked with department and wage and stored using a JSON lightweight data-interchange format:

```
{
    "name" : "John",
    "type" : "Doe",
    "info" : {
                department : "AB12345",
                wage : 1500
              }
}
```

For the sake of brevity, we don't include the welcome page, which is a basic HTML page, containing the name, surname, department, and wage input text fields, and submits to our Servlet the request.

Now package the web application into a file named `mongoapp.war` and move to the **Files** tab menu. From there, upload your web application as shown in the following screenshot:

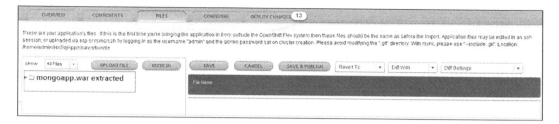

We are almost done. Now, click on the **Deploy changes** tab and choose **Save and Publish** to publish your application. You application is now published and just need to be started from the main application menu.

In a couple of minutes, it will be up and running; we just need to know how to access our application. If you had a look at the Applications' **Overview** tab, you might have noticed that it shows the cluster DNS address where the application can be reached:

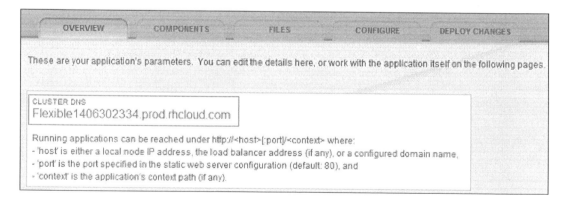

In our example, point the browser to `http://Flexible1406302334.prod.rhcloud.com/mongoapp` and you will be redirected to the application's landing page.

If everything works correctly, you will be able to store and display collection data stored in MongoDB. Nothing fancy, however it's a good starting point for learning how to mix and match different available components.

Going beyond the basics of OpenShift Flex

We have just mentioned some of the most interesting features of the OpenShift Flex platform. Although we cannot describe all the available options in one single chapter, we will mention two of the most interesting features, which are application **scaling** and **monitoring**.

Application scaling can either be carried out manually by adding more servers to the cluster, as shown by the following screenshot:

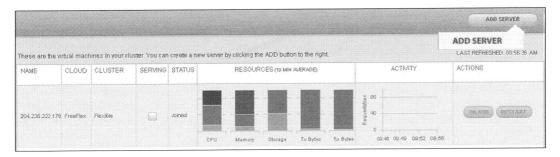

Or you can enable the advanced **auto-scale** option, which is available in your **Cluster** subsection. Auto-scaling will automatically add or remove nodes to your cluster as required to meet the application demand of resources. This can be exceptionally useful to save expenditures in servers machines.

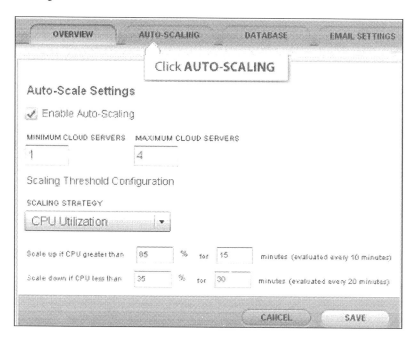

Monitoring is another key element of the Flex platform. Using the OpenShift Flex performance monitor tool, you can monitor the performance of each cloud container and its elements. You can view both current and historical performance data and charts for each element in your cloud environment.

The performance charts can be reached within your cloud environment at the **Performance** panel. The **Performance** screen displays five charts as defaults. You can, however, customize these charts to fit your cloud container view.

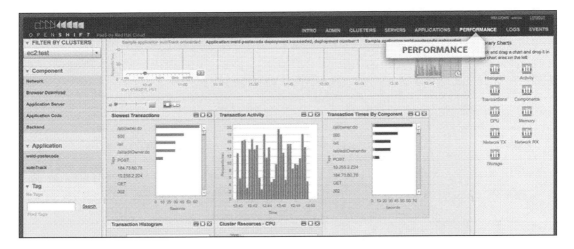

From the **Performance** panel, you can choose a timeframe by simply selecting a portion of the graph, which may identify, for example, a peak in the server activities:

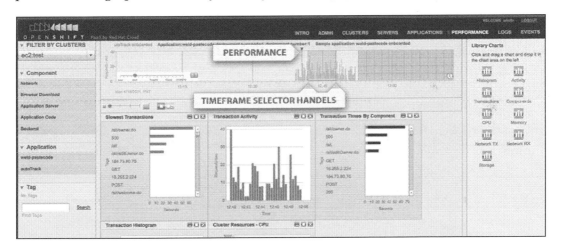

The entire performance window is organized as a drag-and-drop portal where you can add or remove charts to your liking:

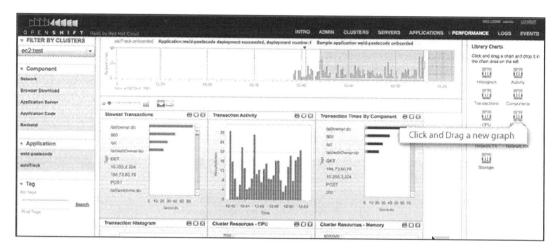

You can view more details about the performance with the performance transaction charts. For example, in the **Transaction Times By Component** chart, you can identify which transactions take the longest time to complete. Move over to various segments in the bar graphs to view the time taken by each software component for each transaction.

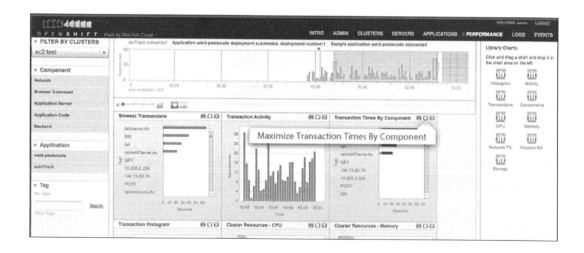

Summary

In this chapter, we have expanded the point of view of your applications from your company's farm to the cloud environment. The suggested path for AS 7 cloud applications leads to the OpenShift platform, which is a free Platform-as-a-Service that enables developers to deploy to the cloud without having to worry about downloading and managing the stack, writing scripts or installing agents.

The OpenShift platform bears some similarities with other cloud solutions, such as MS Azure. Just like Azure, OpenShift is a service managed and run by the vendor, with platform abstractions layered over the underlying infrastructure.

On the other hand, OpenShift provides the ability to choose from multiple hosts, the support for multiple platforms, and the eventual release of the code as an open source project which is important to prevent vendor locking in.

OpenShift services are divided in two main options: the Express and the Flex solution.

OpenShift Express is mainly developer oriented while the Flex platform is operations oriented. With the free OpenShift Express service, you can use client tools to Git-push your application to OpenShift. This platform lets you deploy applications to a JBoss AS 7 (among others) environment and to customize the AS environment, within some limits.

For those who want more granular control over the environment, there's OpenShift Flex. The Flex services use an intuitive GUI to configure, deploy, and monitor your applications. Besides this, you can have access to advanced features such as application auto-scaling, which lets you reduce the impact of your hardware resources on your budget significantly.

Appendix

In this appendix, we will provide a quick reference for the most common commands and operations, which can be used to manage the application server with the CLI. For the sake of brevity, only the `jboss-admin.sh` script (Linux environment) is mentioned. Windows users should just replace this file with the equivalent `jboss-admin.bat`.

Startup options

The following commands can be useful to startup the CLI in a non-interactive way:

- Pass script commands to the `jboss-admin` shell:

  ```
  ./jboss-admin.sh --connect command=:shutdown
  ```

- Execute a CLI shell contained in a file:

  ```
  ./jboss-admin.sh --file=test.cli
  ```

General commands

The following commands can be used to gather system information and to set specific server properties:

- Read environment information:

  ```
  version
  ```

- Read the JNDI context:

  ```
  /subsystem=naming:jndi-view
  ```

- Read the XML server configuration:

  ```
  :read-config-as-xml
  ```

- Read the services registered on the container and their status:

  ```
  /core-service=service-container:dump-services
  ```

- Set a system property:

  ```
  /system-property=property1:add(value="value")
  ```

- Read a system property:

  ```
  /system-property=property1:read-resource
  ```

- Read all system properties:

  ```
  /core-service=platform-mbean/
  type=runtime:read-attribute(name=system-properties)
  ```

- Remove a system property:

  ```
  /system-property=property1:remove
  ```

- Change a socket binding port (for example, http port):

  ```
  /socket-binding-group=standard-sockets/socket-binding=http:
  write-attribute(name="port", value="8090")
  ```

- Read the IP address of the public interface:

  ```
  /interface=public:read-attribute(name=resolved-address)
  ```

Domain mode

Prefix the host name (and if required, the server name) to indicate on which host (or server name) you are issuing the command. Examples:

- Read the XML configuration from the host master:

  ```
  /host=master:read-config-as-xml
  ```

- Read the IP address of the public interface for the server-one running on the host master.

  ```
  /host=master/server=server-one/interface=public:
  read-attribute(name=resolved-address)
  ```

Deploy commands

The CLI can also be used to deploy applications. Here is a quick reference to deploy commands:

- List of deployed applications:

  ```
  deploy
  ```

- Deploy an application on a standalone server:

  ```
  deploy MyApp.war
  ```

- Re-deploy an application on a standalone server:

  ```
  deploy -f MyApp.war
  ```

- Un-deploy an application:

  ```
  undeploy MyApp.war
  ```

- Deploy an application on all server groups:

  ```
  deploy MyApp.war --all-server-groups
  ```

- Deploy an application on one or more server groups (separated by a comma):

  ```
  deploy application.ear --server-groups=main-server-group
  ```

- Un-deploy an application from all server groups:

  ```
  undeploy application.ear --all-relevant-server-groups
  ```

- Un-deploy an application from one or more server groups:

  ```
  undeploy as7project.war --server-groups=main-server-group
  ```

- Un-deploy an application without deleting the content:

  ```
  undeploy application.ear --server-groups=main-server-group
   --keep-content
  ```

JMS

Here you can find the JMS alias commands that can be used to create/remove JMS destinations:

- Add JMS queue:

  ```
  add-jms-queue --name=queue1 --entries=queues/queue1
  ```

- Remove JMS queue:

  ```
  remove-jms-queue queue1
  ```

- Add JMS topic:

```
add-jms-topic --name=topic1 --entries=topics/topic1
```

- Remove JMS topic:

```
remove-jms-topic topic1
```

Datasources

This is a list of handy datasource commands that can be issued using the datasource alias:

- Add datasource:

```
data-source add --jndi-name=java:/MySqlDS --pool-name=MySQLPool --
  connection-url=jdbc:mysql://localhost:3306/MyDB --driver-
  name=mysql-connector-java-5.1.16-bin.jar --user-name=myuser --
  password=password --max-pool-size=30
```

- Remove datasource:

```
data-source remove --jndi-name=java:/MySqlDS
```

Datasources (using operation on resources)

You can also operate on a datasource using operation on the datasources subsystem:

- List installed drivers:

```
/subsystem=datasources:installed-drivers-list
```

- Add datasource:

```
/subsystem=datasources/data-source=testDS:add(jndi-
  name=java:jboss/datasources/MyDB, pool-name= MySQLPool, driver-
  name=mysql-connector-java-5.1.16-bin.jar, connection-
  url=jdbc:mysql://localhost:3306/MyDB)
```

- Add XA-datasource (using operation):

  ```
  /subsystem=datasources/xa-data-source=
  "MySqlDSXA":add(jndi-name="java:/MySqlDSXA",
  driver-name="com.mysql", pool-name="mysqlPool")
  ```

  ```
  /subsystem=datasources/xa-data-source=
  MySqlDSXA/xa-datasource-properties=ServerName:add(value=localhost)
  ```

  ```
  /subsystem=datasources/xa-data-source=
  MySqlDSXA/xa-datasource-properties=PortNumber:add(value=3306)
  ```

  ```
  /subsystem=datasources/xa-data-source=MySqlDSXA:enable
  ```

- Remove datasource (using operation on resource):

  ```
  /subsystem=datasources/data-source=testDS:remove
  ```

Mod_cluster

Mod_cluster management can be carried out using the following CLI operations:

- List proxies connected:

  ```
  /subsystem=modcluster:list-proxies
  ```

- Read proxies info:

  ```
  /subsystem=modcluster:read-proxies-info
  ```

- Add a proxy to the cluster:

  ```
  /subsystem=modcluster:add-proxy(host= CP15-022, port=9999)
  ```

- Remove a proxy:

  ```
  /subsystem=modcluster:remove-proxy(host=CP15-022, port=9999)
  ```

- Add a web context:

  ```
  /subsystem=modcluster:enable-context(context=/myapp,
    virtualhost=default-host)
  ```

- Disable a web context:

  ```
  /subsystem=modcluster:disable-context(context=/myapp,
    virtualhost=default-host)
  ```

- Stop a web context:

  ```
  /subsystem=modcluster:stop-context(context=/myapp,
    virtualhost=default-host, waittime=50)
  ```

- Add a metric:

  ```
  /subsystem=modcluster:add-metric(type=heap)
  ```

Batch

Here's how to handle Batch processing with the CLI:

- Start command batching:

  ```
  batch
  ```

- Pause batching:

  ```
  holdback-batch
  ```

- List of batch commands:

  ```
  list-batch
  ```

- Clear the batch session of commands:

  ```
  clear-batch
  ```

- Execute list of batch commands:

  ```
  run-batch
  ```

Snapshots

Snapshots allow the storage and retrieval of the server configuration:

- Take a snapshot of the configuration:

  ```
  :take-snapshot
  ```

- List available snapshots:

  ```
  :list-snapshots
  ```

- Delete a snapshot:

  ```
  :delete-snapshot(name="20110726-223444446standalone.xml")
  ```

Index

Express 309
extensions, application server 29

F

Facebook 308
FacesServlet 96
farm deployment 211
Fedora 14, 310
file
  CLI script, executing 192
file-encoding property 92
file-store path 228
fire-and-forget asynchronous void methods 64
Flex 309
formatters 41
forward-when-no-consumers element 238
fully-qualified-classname-of-the-remote-interface parameter 108

G

Gartner Group
  URL 306
generate-strings-as-char-arrays-attribute property 94
getCallerPrincipal() method 276
getConnection() method 53
getUserPrincipal() method 276
global modules
  setting up 166
Google Guice 72
Google Web Toolkit (GWT) 198
grid 304
grid computing
  about 304
  versus cloud computing 304, 305

H

H2 open source database engine
  URL 54
handlers 41
ha-sockets group 216
help command 190
Hibernate 4.0 115

hibernate cache, Infinispan configuration
  about 231, 232
  configuring 231-233
  replication, using 234
hibernate.transaction.factory_class property 268
high availability 207, 224
history command 197
holdback-batch command 191, 192
horizontal-scaled cluster 208
HornetQ
  about 236
  acceptor/connector 74
  URL 72
HornetQ clusterable implementation 207
HornetQ clusters 236
HornetQConnectionFactory 77
HornetQ integration 73
HornetQ persistence configuration 80, 81
HornetQ server
  diagrammatic representation 73
host 124
Host 2 135
host controller 118
host parameter 76
host.xml file
  configuring 124, 125
HTML 142
http administrative interface 125
HTTP communication
  securing, with CA signed certificate 299-301
  securing, with self signed certificate 298, 299
HTTP connector
  configuring 89
HTTP level 296
HTTP Request element
  creating 260
HTTP Session 225
hybrid cloud 306

I

IaaS 307
identity, login module 278
idle-timeout-minutes element 57

process controller 118
profile element 186
profiles, application server 31
programmatic security 275
properties, destinations
  address-full-policy 80
  dead-letter-address 80
  expiry-address 80
  max-delivery-attempts 80
  max-size-bytes 80
  message-counter-history-day-limit 80
  page-size-bytes 80
  redelivery-delay 80
protocol parameter 88
protocol servers 74
protocol stack
  customizing 223, 224
proxy_http_module module 258
proxy-name parameter 88
proxy-port parameter 88
public 125
public cloud 306, 307
public key certificate. *See* **digital certificate**
public key cryptography. *See* **asymmetric cryptography**
public key encryption. *See* **asymmetric encryption**
public network interface 31
Publish-Subscribe messaging 71, 72

Q

queries
  caching 270
Queueless Thread Pool
  about 39
  configuring 39
Queue messaging 71
queue size 38

R

Random 238
RAR file 142
read-attribute command 181
read-children-names command 181

read-children operation 184
read-children-resources command 181, 184
read-children-types command 181
READ_COMMITTED isolation level 227
read-only property 93
read-operation-description command 181
read-operation-names command 181
read-proxies-info command 253
read-resource command 181, 182
read-resource-description command 181
recompile-on-fail property 94
recovery subsystem 83
recursive=true parameter 182
redelivery-delay property 80
re-deploy command 192
RedHat 12, 309
Red Hat Enterprise 6, 310
redirect-port parameter 88
Relative Distinguished Name (RDN) 283
relative-to property 145
reload command 16
RemoteConnectionFactory 78
Remote EJB client
  adding, to Web application 106-109
remote machine
  JBoss, stopping on 16
Remoting framework 107
remove-batch-line command 192
remove-metric command 262
remove parameter 189
remove-proxy command 255
REPEATABLE_READ isolation level 227
replicated-cache 226
resources 25
REST-based APIs 306
retrieve-result-later asynchronous methods
  64
retry-interval 238
right driver deployment strategy
  selecting 60, 61
RMI level 296
roleAttributeID 286
roleFilter 286
RoleMapping, login module 278
rolesCtxDN 286
roles.properties 279

Thank you for buying
JBoss AS 7 Configuration, Deployment, and
Administration

About Packt Publishing

Packt, pronounced 'packed', published its first book "*Mastering phpMyAdmin for Effective MySQL Management*" in April 2004 and subsequently continued to specialize in publishing highly focused books on specific technologies and solutions.

Our books and publications share the experiences of your fellow IT professionals in adapting and customizing today's systems, applications, and frameworks. Our solution based books give you the knowledge and power to customize the software and technologies you're using to get the job done. Packt books are more specific and less general than the IT books you have seen in the past. Our unique business model allows us to bring you more focused information, giving you more of what you need to know, and less of what you don't.

Packt is a modern, yet unique publishing company, which focuses on producing quality, cutting-edge books for communities of developers, administrators, and newbies alike. For more information, please visit our website: www.packtpub.com.

About Packt Open Source

In 2010, Packt launched two new brands, Packt Open Source and Packt Enterprise, in order to continue its focus on specialization. This book is part of the Packt Open Source brand, home to books published on software built around Open Source licences, and offering information to anybody from advanced developers to budding web designers. The Open Source brand also runs Packt's Open Source Royalty Scheme, by which Packt gives a royalty to each Open Source project about whose software a book is sold.

Writing for Packt

We welcome all inquiries from people who are interested in authoring. Book proposals should be sent to author@packtpub.com. If your book idea is still at an early stage and you would like to discuss it first before writing a formal book proposal, contact us; one of our commissioning editors will get in touch with you.

We're not just looking for published authors; if you have strong technical skills but no writing experience, our experienced editors can help you develop a writing career, or simply get some additional reward for your expertise.

JSF 2.0 Cookbook

ISBN: 978-1-847199-52-2   Paperback: 396 pages

Over 100 simple but incredibly effective recipes for taking control of your JSF applications

1. Discover JSF 2.0 features through complete examples

2. Put in action important JSF frameworks, such as Apache MyFaces Core, Trinidad, Tomahawk, RichFaces Core, Sandbox and so on

3. Develop JSF projects under NetBeans/Glassfish v3 Prelude and Eclipse/JBoss AS

JBoss AS 5 Performance Tuning

ISBN: 978-1-84951-402-6   Paperback: 312 pages

Build faster, more efficient enterprise Java applications

1. Follow the practical examples to make your applications as efficient as possible

2. Written to version 5.1 and includes advice on upgrading to version 6.0

3. Accurately configure the persistence layer and clustering service

4. Learn how to tune all components and hardware

Please check **www.PacktPub.com** for information on our titles

jQuery 1.4 Reference Guide

ISBN: 978-1-84951-004-2   Paperback: 336 pages

A comprehensive exploration of the popular JavaScript library

1. Quickly look up features of the jQuery library

2. Step through each function, method, and selector expression in the jQuery library with an easy-to-follow approach

3. Understand the anatomy of a jQuery script

4. Write your own plug-ins using jQuery's powerful plug-in architecture

Learning jQuery, Third Edition

ISBN: 978-1-84951-654-9   Paperback: 428 pages

Create better interaction, design, and web development with simple JavaScript techniques

1. An introduction to jQuery that requires minimal programming experience

2. Detailed solutions to specific client-side problems

4. Revised and updated version of this popular jQuery book

Please check **www.PacktPub.com** for information on our titles

Made in the USA
Lexington, KY
10 February 2014

JBoss AS 7

Configuration, Deployment, and Administration

JBoss AS 7 Configuration, Deployment, and Administration will give you an expert's understanding of every component that makes up the JBoss application server, and will show you how to use them, helping you to dramatically cut down the learning curve for this exciting product.

This book will guide you through configuration, management, deployment, and advanced administration in a logical order to avoid the common pitfalls of setting up a new AS. The book dives into the new application server structure and shows you how to install it. You will learn how to configure the core AS services, including thread pools, the messaging system, and the transaction service. Finally, you will learn how to deploy and manage your applications and then tune the performance of your AS to create an efficient, indispensible application server.

Who this book is written for

Java system administrators, developers, and application testers will benefit from this book. The brand new features in AS 7 mean that everyone can get something from this book, whether you have used JBoss AS before or not.

What you will learn from this book

- Understand the new AS infrastructure and how to install, start, and stop AS 7

- Configure the core AS 7 services, including database connections, the JMS subsystem, and transaction service

- Manage the application server using the Admin Console and the new Command Line Interface

- Deploy applications on the AS, using all the available tools and instruments

- Configure and run a cluster of application server nodes and provide high availability to your applications

- Secure the application server and the applications running on it

- Learn how to take your JBoss AS 7 applications in the cloud by leveraging the OpenShift platform-as-a-service

- Tune and slim the application server

$ 49.99 US
£ 30.99 UK

Prices do not include local sales tax or VAT where applicable

[PACKT] open source*
PUBLISHING   community experience distilled

ISBN 978-1-84951-678-5

9 781849 516785
5499

Visit **www.PacktPub.com** for books, eBooks, code, downloads, and PacktLib.